CASPAR JOHN

CASPAR JOHN

Rebecca John

COLLINS
8 Grafton Street, London W1
1987

William Collins Sons & Co. Ltd
London · Glasgow · Sydney · Auckland
Toronto · Johannesburg

BRITISH LIBRARY CATALOGUING IN PUBLICATION DATA

John, Rebecca
Caspar, John
1. Caspar, John   2. Great Britain, *Royal
Navy, Fleet Air Arm* – Biography
I. Title
358.4'1332'0924   VG95.G7

ISBN 0 00 217136 8

First published 1987
Reprinted 1987
© Rebecca John 1987

Photoset in Linotron Sabon by
Rowland Phototypesetting Ltd
Bury St Edmunds, Suffolk
Made and Printed in Great Britain by
Robert Hartnoll (1985) Ltd, Bodmin, Cornwall

To the memory of
IDA NETTLESHIP
and to my daughter Iona,
who never complained

CONTENTS

ILLUSTRATIONS

My dear sweet mother,
         I *am* so sorry father is still bad.
Fancy if I could finish his picture!
Wouldn't that be fine? What a poor fool
I am not to be able to. If I had the
technical power I'm sure I could put
myself into his conception. Strange
audacity!

from: *Ida Nettleship, Piazza d'Arno,
Florence, Italy, 1897 (aged 20)*

NOTE

For those readers who are not familiar
with naval ranks, the order is set out below:

Cadet
Midshipman
Sub-Lieutenant
Lieutenant
Lieutenant-Commander
Commander
Captain
Rear-Admiral
Vice Admiral
Admiral
Admiral of the Fleet

FOREWORD

My father began working on his autobiography in 1981. His working conditions, however, were not easy – he was in a wheelchair and often in great pain – and he was not enamoured of the task of writing about himself. So by the time of his death in 1984, the material he had put together represented little more than an outline of his naval career, with some parts more full than others. I had already become involved with the book, through an exchange of letters and by doing odd bits of research for him; when he died I was fully committed and felt it would be a great pity to allow his efforts to come to nothing.

The chief problem with the writing of the book has been my constant awareness of his dislike of anything inaccurate, but I also remember the silent smile that came to his face whenever he thought of some of the incidents which are here related. Wherever possible I have used his words and have stayed as close as I could to the pattern that he had established.

Caspar was insistent that he did not wish to write a history of the Fleet Air Arm but to tell his own personal story. If he had felt otherwise, I would not have undertaken the task. His life, however, was so bound up with the development of the FAA that it inevitably plays a large part in these pages. I could not have begun to tackle these passages if it had not been for the encouragement and assistance of those who could speak with authority on the subject.

In particular I must thank Rear-Admiral Dennis Cambell, Vice Admiral Sir Richard Smeeton and John Millar who served with Caspar in Washington during the war; Admiral Sir Desmond Cassidi who made it possible for me to visit the aircraft carrier HMS *Illustrious*; Rear-Admiral Roger Dimmock, Naval Secretary, whose help and advice has been unstinted; Commander Sam MacDonald-Hall, one of Caspar's closest friends, who served with him in HMS *York*; and the late Captain John Henry Wood, who let me see Caspar's many letters to him.

Many other naval officers have also made vital contributions, in particular Admiral Sir John Hamilton; Admiral Sir Nigel Henderson, who served in HMS *Ocean*, as did Guy Hughes and James Stewart-Moore; Vice Admiral Sir Geoffrey Norman, who was a lieutenant in HMS *Iron Duke*; Rear-Admiral William Selby; and the late Commander Harry Smallwood, a contemporary of Caspar at Osborne.

Further valuable information was provided by Richard Barrett, who was in China with Caspar; and Sheena Weston, who as a Wren took passage in HMS *Ocean* in 1946. I am indebted to John Shepherd for his reminiscences of life in the desert, and who served with Caspar in HMS *Courageous*.

Chapter 11, 'First Sea Lord', has been helped immeasurably by the contributions of Rear-Admiral Colin Dunlop, Caspar's secretary at the time: to him I owe a special thanks. Admiral Sir David Williams was my father's Naval Assistant during that time and gave me constant encouragement.

I would like to thank Judy Pugh for details on Caspar's private flying trips with his great friend Dick Pugh, and Betty Walker at the Admiralty for her assistance with a number of queries.

I could not have written the book without the support of my mother, who provided help when it was needed, but otherwise did not interfere, as was the case with my sister Caroline and brother Phineas. Caspar's half-sisters Poppet and Vivien were both generous in sharing their memories of their brother, and Caspar's late half-brother Romilly made some helpful suggestions, particularly about the early stages. My cousin, Nathalie Protopapa, kindly supplied information from the Nettleship papers, and her sister Anna John helped convince me that I should write the book. Tom Tudor-Pole remained his optimistic self throughout.

For their generosity, I must thank Thelma Cazalet-Keir, who played a great part in persuading Caspar to write his memoirs and made certain that I continued after his death; and Commander Dennis White, Director of the Fleet Air Arm Museum, Yeovilton, who also helped out on a number of diverse issues. A grant from the Hélène Heroys Literary Foundation, Geneva, enabled me to finish the book free of financial burden: no thanks are adequate.

Evelyn Morrison was a great help to my father at the end of his life and undertook much of the typing for him. I would also like to express my gratitude to Mrs Wilbur for her miraculous retyping of the manuscript, and for additional help at the earlier stages of the typing I would like to thank Valerie Woulfe.

A number of friends expressed interest and support, among whom I would like to mention Raynes and Patrick Minns, Deborah James, Victoria Barclay, Heather Joshi, Joanna Bird, Helen MacDonald-Hall and Jane Rainey. I must not forget here the vital part played by a large, airey London house, an excellent place of work; to Pat Kavanagh and Julian Barnes all my thanks.

Lastly, for his faith and tactful guidance throughout a period of three years, I offer warm thanks to my editor, Philip Ziegler.

I

One father, two mothers, nine children

Throughout his life in the Navy, Caspar John was asked a recurring question: what was it like to be the son of Augustus John? He would invariably answer with the reverse question: what would it be like not to be the son of such a man? But surely, his questioners insisted, it must have been difficult for an unorthodox man 'like you' to conform to the strait-laced ways of the Navy? On the contrary, Caspar would reply, it gave him the ability to see through much of what the Navy held to be sacrosanct, much of which was absurdly outmoded. Whether by direct example, or by reaction, his father's influence was always apparent in Caspar's life.

Although too young to remember the event, Caspar sometimes felt a little sadness when he reflected that his mother, Ida, had died when she was only thirty, and he just brushing the age of four. 'We should doubtless all have been better men had she lived on,' he once wrote to his elder brother David, who deplored the spotlight which invariably played on their male parent, and who became an ardent supporter of anything to do with the Nettleships, his mother's family. Caspar had been able to learn something of Ida's youthful character by reading a small collection of her letters written home from Italy and France when she was a student of art in the 1890s. Her writing revealed a spirited, whimsical creature, and, although devoted to her work, she would make fun of herself and her activities. 'I am so bold and unafraid in the way I work', she wrote from Florence in 1897, 'that all the keepers and all the copyists come and gape. I think they think I'm either a fool or a genius . . . When they find I'm a *genius*, O HO! They will all fall flat like Jericho.' She began to develop an insight into human nature which seems to have been rooted in religious and philosophic beliefs: 'To live up to the best your mind conceives – that is living truly,' she wrote to an elderly aunt when she was barely twenty-one. 'Dear, tho' you may not see the use of your being alive, neither does a rose or any flower. I know it is harder because a flower has no consciousness.'

Caspar was to become very attached to Ida's sisters, Ursula and Ethel, and through conversations with them he learnt of his mother's struggle to remain broad-minded in the face of Augustus's behaviour, and how she held her head up through the domestic turmoil that he and his three brothers created.

Like her father, Jack Nettleship, an artist who specialized in painting wild animals, Ida had attended the Slade School of Fine Art, and by winning a scholarship was enabled to remain there six years, spending the spring of 1897 in Florence and some months of 1898 in Paris, where she indulged her love of Old Master painting and enjoyed the company of her fellow students from the Slade, Ursula Tyrwhitt and Gwen John. Here she concerned herself with all the usual problems that occupy a young girl when staying away from home for the first time: finding decent rooms to lodge in, making friends, worrying about her dress. This last was of particular importance, for her mother, Ada, was a professional dressmaker, specializing in costumes for the theatre. 'Will you send me some sort of evening dress,' Ida wrote to her, 'because there is perhaps going to be a dance at Whistler's studio. If you have had anything done to the little grey blouse, or if not my old green evening dress would do quite well. If you do not want to send anything or are very busy, I will buy some cream muslin and Madame will make it up for me, with old gold-coloured ribbons.'

Ada Nettleship was highly disciplined in all her business affairs, and it was she who determined matters at home. After the death of her husband in 1902, she continued to rule the house and kept a strict eye on each of her three daughters.

Augustus too came from a home dominated by Victorian discipline. His father, Edwin John, had practised as a solicitor in Haverfordwest, Pembrokeshire, but the death of his wife, when Augustus was six, plunged him into crisis and he temporarily abandoned his business. They moved to Tenby: Augustus, his brother Thornton and his sisters, Winifred and Gwen, were thenceforth brought up in an atmosphere of deathly gloom by their father and a succession of housemaids, nurses and governesses.

A talent for drawing and a love of art brought Ida and Augustus together at the Slade in the mid-1890s. Ida's beauty – dark with slanting brown eyes – immediately attracted Augustus; he himself was astonishingly handsome and there was something about him that fired Ida's imagination. In 1901 they were married. Her parents were appalled, especially Ada, who could not come to terms with the fact that her favourite daughter had fallen into the arms of an unwashed artist who *wore an earring*.

Caspar was their second son, born in London on 22 March 1903 at 18 Fitzroy Street, W.1., in the heart of the area that came to be known as Fitzrovia. They had wanted a girl and decided to call the unborn baby Esther; 'but instead of Esther a roaring boy has forced admittance to our household,' Augustus told a friend. Years later, Caspar commented gloomily in his unfinished autobiography, 'I was saddled with the name Caspar, awkward enough on its own without the addition of the surname John, a combination which harried me for life.' Describing the circumstances of his birth, he wrote, 'I emerged into a melodramatic scene of human frailty. Queen Victoria had died, her son Edward VII was King, and the whole of society was trying to adjust to the new "order". That, as yet, had nothing to do with me.'

His father was twenty-five years old at the time and becoming a well-known painter in oils; when Caspar was born he was exhibiting his recent work at the Carfax Gallery in St James's. It was at this show that, among his forty-five, three works by his sister Gwen made a discreet appearance; 'the rarest of blossoms from the most delicate of trees,' declared Augustus. He was shortly to be elected to the New English Art Club and in the autumn was made co-principal of the newly founded Chelsea Art School at Rossetti Studios in Flood Street. And it was in this year that he began drawing Dorelia McNeill. Like Ida, she was dark with brown eyes, but her beauty was hypnotic, mysterious; her nature taciturn. Augustus drew her obsessively over the years to come – never naked, but clothed in her long handmade dresses in a breathtaking variety of poses: 'She must have scored a lasting world record in the number of times she posed,' Caspar later remarked.

In 1903 she was living in a basement in Fitzroy Street and had become friends with Gwen; that autumn the two girls set out to walk to Rome. They got no further than Toulouse, where they spent the winter, and Gwen painted a series of oil portraits of Dorelia: she too found her a fascinating model. Three of these portraits now hang in the Tate Gallery, the Manchester City Art Gallery and in the collection of Mr and Mrs Paul Mellon in Virginia, USA. Among those few people to have known Gwen, Augustus was the first to appreciate her work. Her present reputation – that of being one of the greatest female artists of the century – has had some silly repercussions on Augustus's standing as an artist, although he himself would only have chuckled at this turn of events: long before he died he confidently predicted that he would one day become known as the brother of Gwen John.

Augustus was already in love with Dorelia when he and Ida moved to Matching Green, Essex, the following year. Ida adored the company of her girlfriends, and had become quite attached to Dorelia, who helped with the children and was of some comfort to her in her impossible role of wife to Augustus. 'I shall never consider myself a wife – it is a mockery,' Ida once wrote to Dorelia. Augustus lacked any kind of understanding of, or indeed interest in, what she and the children needed. He could not abide the domestic scene for more than a short period at a time and so would absent himself to work on his portraits or join some social adventure which sometimes lasted for days.

But Ida also felt trapped by domesticity; especially after the birth of her third son, Robin, in October 1904. It was not long before she too was plotting an escape – to Paris. There she would be close to her happy memories of student days; memories that she hoped to share with Dorelia. In the spring of 1905 Dorelia gave birth to Augustus's son Pyramus, in a caravan on Dartmoor. Ida and the children, having joined Dorelia on Dartmoor, decided to spend the summer there, and it was during this time that the two women grew extraordinarily close and planned their flight to Paris. 'Dorelia was already *persona grata* in our household and stayed with us in our Parisian lodgings,' Caspar wrote. 'There seemed to be a happy understanding that that particular *ménage à trois* did work, despite raised eyebrows in the Nettleship family.'

Ida was pregnant with her fourth child when, in the late summer of 1905, the two women, accompanied by Augustus, the four boys and Bobster the dog, left England for Paris.

*　　*　　*

'Safely arrived and not a bit tired,' Ida wrote to her mother, 'Caspar, Robin and Dorelia were seasick . . . Caspar slept after it, so did Bobs. They were all so good. We were on deck. It was fairly rolling . . . Capper remarked on the boat when it began to roll, "We'd better go back."' Capper was his family nickname which eventually died out, as did 'Caper Sauce'.

After a brief stay in a hotel, they moved into 63 rue Monsieur le Prince, just in time for the birth of Ida's son, Edwin, in November. At each successive birth, Ida would announce 'the mixture as before', resigning herself to the fact that she still had not produced a girl.

From the age of two and a half to four, Caspar grew up in Paris. He and his elder brother David were sent to school for the first time, to the École Maternelle Communale. 'We were dressed in black wide-pleated pinafores, the hallmark of young Parisian school children, and learnt to speak French at an early age – with a French accent.' They were taken regularly to the Jardin du Luxembourg where they spent many hours under the eye of their maid Clara.

The household now consisted of three women coping with five boys – David, Caspar, Robin, Edwin and Pyramus – under the age of five. Early in 1906 they moved again, to new lodgings at 77 rue Dareau, where they were joined by Augustus. He was to come and go ceaselessly between England and France at this period, and indeed over the years preceding the First World War.

'Caspar has just come up from the studio, very hot, remarking "He gave me a penny",' Ida wrote to a friend that year. 'I suppose he's been sitting. You would adore him. He is still very fat and solid, and can't run at all quickly.' He was three years old.

Augustus frightened his sons with his sudden changes of mood, so that at an early age they were reduced to silence in his presence. He only really paid attention to them when he was drawing or painting them: in view of this, it is ironic that Augustus's children inspired him to produce some of his loveliest drawings.

Caspar's sole memory of his mother was of sitting on her lap in a horse-drawn tram somewhere in Paris. One week short of his fourth birthday, on 14 March 1907, she died after giving birth to her fifth son, Henry. Ada Nettleship had rushed to the scene. 'It was all very peaceful at the end,' she wrote to her daughter Ursula. 'The nurses folded her hands with a bunch of violets Gus had brought her and I put a crucifix and candles by her side.'

'I'm glad she died when she did,' Ida's sister Ethel wrote years later to Caspar. 'She was very unhappy and her pathetic struggle to be broad-minded, and having the "new woman" to live with them . . . made it an impossible situation, and she was much better out of it. A man like Gus was bound to eat up a few women in the course of living.'

*   *   *

'So there we were,' Caspar wrote, 'five very young boys including a baby in arms in mid-Paris. The Nettleships had to come to the rescue – and with a will.' Ethel and Ada shepherded the three eldest boys back to London, to 28 Wigmore Street, leaving Dorelia in charge of Edwin and Henry, and her own two sons, Pyramus and Romilly. Dorelia's second son, Romilly, was born in France in 1906.

During the four years that followed their mother's death, Caspar and his brothers journeyed constantly between London and Paris, according to the seasons of the year and Augustus's whims. Their London base alternated between Wigmore Street and Church Street, Chelsea; eight times they crossed the Channel and twice trekked across England with horse-drawn carts and caravans to the north Norfolk Coast and North Wales. It did not ever seem important to Augustus and Dorelia that they should settle in a permanent home: sometimes together, sometimes apart, they pursued an outdoor life with the children trailing along as best they could behind. The Nettleships' house in Wigmore Street was the nearest the children knew to having a home such as other children had. It was a Victorian house with basement and four stories, the lower two occupied by the dress-making business and thirty-odd seamstresses.

'It was quite a struggle to conform to the system in the Nettleship household. I think that initially Ursula, who was the elder of the two and felt more directly responsible for the young male family of her sister Ida, viewed her four ragamuffin nephews with apprehension, to be pitied for having lost such a lovable, if wayward, mother. We had a healthy respect for Grannie Nettleship, who treated us generously, if a little severely.' Old

Mrs Nettleship, a tough, tubby woman with grizzled hair and a round face, was strict with her grandsons. She took great pride in her work, and was gratified when some of the more well-known figures from the theatre came to her for their costumes. Caspar remembered one such occasion: 'I was thrilled one day to be introduced to Ellen Terry in one of the workshops. She seemed, to my young eyes, to be beautifully attired.

'We had to wash and scrub thoroughly in preparation for an inspection by Ursula before being accepted as adequately clean,' Caspar went on. 'We wore shoes and socks regularly and had our straggling locks cut short. She influenced our social deportment to reflect the physical cleanliness that she had rightly imposed on us; indeed we needed her help to balance our more customary unorthodoxy.'

This was much to Augustus's distaste, and there followed years in which the boys' upbringing was divided between his eccentric and irresponsible existence, and the orderly, bourgeois life of the Nettleships. Ada wanted full responsibility for the boys, but Augustus strongly resisted a Nettleship takeover: 'I distinctly object to the way they are being brought up with you,' he wrote to Ada in 1908, one year after Ida's death, 'as I can see quite clearly it is *not* a good way, nor their mother's, Dorelia's or my way. I am going to take them away at once . . . I believe you want nothing but the good of Ida's children, so there is no need to quarrel if you will only realize that. I know best what she would have wished.'

This was open warfare, with the children's upbringing as the *casus belli*. Ada Nettleship stood her ground. She did not think that he and Dorelia were capable of looking after Ida's sons, and in any case had a strong dislike for both of them. She ignored an ultimatum from Augustus, ordering the return of all his children the following morning. When no children arrived, Augustus marched round to Wigmore Street. He described what happened next in a letter to Wyndham Lewis. Mrs Nettleship, he said, tried 'to take refuge in the zoo with my three eldest boys and only after a heated chase through the monkey house did I succeed in coming upon the guilty party immediately behind the pelicans' enclosure. Seizing two children as hostages I bore them off in a cab and left them in a remote village for a few days in charge of an elderly but devoted woman. The *coup d'état* was completely successful of course. Dorelia appears on the scene with almost miraculous promptitude and we take off the bunch of four tomorrow morning . . .'

They left for Paris, from where Augustus had planned to go to Brittany with the children for the summer. The painter Henry Lamb had joined them in Paris, and agreed to relieve Augustus and Dorelia of one of their band of six boys; they were to meet at Cherbourg. Augustus and his flock, having reached Rouen, took a boat to Cherbourg. Lamb, however, walked, carrying the five-year-old Caspar on his shoulders. They slept overnight at various wayside inns, which Lamb would offer to pay for with one of his drawings. To make things a little easier, he fitted himself with a sack – like the present-day sling – for Caspar to sit in when the child began to find walking a bit too much for him.

The party stayed in rooms at Dielette from July to September. Augustus felt proud; the children looked healthy and commendably wild, and the place was 'lovely – so varied – sandy beaches, rocks and harbours with prehistoric landscapes behind.' He was also painting energetically, which he remembered in his autobiography, *Chiaroscuro*, forty years later: 'I made some headway at Dielette, where I employed with advantage the method of restricting my palette to the three primary colours represented by ultramarine, crimson lake and cadmium, with green oxide of chromium.'

*   *   *

In October they all returned to London, this time to Augustus's new headquarters at 153 Church Street, Chelsea. Nearby lay a patch of waste ground bordering the King's Road; littered with bricks and bushes, it was the perfect setting for games of cowboys and indians. A few years later it became Mallord Street, where in 1914 Augustus commissioned a Dutch architect to build a house and studio.

The sculptor Jacob Epstein kept a studio in neighbouring Beaufort Street. Twenty-eight years old at the time, he was studying Greek and Roman sculpture, spending many hours in the British Museum. On visits to his studio, Caspar and David would help themselves to his clay, which he kept in metal bins, and roll it into pellets to flick at each other. Occasionally Lady Ottoline Morrell, a formidable new acquaintance of Augustus, would conduct the boys up to Hampstead Heath to practise the art of kite-flying. 'I could not claim much proficiency,' Caspar remembered, 'but "Ottofat", as we boys called her, helped to get the kites airborne. We never ceased to marvel at her striking appearance.'

In the summer of 1909, Augustus announced that he intended to travel by caravan to Cambridge, where he had portrait-painting to do. He had acquired two vans, and six horses – including a black hunter, for him to ride on ahead and find suitable night-stopping places. The vans were what were popularly known as 'gipsy caravans', brightly painted, one bright blue, the other canary yellow, and each containing a somewhat cramped, raised double-bunk at the rear of the cabin, under which was a dark space for the children to sleep. 'We regarded it as a cave,' Caspar wrote. 'On one side of the cabin was a small coal-fired range, with storage lockers under a wooden seat opposite. Outside the "front door" was a platform for the driver and those of us who suffered from claustrophobia. On fine nights a couple of hammocks would be slung between the axles to relieve pressure in the cave.'

Normally the van would be drawn by one horse, the second following behind on a halter, ready to help on the steeper hills. There was little enough for the children to do; often they lined up behind one of the axles and added their modest weight to the horses' pull. Sometimes the van, brakeless and packed with children, would career down steep hills, but miraculously there were never any fatal or even serious accidents. When Augustus was riding ahead, Dorelia was left in charge, and proved herself very efficient at it.

One evening, the troupe pulled into a wayside inn near Watford, having been rejected at a public house a little further back on account of their 'class'. They stayed here several nights, unable to tear themselves away from their genial host. Every evening this paragon among innkeepers transformed himself from landlord into clown, dressing himself up in outlandish costumes and entertaining his customers with a range of bizarre routines.

Eventually the family arrived in a field near Grantchester where they set up camp on the bank of the River Cam. They were joined by Rupert Brooke, who endeared himself to everyone by letting the children clamber all over him and taking them rowing on the river. Ottoline Morrell too turned up for twenty-four hours; this was awkward for no one really knew what to do with her. 'We did treat her badly,' Dorelia remembered half a century later. 'We couldn't imagine what to give such a grand lady to eat, so all she got was an apple. Heard after that the poor dear's favourite dish was kippers.'

Augustus's main task was to paint the portrait of Miss Jane Harrison, a Greek scholar at Newnham, who posed for him reclining on her couch while she smoked innumerable cigarettes. Once this was done, the party moved on to Norwich, and thence to sand dunes near Palling. At this point Augustus typically abandoned his family and took a train to Liverpool where he had been commissioned to paint a portrait of the Lord Mayor.

When he rejoined his family a few weeks later he found that morale was low. Whooping cough had broken out with Caspar among the victims; caravan life was even less comfortable than the children were used to. It was not long before they reversed their tracks to the southwest, finishing up at Church Street, Chelsea.

25

There followed a period of ill-health and discontent, and in January 1910 Augustus once again took off, this time for France and Italy. During his wanderings in the vicinity of Marseilles, he discovered Martigues, 'a little republic of fishermen', as he described it, wholly untouched by fashion and inhabited by craftsmen who got on with their own lives and let their visitors do the same. Martigues stood on the shores of the Étang de Berre, a spacious salt-water lagoon. Their home that summer and for future summers was fixed; the Villa Ste Anne was to remain in the family until 1928. In July, Caspar and his two brothers David and Robin made their first trip by train to Provence.

In a letter to his Aunt Ursula, Caspar attempted to describe their activities. 'There is a rock we play on. Sometimes we play boats. We found a lot of blackberries and Edie [Dorelia's sister] made some jam. We went out very early in the morning and I saw two shooting stars and flashes of litning all the time. The Donkey fell in the ditch. We went for another drive by a canal and a little tiny engine run . . . we go out for walks and get fir cones to lit the fire with and we got a great bunch of lavendar.' The unfortunate donkey had been purchased from a gypsy accompanying a pack from Algeria.

Here, on the shores of the Étang, the children ran about naked, and made the acquaintance of their landlord. Monsieur Bazin was one of the tiny number of men at that time whose passion was flying, even though it was impossible for him to indulge in it. He devoted all his time to constructing primitive aeroplanes; but, unfortunately, every time he succeeded in getting off the ground he found himself almost immediately splashing into the Étang de Berre. This was the tender age of aerial experimentation, and those pioneers who dedicated their lives to the dream of flight – of whom there were some notable examples in France at this time – worked largely in isolation from one another.

In the year that Caspar was born, the brothers Louis and Orville Wright had spent months hopping like wounded birds among the sand dunes of North Carolina, then triumphed in December with the first ever powered flight lasting fifty-nine seconds. Five years later, in 1909, Louis Blériot flew across the English Channel. They were heroes, and duly honoured, but the Bazins of that time were regarded at the best as cranks, at the worst as mad men. Quite often they were both.

M. Bazin was a crank but he was not mad. His efforts to become airborne were closely watched by a starry-eyed Caspar and his brothers. Augustus was equally enthusiastic and came to the rescue financially. Thinking that an American would be sure to appreciate such an enterprise, he approached the New York art patron John Quinn for further funds. Quinn, however, was already sending monthly contributions to Gwen John in Paris, and had to decline. 'Personally I can't afford to "take a flyer" now myself,' he explained.

'Our host still dreamt of flying,' Augustus wrote in his autobiography, 'and had a new apparatus in view: once it was perfected, he proposed that I should be its "jockey" and try it out over the Étang de Berre. Through shortage of funds, however, this project had to be deferred.' As luck would have it, the second Madame Strindberg, wife of the Swedish dramatist but relentlessly pursuing Augustus, suddenly presented him with an embarrassing £300. Perhaps fortunately, Augustus was by then out of France, but he decided it would be a proper use for this windfall to send it to Bazin to aid him in his researches. Bazin was delighted by this unsolicited donation, but Augustus never heard that his experiments were any further advanced as a result. A number of letters had been exchanged between the birdman and the artist, and over fifty years later Caspar arranged for their correspondence to be given to the Musée Aeronautique in Paris.

*   *   *

The return journey from Martigues at the end of that summer was the last time that Caspar was to cross the Channel before joining the Navy. Back at Church Street, it was becoming increasingly obvious that a permanent home large enough to accommodate six children, and a fluctuating number of adults, had to be found. Despite the hostility that simmered between Augustus and the Nettleships, Caspar and his brothers continued to spend time at Wigmore Street. From there they were taken on the ritual round for middle-class London children: to the parks, to the zoo, to Madame Tussaud's and the pantomime – usually in horse-drawn four-wheelers or a convoy of hansom cabs. On the way to *Peter Pan*, Caspar asked Ursula to scatter 'fairy dust' over his shoulder blades so that he could grow wings and fly. M. Bazin could have done with some of that, too.

Ethel and Ursula were complementary as aunts. 'They were for us, I believe, a partial mother substitute, at any rate for me,' Caspar wrote. 'I say that with no disrespect for our stepmother, Dorelia, who was a wonderful woman.' Wonderful though she may have been, Dorelia was detached, and lacked the warmth that Ida's sisters were able to give their nephews. 'Blood being thicker than water, it exerts an emotional pull. Both Ursula and Ethel kept open doors to us throughout their lives. Later I sought their stabilizing influence, an encouraging one to me, by then in the Navy and often cut off from the world.'

Apart from the boys, Ursula's principle preoccupation was with English music. She continued to teach singing until she died in her eighties in 1968. She was no mere dilettante; after Benjamin Britten and Peter Pears stayed with her during the war, she became involved with the Aldeburgh Festival and was a formidable choir trainer during the Festival's early years. A foot-bridge which spans some rushes at the Maltings, Snape, has been named in her memory. She was also passionate about mountain-eering and fearless in pursuit of this passion. Perhaps she had inherited her love for this intractable activity from a paternal uncle, Lewis Nettleship, who had been a philosophy tutor at Balliol College, Oxford, and perished from exposure on the slopes of Mont Blanc in 1892.

Warm-hearted, possibly more broad-minded and with a less

tidy nature, Ethel was equally musical and became an accomplished 'cellist. She joined the VAD in the First World War and drove a Red Cross ambulance in Flanders and Italy, then nursed in an Army Hospital in Malta. She was a good driver and used to motor around in an open Austin which she sometimes ran as a taxi. After the war she became a hand-bobbin lacemaker, holding her own with the experts in Brussels. She wrote an unpublished manuscript on the technique, including a design which was charmingly inspired by a passage from the music of Delius, and another by the patterns made by butter when spread on a slice of bread.

In 1958, two years before her death, an 'Exhibition of Twentieth-century Pillow-lace and Bobbinwork by Ethel Nettleship' was held (under the patronage of Augustus) in Westbourne Grove, London. 'This is a Pioneer Exhibition,' Ethel declared in the catalogue. 'Till now we have made only what the Hugenot refugees taught us or what we have learned from other countries. These three Books are to be the foundation of an Industry – our own – an English Industry.' Bobbinwork was the expression of perpetual movement, needle lace an expression of repose; Ethel's designs revealed both the whimsical and down-to-earth sides of her personality: 'Passing the Time of Day' was a table centre and mat 'intended to promote conversation at the beginning of a dinner party'; 'Sally' was designed after hearing Gracie Fields sing it, and 'The Birds in the Spring' 'after hearing my sister, Ursula, sing it'. There was a bedspread, 'Aloes and Prickly Pear', and a piece of edging with the title 'Fish and Chips', which she had made for a curtain in a fish and chip shop. Birds in flight recur through her designs, but there are no marine themes.

The two sisters remained very close. In the 1930s, Ursula had a house built to her specifications in Cheyne Walk. It incorporated a vast, beige music room which she kept bare for acoustical reasons and for the regular concerts she held at home. Here, Ethel would come and play her 'cello, and traces of her life's work would sometimes turn up beneath a cushion: a piece of crumpled lace. Caspar described her 'as gay and untidy', and she un-doubtedly set him a feminine example.

Ursula had reacted strongly against Ida's decision to live in Paris with Dorelia; it was, quite simply, unclean. She wrote to Ida saying that, unless she was prepared to reform her 'ménage', she would have no alternative but to renounce marriage for herself and never see Ida again. Within two years of this outburst, Ida was dead, but Ursula, either because of this painful memory or for other reasons, remained a spinster for life. So did Ethel, though she was certainly not deterred by her sister's example, viewing Ida's activities with tolerance and considerable sympathy.

*   *   *

Dorelia was beginning to tire of the gipsy life, but she did not find London any more congenial. The children, too, clearly needed somewhere to settle. Augustus still felt that conventional school-ing was unnecessary, if not actively harmful, but even he could see that the nomadic life had its limitations. The search began for a country base. It ended in the summer of 1911 with the discovery of Alderney Manor near Parkstone in Dorset. This was a one-storey building in Strawberry Hill, Gothic style, with castellated parapet and pointed windows, built by an eccentric Frenchman. There was a coach house, which Augustus turned into a studio, a cottage for overflow, and various caravans dotted around the property to accommodate those who overflowed even from the cottage. Around the house were fifty acres of varied pasture, heath, woodland and marsh – ideal surroundings in which to grow up.

Dorelia, or 'Dodo' as she had now become – she was rarely referred to as Dorelia in later life – created an enchanting environment now that she had the chance. A local woman, Mrs Cake, turned up, and was promptly engaged as the cook. Her husband, an ex-cowherd, taught the boys how to milk a cow; a Jersey had arrived, and in time a large black sow, two New Forest ponies, swarms of bees, chickens, ducks, red setter dogs and Siamese cats joined the throng. Flower and vegetable gardens flourished. 'It is very nice in Dorset at the new house,' the eight-year-old Caspar wrote to Ursula that July, '. . . there is no cow parseley here but there are Rhodidandrums. In the garden we grow some tomatoes radishes cucumbers lettises green peas onions potatoes mint and gusberis.'

They had a good grounding in animal and plant life. Dressed in colourful blouses and shorts, mostly bare-footed, frequently topless, and sometimes naked, they roamed the countryside, catching their stray ponies, counting piglets, trying to milk the cow, collecting firewood, looking for chicken and duck eggs and performing the numerous other chores that were thought up for them. David and Caspar did all the stabling at Alderney. 'We'd groom and harness the ponies into their traps, ready to drive up to the front door where Augustus and Dodo would be waiting, he for a round of the nearer public houses, she for a round of the shops. We two would sit on the tail boards, ready to feed and water the ponies at each stop, most of which they knew without being reined.'

As well as looking after the ponies, one of Caspar's earliest skills in life was to make butter: 'In turns with my brothers, we'd skim the cream out of shallow metal vats, where the milk had been left overnight in the cellar for the cream to rise. Then we poured the cream into an eccentric hand-rotated churn, which we turned for twenty minutes to half an hour, waiting for the 'bomp', 'bomp', 'bomp' when we knew the cream had solidified. We then took the lump into the kitchen and squeezed out all the buttermilk with rolling pins and patted the butter into rounds or cubes.'

Soon after the family was installed at Alderney, the question of the boys' education arose. Apart from a short spell in Paris and Chelsea, none of them had been subjected to any systematic course of schooling. Augustus felt that this was as it should be. Determined to avoid the debilitating effects of traditional British education, he decided to have recourse to a private tutor. One duly arrived from Turkey, pushing a child's pram full of rare books which he had come by in the Middle East. John Hope-Johnstone was devoted to worldwide travel, something which suited the John household; when his time was up as tutor – Augustus quickly tired of too much of the same company – he left, pushing his pram in the direction of China. 'Besides being scholarly and a first-class mathematician,' Caspar remembered, 'he was also a good cook, in the French style. Eccentric, yes . . . and considered by Augustus to be a worthy tutor for David and me. We quickly learnt to recite accurately and at length from the Book of Kings, and to write Gothic script with calligraphic pen and black ink.'

*   *   *

At the time of moving into Alderney Manor, Augustus had also acquired a cottage in North Wales. He had spent some months painting the landscape there with his friend Dick Innes, and had wanted to find a permanent base so as to make his working conditions a little easier. That summer, John Hope-Johnstone set out from Dorset in a pony trap to join the family there. He was accompanied by David and Caspar. They travelled some two hundred miles. While their tutor sat upright in the trap, the two boys trotted along barefoot behind, on steep hills helping to hold the trap back or push it up. It was a rough journey, but this was something to which they were quite accustomed. At night they slept on the grass verges between the wheels.

The cottage, called Nant Ddu, was situated in a desolate valley not far from Snowdon and Bala Lake. It was surrounded by stacks of peat which David and Caspar used to rob for the fire. A local train ran through the valley, and the boys used sometimes to be taken to the stop called Cwm Prysor, about a mile away, and introduced to Mrs Evans, the station-mistress. 'She would always go to the oven and pull out some lovely hot cakes – beautiful they were!' Dodo gave two of the boys a job to do every morning, which was to cross the valley to the farm and fetch a supply of milk. This involved fording a stream, and once, on the way back, Caspar slipped on a stone and out poured the milk. 'I lied to Dodo that the cow had given no milk that morning.' Caspar was conspicuous in later life for his inability to misrepresent the truth. This early fall from grace suggests that he must have feared Dorelia's reaction if he was unable to tell her about the mishap.

They had returned to Alderney in the comfort of a steam train, and there they began a new existence, 'turbulent and happy-go-lucky' Caspar described it, 'against the background of Augustus's wild eccentricities.' There was a stream of visitors from Europe and the Americas, attracted by the way of life at Alderney and the character and reputation of Augustus. A poet from Iceland turned up, 'an irrepressibly cheerful little man', as Caspar's younger brother Romilly described him in his autobiography, *The Seventh Child*; Jan Sliwinski, known as 'the Pole', a musician with a fine and powerful voice which set the furniture quivering; an ex-heavyweight boxer and painter from South America called Alvaro Guevara, and known as 'Chile', Uncle Thornton blew in from Canada, and from South Africa came the poet Roy Campbell.

Caspar made a particular friend of Trelawney Dayrell-Reed, another frequent visitor at Alderney. Trelawney had just come down from Oxford. He was a strange mixture; flamboyant at one moment, behaving like a Dorset yokel the next. Always dressed in loud checks and red socks, 'distinguished and peculiar' was Romilly's description, he enjoyed being at the centre of events. He much impressed the boys with his writings on Wessex. Two slim volumes of these were published during the Second World War and in 1947. 'I am one of the infinitesimal minority that views the period that witnessed the relaxation of the Roman grip on Britain as one of the most exciting and important in our history,' he wrote in his *The Battle of Britain in the Fifth Century: an Essay in Dark Age History*. In spite of his stammer, he used to read aloud passages from Thomas Hardy. Caspar listened avidly, and remained fascinated by the novelist and his work throughout his life. Trelawney was also a very good left-handed shove-ha'penny player; indeed he wrote a treatise on the game. He remained friends with Caspar until he died in the 1950s, by which time he had taken to hibernating. When the weather grew cold he would retreat to his bedroom and remain there, with a fire blazing and a couple of spaniels at the bottom of his bed, until assured that spring had come. He had a sister, who became rather confused. She was apt to put the hot water bottle in the oven and the leg of lamb in the bed.

A frequent outing from Alderney was the five-mile trip to Bournemouth. The boys would bicycle to the top of Constitution Hill, above Poole, and then board a tram for Bournemouth. There they got off at the Square and walked to the roller skating rink, where they had skates strapped to their feet and were let loose on the floor, already crowded with more proficient skaters. After various collisions and falls, it would be time for a change, so they took off their skates and sat at a tea table, facing the cinema screen. A pianist would accompany the silent, flickering pictures while the John boys demolished everything that the waitresses put in front of them.

After some months' 'guidance' from John Hope-Johnstone, even Augustus reluctantly concluded that the time had come for some more conventional schooling. Consequently, one day in 1912, with Dodo at the reins, they set out in a pony and trap in search for a suitable preparatory school. 'David and I were literally *hawked* around the local schools near Poole,' Caspar wrote, 'and eventually drew up at the front door of Dane Court, Parkstone, to be welcomed by the headmaster, Mr Hugh Pooley, and his Danish wife, Michaela; the former, I'm sure, muttering to himself "hair too long . . . odd clothes!"' By now Dodo was short-tempered and would brook no opposition. 'You must take these two boys,' she announced, and added, 'There are three more somewhere – you may as well have them too if I can find

34

them.' She was referring only to Robin, Edwin and Romilly; in March that year her seven-year-old son Pyramus – 'a celestial child' Augustus had described him as – died of meningitis. It was a tragic and moving event, for even as Pyramus was dying, she gave birth to a daughter, Poppet. She was to have one more child, a daughter named Vivien, in March 1915.

In *The Seventh Child*, Romilly describes the agony that children may suffer over their parents' appearance, which reaches crisis point if a father or mother is spotted at the school gate *wrongly dressed*. Augustus and Dorelia could always be relied on to be wrongly dressed, but their appearances at the school gate were rare. Caspar and his brothers, however, had to brace themselves for the extra humiliation caused by their own appearance. But they were lucky in their headmaster, and could not have known that he and his wife were open-minded. 'Their long hair and tunic shirts were certainly picturesque,' Hugh Pooley wrote in the school magazine many years later, 'and did not seem to worry anybody very much.' An ex-pupil of Dane Court described Pooley as being 'a fine teacher, a born leader and a man with the most amazing insight into the mind of a small boy'. His wife, Michaela, was the daughter of the director of the art museum in Copenhagen. She was something of an extrovert; wore astonishing hats, and liked to dress in russets and golds; it was not unknown for her to turn a pair of the school curtains into a garment for herself to wear.

The school, which was entirely gas-lit, had been founded in 1867 by a vicar with a solitary pupil, Henry Rider Haggard. It moved to Parkstone in 1900. There were still only a dozen pupils or so when, in 1912, it was dramatically enlarged by the arrival of Caspar and his brothers.

> We were enrolled as weekly boarders and entered our first experience of orderly living away from the family and the Nettleships. I was just nine years old and wondered what was in store for us. By reason of our long hair, strange clothing and relatively outlandish

35

habits, we became known as The Persians. We completed the blotting of our copybook by being able to speak French – not a good thing in 1912. But we shone on the playing fields, and won many games of cricket and football for the school – without short-pitched bowling or bad temper. Augustus once scored a goal – palpably offside – playing for the parents and Old Boys. Unhappily I was the goalkeeper and was accused of deliberately letting the ball into the net. Physical prowess in English sports being more important than knowledge of a foreign language, we were forgiven our strange ways.

The Nettleships had not lost sight of the boys and came to the rescue during holiday time. 'Holidays were spent with Grannie, mostly at the seaside, with Ursula and Ethel in attendance. Mevagissey, Ashburton, Barmouth and Harlech were some of the places we were taken to. Fresh air, healthy walks, deep breathing were the order of the day, followed in the evenings by games of "Up Jenkins", Racing Demon, Charades, and early to bed. A barber would be summoned and outfits of orthodox school clothing bought.' Soon the John brothers were outwardly indistinguishable from boys with a more conventional upbringing, but inwardly they had a struggle to adapt themselves.

Every week the school had to face the parade-ground discipline of ex-Sergeant-Major Thomas Kelly, who spared the boys nothing in his insistence on the right way to march and turn, followed by a period of physical jerks. David and Caspar were deemed good enough to be enrolled as scout leaders – David with the Kangaroo patrol and Caspar with his Ravens. 'We had many a battle in the nearby woods with wooden staves and rubber balls. Honours were probably even, and we retained some brotherly love.'

*   *   *

In 1916, with the First World War in its second year, conversation both at school and at Alderney Manor frequently turned on the achievements of the Army, the Navy and the Royal Flying Corps. Caspar had been doing well at school although there were few other boys to compete with. 'I was top of my form for the whole term,' he told Ethel, 'but it was not my fault because the two boys who might have beaten me were away for a long time.' He was especially good at Latin grammar, for which he was awarded a leather-bound edition of Dickens's *A Tale of Two Cities*. In his final year he won three prizes, one of which, awarded to the boy deemed to be the 'best gentleman in the school', was the current edition of *Jane's Fighting Ships*. 'Awfully nice,' Caspar said of it to Ethel. It was this somewhat arid work that first gave Caspar the idea of joining the Navy, which seemed to him the most orderly and travelled of the Services. Further, candidates for the Navy were accepted at the young age of thirteen and a half, which for Caspar would be September 1916. He quickly made up his mind that this should be his future.

'I am going to try and get into the Navy,' he announced to Ethel, who was nursing at the Army hospital in Malta, 'but whether I shall succeed is another matter. First I have to go up to the Board of Admiralty and pass my health test, to see whether I am fit and strong enough for the Navy. The Admirals question you on all sorts of things to test you for smartness of answer. If you don't pass the Admirals you don't try for the exam, but if you do, you then go in for the exam and if you pass you go into Osborne College for two years, and after that two years at Dartmouth, then on a training cruiser where you learn either Gunnery, Engineering or Navigation. Everybody must know a certain amount of each, especially Engineering.'

Even before he could embark on these arduous preliminaries, he faced the formidable hurdle of Augustus's opposition. He was not an easy father to approach. The brothers ganged together, united in a feeling of cowed hostility towards him. The wisest course, all agreed, was to avoid him altogether. The day came, however, when Caspar decided he must face his father with the news that he wanted to join the Navy. 'I could only guess at what his reaction might be. I was right. *"What?"* he shouted. "You want to subject yourself willingly and wittingly to the harshest discipline in the world? You must be mad, boy!"'

Augustus had a complete lack of understanding as a father; indeed, scarcely recognized his sons as individuals at all. Although he liked to boast about their unconventional appearance, he did not show any paternal pride in his family; neither did he have any clear ideas about the elder sons' future careers, a career being a minor concern in his view of the world. But he had given the matter some thought. His eldest son, David, had also considered the Navy, though for romantic reasons, and in a letter to Ursula, who was most concerned about her nephews' futures, Augustus set out his ideas on the subject.

> My David has been reading *Coral Island* and naturally wants to go to sea on the chance of getting wrecked in some such charming spot. I believe the training for the R.N. is now awfully severe and awfully good. At D's age I had definitely decided to trap beaver on the Arkansas river, USA, with vague hopes of eventually being adopted by the Antelope-Comanche horse Indians of Texas, but things turned out otherwise. I fancy in another year or two one will be better able to judge of David and Caspar's aptitude – if any. It is very good of you to offer to find out about the R.N. and Merchant Service but I think Dafydd is too vague just yet for either. I hope some of them will come to learn some craft . . . anyhow, I can't see any of them shining in an office – *mais nous verrons*.

Caspar was not surprised or discouraged by his father's reaction when he in his turn suggested the Navy as a career. Instead he beat a hasty retreat and sought the assistance of Mr Pooley. Pooley was entirely sympathetic and promised to try to get Augustus into a more helpful mood. He succeeded, but it can hardly be said that Augustus's attitude was positive. He was, Caspar felt in retrospect, bewildered by his son's choice of career.

'At least that will be one less brat on my hands,' he remarked at the time.

Caspar kept the Nettleships closely in touch with what was going on. Augustus and Dodo were away, leaving Caspar a little anxious. 'Mr Pooley wrote to the Home Secretary about me going into the Navy,' he told Ursula in February 1916. 'He received a thing for him and Daddy to sign . . . Do you know when Dodo and Daddy are coming home?'

Augustus's hostility to his son's proposed career in no way soured Caspar's interest in his father's work as a portrait painter. 'I hear Daddy's picture of Lloyd George is done,' he wrote to Grannie Nettleship, thanking her for a copy of Rudyard Kipling's *Fringes of the Fleet*, a thirteenth birthday gift that March. 'I have seen lots of photographs of the portrait and like it very much. I should like to see some of Daddy's pictures wherever they are next time we come to London.'

Lloyd George was Chancellor of the Exchequer when this portrait was completed in February 1916; he was to succeed Asquith as Prime Minister the following December. The two Welshmen did not get along, and the sittings went badly, though Lloyd George was amused to learn that his father had been the artist's father's schoolmaster at Haverfordwest in Pembrokeshire. 'He asked me to enquire what impression the schoolmaster (who had died rather young) had made on his pupil,' Augustus wrote in *Chiaroscuro*. 'My father's reply was that Lloyd George *père* was a strict but just disciplinarian, earning the respect of all boys, but that his wife had won their *love*. This tribute delighted Lloyd George and was all the more valuable as coming from one ordinarily in the habit of confusing the distinguished offspring of the couple in question with the Devil himself.'

Caspar's entry into the Navy coincided with the commissioning of a portrait of Admiral Lord Fisher, who had been First Sea Lord from 1904 to 1910. Augustus described him in his autobiography: 'Lord Fisher was the very archetype of a sailor. He had started his career in the old wooden ships. He told me his qualifying examinations as a candidate for the Navy consisted in reciting the Lord's Prayer and drinking a glass of sherry. He had no difficulty in passing the test: though he couldn't spell *cat* . . . Like many great men, "Jackie" Fisher loved the simplest jokes and was well stocked with such himself. He liked walking up and down Mallord Street while talking, but no further than the length of a quarterdeck, his ideal ambit. The night before his sittings, he might have been dancing indefatigably, or sitting up till all hours drinking champagne with Winston Churchill; as far as I could see he was never the worse for it.'

Jackie Fisher had entered the Navy in 1854, forty-eight years after the Battle of Trafalgar. He had served in the Baltic during the Crimean War and as a midshipman in China in 1859. After 1860 there was no major war at sea in which the British Navy took part and when he became First Sea Lord in 1904 (the year following Caspar's birth) the Navy was, as Caspar described it in a speech he gave in 1967, in the main, 'psychologically stagnant in foresight and out of date in material. Naval tactical ideas were still in the bow and arrow era. Spit and polish, sail drill and ceremonial were considered far more important. Into that complacent environment Lord Fisher plunged head first, and the controversial job of producing a Naval renaissance. He needed all the arrogance, energy, perseverance and ruthless strength of character which he had at his command.' He introduced sweeping and often unpopular reforms, and, like most radicals, he made a lot of enemies.

One day, at the studio in Chelsea, the thirteen-year-old Caspar was introduced to Lord Fisher. He inspired me at once. He hung his Bath Insignia around my neck and said, 'You'll wear one of these one day, boy,' and gave me the advice: 'Look forward, not backwards.' Caspar never forgot Fisher's words and made the Admiral his personal hero, for not only did Fisher see that reforms were needed after so long a period of peace, but he was the first naval officer of high rank to realize the future importance of flying at sea.

The day of reckoning approached. 'Daddy received a paper from the Admiralty the other day, asking me to go before the Admirals on the *1st June 1916* at two o'clock *precisely!*' Caspar told the Nettleships. 'I take my exam on the *11th and 12th July 1916*. I believe I am going to get a new suit to visit the Admirals with!' Oddly enough the ordeal of his appearance before the Admirals left no impression on him, and in later life he could recall no detail of the interview. Possibly his memories were clouded by the fact that the family was struck down by chicken-pox a few days later and Caspar with the others was miserably ill.

On 23 June, he wrote to Ethel: 'The Admirals told me that I should hear some time at the end of this month.' The news came the following day. 'I've passed the Admirals all right and now I've got to work up like a demon for my other exam to get into Osborne,' he wrote exultantly to Ursula. He was referring to the Admiralty's stiff physical, oral and written exams. There was no time to think about what might lie ahead if this hurdle was surmounted; Caspar concentrated on what he had to face, and managed to pass, though with a fairly low mark. Only then did he contemplate the future. 'I shuddered at what I had done!'

With the day of his entrance into the Navy only weeks away, Caspar realized that he was approaching a violent change of life. 'I had no encouragement at home; I felt a lonely outcast.' The terrible question of *clothes* hung over him – which was not the sort of problem likely to interest either his father or Dorelia. 'I have got a nice trunk and hand bag now for my uniform,' he told Grannie Nettleship. The bag, made of pigskin, was given to him by Augustus. An experienced naval outfitter took care of the rest, and kitted him up with naval cadet's uniform – a formidable array of garments in spite of the insignificance of the role. 'You must try and see me swanking in my uniform sometime,' Caspar wrote proudly to Ethel. In September 1916 he rode in a pony and trap from Alderney Manor to Portsmouth, the first thirty-five miles of the journey to the Royal Naval College Osborne, on the Isle of Wight. Dodo sat at the reins in her long skirts, Caspar beside her in his smart new uniform. Eventually they arrived at Portsmouth. 'I was dumped through the dockyard main gates together with my fellow embryo Nelsons, inspected for the first time by the Commander-in-Chief, and taken in a paddle-wheel tug across the Solent to Cowes. Here we assembled ashore and marched the mile or so to Osborne. I felt like a fish out of water and probably looked it.'

2

Cadet and young officer

To understand the training of a naval cadet in those days, it is important to know something of the Term system. The term was not unlike the house in the traditional English public school. There were four terms, each consisting of a hundred boys who had all passed the same type of examinations at the same time. Each term was named after a well-known naval figure – in Caspar's year they were Drake, Blake, St Vincent and Hawke – and each term member was numbered in alphabetical order. Thus Caspar became H.51 in Hawke Term – named after Admiral Hawke who had won the Battle of Quiberon Bay against the French in 1759.

Throughout the College each cadet held a strong allegiance to his term name, which became the focus for intense rivalry both in the classrooms and on the sports grounds. Physical competition was part of life; rugger, squash, running and boatwork were all eagerly practised, and the teaching and training of all forms of sport was highly organized. 'Hawke's' acquired a reputation for producing the best athletes of their year, winning the Arbuthnot Trophy for the twelve-mile cross-country run at the first attempt. Caspar, who remained small in his early teens, finished up at 6 feet 1 inch tall and, being light-boned and tenacious, became one of Hawke's fastest long-distance runners.

He soon managed to adapt himself to the routine of College

life, which began daily with reveillé and a cold plunge bath. What was strange for most of the new cadets was for Caspar revolutionary. Everything happened at a set time and place, something he had never encountered at home. 'Naval discipline came as something more than a shock to me, but I quickly decided to master the very strange surroundings; after all, it was my choice. My main difficulty concerned my stiff white collar with studs and black tie, an infernal jigsaw puzzle to one who had never encountered such sartorial complexities.'

In a letter he wrote to Grannie Nettleship a few days after term began, he said:

> I am sure I shall be very glad that you are slow when I come home. It will be a great relief! All the Cadets have just been reviewed by the Commander which happens every Sunday. We have two very short services every day which are called Divisions. And on Sunday we have morning and evening service in a huge hall called 'Nelson' which is made into a Chapel every time. I have a prayer book but I haven't got a proper Bible. There is a very nice canteen where you can't spend too much money. You always wish you were a millionaire there! They give you very good food.

After his first Christmas leave, spent at Wigmore Street, he returned to Osborne in a special train from Waterloo for the start of the second term. 'There was a frightful crush,' he told Ethel. 'I am *very* bored *indeed* to be back and wish it was the end of term again . . . It's lovely, though, *not* being a first termer, and awfully funny to see the new first term helplessly wandering about, although you were just like it once yourself.'

Even though the First World War was in its second year when Caspar joined the Navy, it had hitherto meant little to him. His father had been unfit to serve because of a knee injury suffered while jumping a fence in Ireland – 'My grasshopper days,' he joked in *Chiaroscuro*. But in 1918 he was created an honorary major in the Canadian Army and despatched to the front as a war artist. Caspar may have received news from him, but Augustus was guarded against becoming a war bore, and did not like to elaborate on the theme. Caspar had certainly chosen the Navy because he wanted to fight for his country, but it was a generalized ambition and, aged thirteen, he knew little about the day-to-day progress of the war.

Now, suddenly, it was in the forefront of his daily life and uppermost in his mind. Every cadet followed avidly the exiguous news of the war at sea; the exploits of the more recent Osborne heroes were discussed proudly in every detail. Reminders of the war were omnipresent. Nearby there was a yard where destroyers were being built, and a number of hydroplanes lined up. Shells sent up by anti-aircraft men in practice would burst into small black patches, then grow bigger and lighter until they vanished.

Realistically the cadets knew that it was unlikely the war would go on long enough for them to take an active part in it, but realism was never a prominent part of the average small boy's make-up. Caspar, like all his contemporaries, prayed for the day that he would go to sea and dreamt of the glory that would then be his. On the rare occasions that a naval engagement took place, the cadets cursed the fate that had doomed them to watch from the sidelines. Of Jutland, the thirteen-year-old Caspar wrote that it was a most 'bloodthirsty Battle, but very glorious. I should have given lots to be in one of our ships.' In due course he was, when he served in a veteran of Jutland, the battleship HMS *Iron Duke*, but this was three years after the First World War had ended.

Practical instruction took place on the river – 'we are allowed to go for rows this term but there is no bathing which is horrid,' Caspar told Grannie Nettleship – and in the coppersmith's shop, where the cadets learnt to make moulds and castings: 'awful fun'. Here they were instructed by an ex-naval engine room artificer, who one day delivered a piece of advice to his pupils which was to stick in Caspar's mind for life, and never failed to raise a wry smile when he thought of it: 'You cannot solder without a flux. I've tried, and I can't, so you can't.'

Osborne trimmed the rough edges of his unorthodox up-bringing. But he still had not been to sea when, at the end of that first year, circumstances forced the College to close down. 'It was a horrid term last term,' he wrote to his grandmother. 'Every kind of disease ... measles, pneumonia, chickenpox, German measles, influenza. Six boys died.' Cowes was often designated out of bounds because of the fear of infection, and there was always the worrying possibility that the water would become contaminated. The authorities did their ineffectual best, but disease spread and the cadets were transferred to the Royal Naval College, Dartmouth.

Here, academic studies continued but increasingly were over-taken in their importance by the teaching of Naval Tradition, Custom and Usage, supported by practical seamanship instruction on the River Dart and in the engineering workshops of the College. Caspar continued to write home regularly to the Nettleships, who were always at the ready to help out with the tricky matter of clothing. 'You need not bother about the shoes,' he told Grannie Nettleship, 'because a man from Gieves comes down twice a term and I can order from him.'

Home seemed all the sweeter because it was so different from his life at College. 'Daddy is quite well known here,' he wrote in some surprise. 'Do you think there will be any of his pictures to see when I come to London? Because I should like to very much.' He always looked forward to spending leave in Wigmore Street: 'How I wish it was the end of term again and that we were with you having a nice time!' he told his grandmother. Aunts Ethel and Ursula continued to arrange visits to the theatre, and any Charlie Chaplin film. To them he was something of a hero, but at Alderney, small interest was taken in his activities. If anything, this confirmed him in his conviction that he had taken the right course. 'I was happy to have flown the nest as early as I did,' he wrote long afterwards. 'I gave no heed other than to the affairs of the Navy, and I counted myself lucky to be, or about to be, part of that great service.'

The officers and cadets at Dartmouth College were among the first people in England to hear that peace had been declared on 11 November 1918, having received the news direct by wireless from Portsmouth. 'We did have a fine time,' wrote Caspar. 'We had the feed of our lives at a farm. We had a huge rag in the evening on the quarterdeck, also a concert. Everyone went very mad! and raced about everywhere . . . I have been training like a Spartan lately, running all over the country and playing rugger.'

The peacetime celebrations seem to have underlined questions in Caspar's mind about the quality of life at Dartmouth with its rigid discipline and relentless regime of study, sports and prayer. 'As a matter of fact I don't think I shall stay in the Navy much longer, the life isn't free enough,' he wrote to Grannie Nettleship. 'I shall become an animal trapper or something. I should love to go out to Canada and have a little hut miles from anywhere and trap bears and live on my own produce . . . I'm getting more and more sick of this beastly place every day. I've never wanted to see the last of it so much before.' Perhaps Augustus had talked to his sons about his own boyhood dream of becoming an animal trapper in the wilds of North America. It was a dream he had shared with his brother Thornton. In the 1890s, when Augustus was at the Slade, Thornton left England for Canada, where he travelled through Montana on horseback, lived in a tent among North American Indians and spent the rest of his life prospecting gold. In 1915 he returned briefly to England and visited Alderney Manor. 'Uncle Thornton came down here for a week or so,' Caspar had written to Ethel. 'He has been out in Canada fishing in the Pacific Ocean.' Thornton's descriptions of his outdoor life in the Canadian prairies and mountains so impressed Caspar that the idea of going out there himself remained at the back of his mind for many years, but with the exception of a brief visit during the war, he was not to set foot

47

in Canada until he was a full Admiral and Vice Chief of Naval Staff in 1957.

It would be difficult for anyone to pass through a training as rigorous as that of naval cadet without experiencing moments of doubt and disillusion. Caspar's do not seem to have been frequent or seriously felt – certainly he made no attempt to escape from his chosen career when he finished his time at Dartmouth.

The final term at Dartmouth was not particularly glorious. He passed out successfully but was placed only eighty-third out of a hundred, hardly the level to be expected from a future First Sea Lord. But he had impressed his superiors by his tenacity and determination and embarked on his new life with every likelihood that he would be successful, even if not remarkably so.

In later life Caspar felt no shame over this indifferent result. Indeed sometimes he seemed actually to take pride in it. 'To all of you who find yourselves lowly placed in examinations,' he told the young gentlemen at Dartmouth when he visited them as Vice Chief of Naval Staff, 'I offer you this encouragement. I was, throughout my studies here, conspicuously close to the lowest acceptable standard. But academic standards are not the whole answer to a naval officer's problems, and we do not all develop grey matter at the same rate. This seems very wise of us, and judging by the amount of brass on my arms today I do not seem to have suffered unduly by being slow on the uptake as cadet and midshipman.'

As the next stage of his training Caspar was sent with his fellow cadets to an elderly battleship, HMS *Temeraire*, then used as a cadet training ship. For the first time they came into contact with the sea-going Navy, visiting Irish, Scottish and Scandinavian ports, and on into the Mediterranean, which was soon to become a familiar stamping ground. 'We have been inoculated against typhoid and feel absolutely b. . . .y!' he wrote to Ethel, *en route* to the Spanish port of Vigo that September. 'We did 4″ firing crossing and fairly woke the public school chaps up! They thought their last day had come!' Vigo, he concluded, was a

Ida.

Pencil drawing by Augustus
of Caspar, aged about three.

Caspar, Pyramus and David,
c. 1910. Their childhood was
spent mainly out of doors.

Augustus, *c.* 1910.

First time in cadet's uniform, 1916, photographed by Augustus at Alderney Manor.

stinking Spanish hole, but on the way down he was thrilled by the sight of one or two whales and what he lyrically described as the 'time-honoured porpii gambolling i' the waves.'

The first year at sea ended with more exams, after which the successful cadets were rated midshipmen and dispersed around the Fleet. On 7 February 1921, Caspar arrived at Malta to join the battleship HMS *Centurion*, and to begin life as a midshipman, 'the lowest form of human life' as the Navy considered them. The traditional midshipman's nickname was 'Snotty', so called because the buttons on the sleeves of a midshipman's jacket made it horribly awkward for him to wipe his nose on his sleeve. (The buttons were replaced by one gold stripe on promotion to sub-lieutenant.)

*   *   *

The Near East in 1920 was in even more than its usual state of turmoil. New political problems had arisen as a result of the 1914–18 war, the question of the freedom of the Straits being among the most prominent. The Straits were two narrow stretches of water, the Bosphorus, nineteen miles long, which linked the Caspian Sea and Russia with the Sea of Marmora, and the Dardanelles, nearly fifty miles long, which linked the Marmora with the Aegean Sea and northern Greek Islands. The Sea of Marmora divided the two Turkeys, which in 1920 were split between Europe and Asia. Britain, Russia, Turkey, France, Greece and Italy were all involved: what did the future hold for the peacetime or wartime passage of their ships, now that a new Russia and a new Turkey had emerged?

A second major problem centred on the territorial ambitions of Greece and Turkey in Asia Minor and the need to draw a new boundary between these countries in Europe. Although most of the action occurred on land, the outcome would obviously affect the disposition of the Navy, which was increasingly drawn towards Constantinople. The city was under the military occupation of Britain, France and Italy, who had interests in

49

forming neutral zones bordering the Straits. Chanak, at the entrance to the Dardanelles, was a focal point. The anchorage in the Bosphorus opposite Constantinople, and close by the Sultan's palace of Dolma Bagtché, became international, with US, French, Spanish, Italian and Portuguese ships permanently on duty.

But this was not the Navy's only, or even principal preoccupation. When Caspar arrived off Constantinople in February 1921, the British Navy was under orders to support the White Russians against the Reds, following the 1917 Revolution. 'The whole place is seething with Russian refugees who pour in every day from the Black Sea,' he wrote to Ethel from Constantinople that March, 'and vague rumours float about of Bolshy submarines!' Typhus had spread among the refugees, and many, who had never before experienced any sort of deprivation, were now grateful for a cup of cocoa and a blanket. Geoffrey Norman, a senior contemporary of Caspar's, dining one night at the Pera Palace Hotel in the company of an Army Intelligence Officer, watched as a group of Russians virtually became destitute as they ate.

> The centre table was elaborately laid for a big dinner; a party entered consisting of three or four couples who appeared to be young marrieds, wearing dinner jackets and long dresses, which was quite unknown at the time. At the end of the meal, which appeared to be a very happy one, the bill was presented to the host, who instead of paying in the normal way, handed over such things as his wristwatch, note-case and cigarette case; he then sent the Maitre D. to his wife, who took off her wristwatch and together with her fur, handed them to the Maitre D. who politely bowed, and the party disappeared in quite a happy mood. The Intelligence Officer then told me who they were. He'd been dealing with them as distressed Russians on their way to North Africa, and this was their farewell party to civilization. It was a very gay occasion.

At one time the White Russian Generals Wrangel and Deniken came on board *Centurion*. Caspar had heard their names favourably spoken of as deserving British and French support in what had become known as 'The War of Intervention' to combat the Bolsheviks. He looked with interest on these outlandish visitors; the Bolshies were the enemy, so they must be friends, but they did not look much like it.

Apart from the influx of refugees, Constantinople already teemed with hawkers and beggars; watchmen, firemen, money changers, gatekeepers and priests of Russian, Turkish, Greek and Armenian faiths thronged the streets and everywhere roamed countless stray dogs, scrounging a living in their separate territories.

'Constantinople is a very original place and horribly expensive, of course,' Caspar wrote to Grannie Nettleship. 'Once a week ashore keeps most people thinking of where the next meal will come from! I've been into the town a few times and had a look round the various mosques, etc., including the wonderful Sta Sofia . . . by the time we leave here for Malta I shall be sick of the sight of the minarets which stick out of the town.'

On arrival from Malta, *Centurion* had anchored off Cape Helles at the Aegean entrance to the Dardanelles. Here the midshipmen were let ashore to visit the battlefields on the Gallipoli Peninsula – a shocking reminder of the ill-fated Dardanelles Campaign. The walk across the peninsula was approximately five miles, but it was not until they had covered a mile or so that traces of the fighting became apparent. Trenches, barbed wire entanglements and 6" shells lay everywhere – five years after the battles. Further north, roughly dug trenches were spaced not more than ten yards apart, evidence of how the Australians and New Zealanders had fought for the ground inch by inch. 'Whilst struggling over these remains, I felt like relapsing into tears,' Caspar wrote, 'but marvelled at the orderliness of the graveyards established by the Imperial War Graves Com-

51

mission.' These were still being rearranged and constructed ten years after the last soldier fell in 1915.

The first two months aboard *Centurion* in the eastern Mediterranean were taken up with the usual ship routine and visits ashore. Caspar and his fellow midshipmen were allowed on both banks of the Bosphorus and made the most of the plenty there was to see. Haidar Pasha, once the start of the Baghdad-Berlin Railway in Asia, was a burnt-out shell. Skutari, where the military hospital was located during the Crimean War eighty years before, bore little resemblance to what it must have been like in the time of Florence Nightingale.

It was customary at that time for officers to form shooting parties ashore wherever duck and quail were to be found. 'Shooting parties were landed on the marshes in the afternoon,' Caspar recorded in his midshipman's journal. 'I and some others landed and walked to the top of the hill and found a Greek encampment in an old ruin and discussed politics with one or two soldiers who spoke English.' Midshipmen, who were subordinate to every officer on board, generally did not mix with their seniors, and were not included in shooting and hunting parties. This did not worry him much; the world of shooting and hunting never much attracted Caspar.

*   *   *

On 8 April 1921 Caspar joined the battleship HMS *Iron Duke*, flagship of the Mediterranean Fleet. 'This was a very important event for me,' he wrote. 'For the first time, although we junior midshipmen were referred to as the lowest form of human life on board, I felt ready to give something back after all that training. I was eighteen, and able to start thinking about what the Navy was really like. I had little enough to give, beyond a character completely lacking in class-consciousness. Augustus had said to me, 'Take 'em as you find 'em, high or low, wherever they come from,' so I did, and got on well with officers and ratings . . . My only interest was the Royal Navy and, presumptuously, its betterment. A young, but ardent devotee, though unambitious.'

The Mediterranean Fleet of those days was a formidable gathering of orthodox naval power, commanded by Admiral de Roebeck. It consisted of eight or nine battleships, cruisers, destroyers and submarines, but Caspar bemoaned the fact that there was not an aeroplane in sight to raise naval eyes above the fifteen miles to the visible horizon. And yet aircraft had played an important part in the navy's role in the First World War.

Much of the time was spent at sea, improving all-round efficiency. The Sea of Marmora was used as an area for seamanship and frequent gunnery and torpedo practices. 'This usually consisted of firing any gun you can find, amounting to a bloody awful noise and no result,' Caspar told Ethel.

To his father, Caspar reported that he was having 'an extraordinarily fine and untroubled time in the Service. The C-in-C is a great man. I expect we shall go to lunch with him one day. I see you've become on RA. Bit of a lad I s'pose you are now!' Augustus greeted his election to the Royal Academy with bemused surprise. As a member of the New English Art Club, he viewed the Royal Academy with some disdain, and would never have considered sending a picture to it for exhibition. 'In our select circles it simply wasn't done,' he wrote in *Chiaroscuro*. 'In our eyes the RA was so bad that no self-respecting artist would be seen dead in it: and yet among its more outstanding corpses are to be numbered those of Reynolds, Gainsborough, Hogarth, Lawrence, Turner and Constable.' It was presumably the thought of joining the illustrious dead rather than the less distinguished living that led him to accept the honour.

In April 1921 *Iron Duke* was preparing for a May cruise around the eastern Mediterranean and Aegean. 'I expect we shall have a good time all round,' Caspar wrote to Augustus, for not only was he in the Flagship of the Mediterranean Fleet, but Prince George was on board. 'He's becoming most degenerate and does nothing but look after women all day!' – an exaggerated description of his fellow midshipman, obviously aimed more at his father than at the Prince himself. The future Duke of Kent's presence among some half dozen junior midshipmen, carefully selected for their alertness and ability, created an extra responsibility for the Captain and those in charge of the Gun Room. Prince George was not very fit, but his father insisted that he was to have a normal training without privilege. This was all right while he remained on board, but ashore people could be a thorough nuisance, and eventually he was despatched to the hospital ship to recover and get away from Malta.

The cruise, which was to last six weeks in May and June, included stops at Alexandria, Sollum, Jaffa, Cyprus, Rhodes and other Greek islands, and finally Constantinople. All midshipmen had to keep a journal which was periodically signed by the officer in charge. They provide a record of the daily life of the seagoing midshipmen of the time, and Caspar's is illustrated throughout with minutely detailed, coloured ink maps of the coastlines and islands of the eastern Mediterranean, and diagrams of such things as a mechanical smoke-making apparatus, or a Heath Robinson contraption called a Kelvin's Mark IV Sounding machine.

'The water is extraordinarily clear,' he noted at Sollum on 7 May. 'The cable can be seen lying on the bottom. The place is very deserted; a few tents and huts being the main objects. A small oasis on the shore constitutes the only green in sight. A section of the Camel Corps is posted here. A cricket match was played against the soldiers in the afternoon, which we won.' At Port Said a week later: 'We had to go some way down in order to turn, the harbour being rather crowded. We secured the buoys ahead and astern about thirty yards off the offices of the "Canal Suez". We must have had about two feet of water under us when we finally secured.' There followed a joint wardroom and gun room picnic down the Canal and an At Home on board *Iron Duke* for British and French residents.

By 19 May *Iron Duke* had reached Jaffa, the port of Jerusalem. 'The landing from the ship presents rather a problem, as a formidable reef of rocks (believed to be a fossilized dragon) runs right across the entrance. The ship was open to the Greek, French and Italian communities. The whole of the lower classes turned up and swept all opposition before them in their efforts to get fed.'

On 5 June, they anchored at Famagusta. 'Four snotties went to tea and a car ride up the mountains with the Commissioner. A party of officers climbed up thousands of feet to an old castle called St Hilarien, which seemed to cause great pleasure.' Then, on 7 June, they steamed into Rhodes Harbour, 'a very interesting place. Everyone is whispering, "Where is the Colossus?"'

A day in the *Iron Duke* would begin at 5.15 a.m. Midshipmen slept in canvas hammocks, slung in rows fore and aft in the gun room, which was their headquarters. Clothes and equipment were stowed in a sea chest; ready-use articles such as a scrubbing brush lay on top, with uniform, collar and tie; underneath were cap, sextant, telescope and dirk. After breakfast came a period of study, with subjects such as star-sighting and naval history. 'Colours' – raising the Union Jack and White Ensign flags – was performed every morning at 9 a.m. to the accompaniment of the marine band playing the National Anthem.

'We were chivvied about and run off our feet. We used to turn out at 5.15 every morning, scrub the decks with the seamen, and do some physical jerks. In the morning, snow, ice, rain, howling gale; it didn't matter. The whole day was divided up into set routines, immovable to the minute, irrespective of wind or weather or circumstances. We had to do exactly what we were told, precisely, without thought.'

Sports such as hockey, tugs of war, running races, water polo, rowing and regattas generally occupied the afternoons. Caspar became co-champion at racquets with Peter Reid, a fellow Hawke, who remained a lifelong friend. Jobs such as 'painting ship' could take all day; occasionally an afternoon would be devoted to 'Make and Mend', when midshipmen were expected to do their own laundry, stitching, and letter-writing. Pipedown was at 10 p.m. when the whole ship, apart from the watch-keepers, went to sleep.

A Lieutenant-Commander, designated 'snottie's nurse', kept the midshipmen alert and generally looked after their mental and physical wellbeing. They were never allowed to say 'I don't know' when interrogated by a senior officer. In answer to such questions as how to wash a ship's side, raise a sail, fire off a gun, tow another ship, the snotty had to reply: 'Sir, I will go and find out' and *run*. But if a snotty *did* know the answer, he was considered above his station. He ought *not* to know; the officer wanted to see him turn round and run. They were kept down all the time, subordinate to every officer on board, the lowest of the low. But Caspar at least did not resent such treatment. He had never expected anything else. On the contrary, he considered himself lucky to get to sea as a midshipman with a square white patch on his collar – and that was it.

They were nearly always hungry. Occasionally it was poss-ible to fill the gaps with biscuits and chocolate from the canteen on board, and frequent requests were written home for chocolate powder. Ship's provisions would arrive at intervals: 'Took in flour, potatoes, rice, jam etc.,' Caspar recorded in his journal. 'I had no. 2 hold which was stored with sugar, peas, coffee, tea, jams, pickles, milk, chocolate and various minor articles. It was very difficult to distinguish the piccalilli from the walnuts.'

A midshipman's wine bill was restricted to ten shillings a month and it was considered a serious matter to exceed this. They earned £1.15s per month. Beer, although more expensive than spirits or wine, was much favoured, especially a bottled brew from one of the Maltese island breweries.

The gun room pantry, or galley, was inhabited by hordes of cockroaches which the midshipmen used to smoke out at regular intervals. Ship's biscuit or 'hard tack' was riddled with weevils. A blow with the fist would scatter them and this gave rise to 'weevil racing'. All the big ships at that time were alive with rats. Now and again Caspar and his mates would plan a slaughter –

armed with hockey sticks and a blackboard to block any exit holes. One evening, dressed in the midshipman's evening costume of short jacketed 'bum-freezer' and bow tie, they were enjoying a pre-dinner glass of sherry, when Caspar saw a rat running along the beam above him. 'He caught it,' Harry Smallwood, one of his contemporaries, recalled, 'put down his glass of sherry, wrung its neck, threw it into the waste paper basket and resumed his drink.'

Although *Iron Duke* had been fitted with oil-burning furnaces, she was still principally coal-fired. Coaling was filthy hard work, and happened more than often enough. The process began when a floating pontoon carrying the coal was pulled alongside the ship by tugs. The coal was then dug out of the holds and thrown into bags or baskets before being carried on a man's back up a sloping gangplank, or lifted by derrick up to the ship's deck, and tipped into the ship's bunkers. In this way, hundreds of tons would be taken in within a few hours. 'Proceeded to coal with native labour, taking in 1500 tons,' Caspar recorded in his journal on 14 May at Port Said. 'The natives were goaded on to fresh efforts by their Leading Hands, using the lash. Several snotties did some surf bathing after coaling, which was quite good for us under the circumstances.' He retained unpleasant memories of Port Said, and never looked forward to returning there; though because of its strategic position at the head of the Suez Canal, it was a frequent port of call for ships either operating in the Mediterranean or sailing to and from the Far East.

The rigours of coaling or painting ship alternated with the pomp and formality that dominated the seagoing Navy of those years. The presence of royalty, or important anniversaries such as the storming of the Bastille, American Independence Day or a sovereign's birthday, were celebrated with a 21 gun salute, although a foreign anniversary would only be acknowledged in this way if a ship from the relevant nation was present.

8 March 1921: 'Noon, dressed ship to Queen of Roumania who passed down the Bosphorus in Royal Yacht. Fired 21 guns.'

Formerly an English princess, Queen Marie was the grand-daughter of both Queen Victoria and Tsar Alexander II of Russia, and was linked to the recently overthrown Court of Russia as well as the British and German royal families. She had done valuable work for the Red Cross during the First World War and was loved and admired for her beauty and zest for life. In October she was entertained on board *Iron Duke* at Constanza in the Black Sea. She had arrived by train and, in the company of her two young daughters, was conducted around the *Iron Duke* before lunching with the Admiral. She was accompanied by a Roumanian Admiral sporting a big black bushy beard, 'an impressive sight to our young eyes', and one of Caspar's lasting memories.

Sometimes, formality had a comic aspect, as when the Japanese and British navies exchanged visits at Malta on 22 April 1921. 'Everything is being prepared for the Crown Prince of Japan.' On the 24th the Japanese ships *Katori* and *Kashima* were sighted and entered harbour while the British played what they fondly hoped to be the Japanese national anthem. The Japanese promptly replayed it 'in their own style, which rather put our version in the shade.' Members of the *Iron Duke*'s Gun Room then went over to the *Katori* to pay a call. They were looked after well by their opposite numbers and given beans and green tea. In the afternoon Japanese officers were invited to take part in games of tennis, and in the evening a large State dinner was given by the Governor of San Antonio, as well as a dinner at the club for the lesser lights.

Next day the Japanese Gun Room paid a return call on their British counterparts. They were offered sherry, which seemed new to them. A garden party was held in the afternoon, then the officers were taken in cars around the island, after which two Japanese officers boarded *Iron Duke* to present two bottles of wine. Finally, at eight in the evening, all illuminations were switched on at once, including the Japanese ships. 'It was a fine sight. I and some others took a *dghaisa* [Maltese rowing boat] round the Fleet and listened to the band playing in the *Katori* where the C-in-C was dining. It was a very weird noise and extremely nice to listen to.'

The Japanese next day were given a farewell 21 gun salute. They were bound for England. Caspar did not suspect that the Crown Prince would include in his itinerary a visit to Augustus's studio. The idea was that he should have his portrait painted, but as only an hour was allowed the result was somewhat cursory. Still, Augustus was well paid for his pains and was assured that 'if I went to Japan I would be *persona grata* at the Imperial Court, and that if I took the chair my semi-divine model had sat on, I could sell it for its weight in gold. It was quite a heavy chair.'

* * *

In August 1921, Caspar wrote home:

> Dear Daddy,
> It's hot enough out here, specially when we do a spot of engineering in the boiler rooms. One feels really fruity then, and one's garments rot with the smell of sweat.
> Things seem to be fairly quiet now, as far as we are concerned. We're going to put up some barbed wire defences for the Greeks next week on the shores of the Marmora round Maltepe, to make them think we're on their side, I suppose . . . We're sending Prince George home for Christmas to stuff it at Buckingham [Palace].

For those left behind, Christmas turned out to be 'the usual Xmas that always happens in the Navy, one of the most boring days in the year; in which a general feeling of "nothing to do but die" pervaded.' To make matters worse, they were put into semi-quarantine due to an outbreak of influenza, and the Commander-in-Chief arrived on board, 'received over the gangway by a funny party who played the Admiral's salute on various stringy instruments', followed by 'the usual tramp around the mess decks'.

With the onset of the Turko-Greek war in 1922, interest in the war in Russia waned, and reinforcements including 15″ gun battleships arrived from the Atlantic Fleet. 'Mr Lloyd George came down heavily on the Greek side, and it seemed to us that our Government was, for the second time, backing the wrong horse,' Caspar wrote. Naval officers instinctively backed the Turk, a straightforward fighting man, against the Greeks, whom they considered devious and untrustworthy; in much the same way as British officers in the Indian army preferred the Muslim to the Hindu.

Back in London the Geddes axe was falling. Lord Geddes had been instructed to prune the Services in order to reduce national expenditure, and his axe fell on some of the Navy's best officers. 'One of my best friends in *Iron Duke* got it. Why, I don't know. He's a red-hot fellow all round,' Caspar wrote home in August. This was very dispiriting, added to which the harsh winter was about to descend on them. 'But we seemed resilient enough to take these setbacks in our stride; certainly there was no time to ponder them.' There is nothing in Caspar's letters that survive from this time to indicate that his own career might have been threatened by the cutback in the Navy's strength.

On 5 August 1922 Caspar was transferred to the destroyer *Spear*, to gain experience of life in a small ship. He delighted in this new aspect of naval life. 'It's a very fine show in a destroyer,' he wrote, 'quite different to a big ship. Instead of twelve hundred men, you have ninety, all of whom you get to know inside out, which helps a lot to the general happiness of a ship.'

Meanwhile, the situation on land was becoming strained, with General Harrington's troops assembled in defensive positions against the Turkish troops. After a month based in the Sea of Marmora, *Spear* was ordered 'to raise steam at utmost despatch' and proceed to Smyrna [now Izmir], where the Greeks were being driven by the Turks. 'We're all buzzing around like flies over this Greek affair,' Caspar told Grannie Nettleship. 'We get thoroughly annoyed at the beastly little Greek destroyers who come up to watch our movements.' The idea was that *Spear* should be ready to feed and take on board Greek refugees fleeing the Turkish troops, and to convey them to some peaceful district, if one could be found. Smyrna harbour was crowded with refugees, and war and merchant ships from several nations sympathetic to Greece were waiting for the arrival of the Greek army.

It was not long before stragglers were encamped on the quayside, 'very depressed and haggard,' Caspar noted, 'having fed on rice and lamp-oil for the past three months.' One Greek soldier, completely terrified, jumped into the sea and began to swim off towards HMS *Spear*. 'We rescued him halfway, and brought him on board; he explained that he couldn't stay ashore or the Turks would certainly be at his throat.'

The British population was advised to evacuate. Caspar was sent with a couple of able-bodied seamen to guard the northern depot of the British-owned harbour ferry service and prevent any panic-stricken rush on to the ferry boats. 'I have never been so disgusted at the totally absurd behaviour of some of them,' Caspar told his grandmother. 'They would not be persuaded to clear out, saying it would be all right and they weren't afraid. In our section we got so fed up with them that we left them to their own devices until the last moment, when you should have heard the row they kicked up and the temper and panic they flew into because our boats weren't inshore for them. However we got them off (very unwillingly, almost), and were very glad to get rid of the idiots to the refugee ships. Some people are soft.'

The Greeks escaped in the nick of time. Depressed and frightened, the whole Greek army was successfully evacuated into Greek shipping on the night of 8 September, 'though it looked at one point as if one could walk ashore on the backs of drowned soldiers.' Within minutes of the last Greek soldier passing, mounted Turks began to arrive, lances and flags flying, singing and cheering. By 10 September, the Turks were in possession of the town: 'It was very humorous to see the town flutter out into hundreds of Turkish flags as soon as the Greeks had gone,' Caspar told Grannie Nettleship. On the 11th, *Spear* left harbour, having received orders to proceed to Chanak which was neutral zone; on the 13th fires flared up in the Armenian quarter of Smyrna and within minutes the whole town was ablaze. Scarcely two-fifths of the town remained, and the Armenian population was brutally massacred by the Turks. None of those present seemed to know whether the conflagration was Turkish or Greek inspired.

Chanak was occupied by British troops, under the command of General Harrington. The Navy's movements were now dictated by the Army's plan of defence. 'Here we are stuck. All ready for a whack at a Turk and not allowed to,' Caspar explained in some exasperation to his grandmother. Their main duty was to stand by to help evacuate troops if the situation became critical. In due course they were asked by the Army to go to the help of a detachment on the south shores of the Sea of Marmora. 'We landed men to put up barbed wire defences and kept the coast road under observation by daylight and by searchlight at night.' There followed a ceaseless patrol of the straits and sea around, 'deadly dull', and numerous postings offshore watching the movements of the Turks. 'On land the situation has become ludicrous as Turkish cavalry prance about in front of our trenches and take down the wire at night, which after all is rather absurd . . . they pay no attention to England's foolish threats!' Caspar found the situation very trying, having to be constantly on the alert without ever getting truly involved, added to which the weather was physically exhausting, very hot days alternating with cold nights.

By October, peace at last was at hand, a protocol having been signed at Mudaina by General Harrington and Kemal Pasha agreeing on the main points and leaving the remainder to the coming Peace Conference. But subsequent negotiations seemed interminable and *Spear* remained anchored at Constantinople. Caspar wrote to Grannie Nettleship on 17 November 1922:

A worse place to winter is hardly imaginable. It doesn't really start until January and then until the end of March it's one long snow, wind, rain and general foul weather. It's bad enough here now, having rained and blizzarded for ten days on end and with no sign of it stopping! Which reminds me, you are to knit that scarf with all despatch both long, thick and broad to wind round, down and up my neck 99 times at least!

As for my Xmas present, I should very much like a box of the most exquisite instruments that can be bought . . . Preferably a wooden box not more than 7″ or 9″ long or broad, smaller if possible, containing at least the following:- 2 pencil compasses large and small; 2 ink compasses large and small. Dividers. Ink pen, etc., etc. . . .

The kettle is going most wonderfully, and has put heat into many a cold body! You got the very best type owing to its being able to work on two voltages. I could use it in destroyers as well as here. Most wonderful foresight on your part!

Let me have your views on the election and who you voted for. Lloyd George I hope.

In his surviving letters, this is the only evidence that he took any interest in British politics, or supported any party. *Prima facie* it is surprising that he should have supported this somewhat maverick figure against the staider Conservative, Bonar Law, even though Lloyd George was now remembered as the great war leader rather than the radical Chancellor of the Exchequer who had baited the rich. Possibly Caspar was influenced by the fact that his father had painted Lloyd George. In all events his support proved valueless; Lloyd George and the Liberals were roundly defeated in the election of October 1922.

The date of this letter is significant; his journal entry that day reads: 'Meanwhile, the Sultan, fearing the dangers of Constantinople, decided to leave and applied to Britain for protection, which was afforded him, and he was embarked in the *Malaya*, having been guarded by Lt-Commander Dickenson and an armed guard down to the boat. *Malaya* sailed for Malta.' This puts it rather simply. In fact the British Army and Navy had had to devise a Buchan-like plan to allow Mehmed VI, Vahid ed Din, Caliph of the Mussulmans, to flee his palace, leaving Constantinople without a Sultan for the first time since the fifteenth century and bringing to an end the House of Osman, once the most powerful dynasty in the world. In pouring rain, he left the palace under an umbrella and climbed into the back of an army ambulance to be conveyed down to the waterfront. On the way, they had a puncture, which cannot have done much to calm the nerves of those who had planned his secret escape; but once safely aboard the C-in-C's launch, the Sultan found himself in the company of General Harrington. 'I perhaps hoped that he might give me his cigarette case as a souvenir,' David Walder quotes Harrington as recalling in his detailed account, *The Chanak Affair*, 'instead he suddenly confided to me the care of his five wives!'

In April 1923 *Iron Duke* was back in Malta for a refit and a welcome relief from a near warlike routine, 'not to mention the sight and smells of Constantinople,' as Caspar commented. In the meantime the Navy had begun work on two new battleships. 'They are a funny design,' Caspar told Grannie Nettleship, 'as they have to be very powerful from the gunnery point of view and at the same time very light [in accordance with the Washington Conference which limited the tonnage of warships]. One reads a great deal about the Americans and Japanese etc., building wonderful new up-to-date fast ships and aeroplanes, but it's no good doing that unless they've got good men to put in them to fight. An American sailor rarely does more than three or four years' service. He only joins in order to go abroad.'

Caspar had grown fond of Malta, 'an extraordinarily nice place to get back to, after a long time away'; and although the weather had become hot and muggy, making everyone feel dismal, sporting events, visits to the opera and a variety of other entertainments kept their spirits up. 'I've been to the opera quite a lot. They do some quite good ones – *Madame Butterfly*, *Faust*, *Rigoletto* . . . One thing I've never seen and that is a Gilbert and Sullivan, a great error.' Opera, theatre and film never played an important part in his life, but he loved classical music. When, later, he became a Captain, he kept a number of 78 records with a wind-up gramophone in his cabin; still later, he became devoted to the music of Monteverdi, and would spend whole evenings listening to it. Visits to the cinema were rare; of the few films he did see, *The Third Man* was the one he always referred to as having enthralled him. Eventually he refused to go at all. 'There is enough drama in life without the moving pictures,' he'd say.

3

Aviator

It was at this time, the end of 1922, that rumours started about the future of the Fleet Air Arm, successor to the Royal Naval Air Service after the formation of the Royal Air Force on 1 April 1918. It was suggested that the Navy should regain control of its own air arm and eradicate what seemed to Caspar the folly of dual control between the Admiralty and Air Ministry. It was to take some fifteen years before this was actually done, but for the moment it was enough for Caspar that the subject was even being debated. 'To be honest, I was a bit fed up with the Pomp and Circumstance of battleship life,' Caspar wrote. Priority was given to surface gunnery and underwater weapons, and it seemed to him that the Navy was neglecting the air. Yet this was a medium in which he felt sure it was destined to do much of its fighting. The First World War had established the aircraft as an important element of the Fleet, yet now the experience had been forgotten. In spite of its worldwide deployment, the Royal Navy seemed to Caspar to be blinkered, professionally introvert.

'I was the angry young man of the day,' he wrote many years later. 'I made up my mind that the enormous battleships which cluttered up the Navy were outmoded and outdated; but it was very hard to escape the great naval traditions that were upheld and thought wonderful, and the battleship lingered on as a naval tradition far beyond its time.' What Caspar envisaged was a built-in organic air power for the Navy as a substitute for the enormous vessels for which he could see little use. He was not a great promoter of tradition for tradition's sake, and would question whether the fact that something had been done in a certain way for fifty or a hundred years necessarily proved that it should be continued. Indeed, he was inclined to think that it was evidence that it should be stopped at once, a heretical point of view which earned him bad marks among the more conservative members of the naval establishment.

But in 1922 there was no way in which his voice could be heard. He was left to nourish his doubts in solitude. 'I was put in my place as a cog in the great battleship's wheel,' Caspar summed it up. 'A reasonably competent youngster, who should keep both feet on deck and not question the future with thoughts about what the air above us might have in store.'

*   *   *

'I'm trying to ram a little knowledge into my head for the coming exam in May,' he told Grannie Nettleship in April 1923, 'which will decide whether we get a stripe on our arm or not!' The examination would include such diverse subjects as Navigation, Engineering, Torpedo and Gunnery, and a jigsaw puzzle of practical seamanship comprising such things as knots and splices, and sextant sights of sun, moon and stars. The sextant was a most important instrument; every midshipman had to have one, and prior to 1924 they were not provided by the Navy. Caspar therefore had to go to his father:

'Dad, I need a sextant.'

'What the devil's a sextant?' Caspar explained that it was an instrument for measuring the angle from the visible horizon of the sun, moon, planets and stars. 'And who the devil wants to know that?'

'Seafarers do, to reckon their position,' said Caspar.

'Oh, a pity Columbus didn't have one, or he might have steered a different course!'

In spite of these somewhat unhelpful comments, Caspar got his sextant. It was an expensive instrument, but Augustus was never mean, and was always ready to give financial help to others with the same insouciance as he demanded it himself.

Having gained all the qualifying certificates, Caspar was made an acting Sub-Lieutenant. He was now due for some leave and was told to make his own way home from Malta. He did this using the ferry boats to Syracuse and across the English Channel, travelling through Italy and France by train. He returned to Alderney Manor, which had not changed much. 'I was treated as though from another world, not far wrong.' He proudly put on his new Sub-Lieutenant's uniform and received a reasonably favourable reaction from Augustus, who at once started a full-length oil portrait. When later it was finished, the canvas was leant against a tree in the garden to dry in the sun. Ruth, a large black Berkshire sow, out foraging, got wind of this, and was so attracted by the smell of wet oil paint that she rubbed her snout up and down the canvas. 'The result might have had some surrealistic value,' Caspar commented, 'but this was not Augustus's line, so I returned to the Navy artistically unrecorded for the moment.'

Caspar was now faced with the prospect of four three-month courses, each with an exam, before he could qualify for the next step in the ladder, the rank of Lieutenant. These took place at shore establishments in Portsmouth, followed by a spell at the Royal Naval College, Greenwich. These courses were comprehensive and required a great deal of application of mind to reach the required standards. The knowledge they imparted followed directly from what the officers had learnt at sea, though at a considerably higher level. To gain a certificate in Pilotage – navigation in dangerous waters – for example, they were examined on some dozen related subjects, including: Magnetic Compass and Terrestrial Magnetism; Astronomical Navigation; Chronometer Work; Meteorology; Winds and Currents;

Surveying; Tides; Ship and Fleet work; General Navigation and Pilotage.

In the Gunnery Course they had to decipher ballistic formulae, fire a rifle or revolver accurately, dismantle and reform a 4″ gun breech mechanism, learn to operate a range-finder and, somewhat irrelevantly, learn how to create an orderly parade from a shambles of young seamen.

At the Torpedo School they were required to understand the intricacies of a warship's electrical system, as well as the motive power of a torpedo, with a detailed grasp of how to defuse a variety of mines.

Almost everything, it seemed, was covered – except the role of the aircraft in naval warfare. Caspar did well, winning First Class certificates in Gunnery and at the Torpedo School. But his pleasure in his achievement was dampened when he was lined up to be congratulated by Matthew Best, the Captain at the Gunnery School. Captain Best surveyed the successful candidates. 'Well done,' he said. 'By the way, are any of you young officers *not* intending to specialize in Gunnery?'

'Foolishly I took a step forward,' Caspar recalled. 'The Captain halted in his stride, and said, "I will see that young man later." I was led into his office to confess my crime of preferring aeroplanes to big guns. My written request to be trained as an aircraft pilot was handed to the Captain. He read it quickly, shuddered and tore it into little pieces, muttering, "another soul saved" . . . A fair reflection of the attitude of the Navy of those days.'

At that time, indeed until comparatively recently, an officer had little hope of getting anywhere near the top of the naval hierarchy unless he had specialized in Gunnery. Caspar had passed that subject with ease and so could reasonably hope to have his path clear before him. Instead he chose to reject the easy and traditional way. The air, as an element to explore and conquer, had caught his imagination and nothing less would satisfy him. If it meant that his career prospects were blighted, then so be it. If the worst came to the worst there was a world outside the Royal Navy. He remembered Jackie Fisher's advice to 'look forward', and he therefore always looked towards the future. It was to the world of naval aviation, merely ten years old and still struggling for an identity, that he turned his attention.

Caspar once referred to the Fleet Air Arm as 'an awkward child for which no legal birth certificate exists'. The Royal Naval Air Service had been formed in 1914 but had been amalgamated with the Royal Flying Corps on 1 April 1918 to form the Royal Air Force. The Navy surrendered its expertise in aeronautical matters, and it was not until 1924 that naval flying was restored, with the opening of the first Naval Officers' Flying Course at Netheravon on Salisbury Plain. Even then the course was run by the RAF, and from 1924 until the day of liberation in 1937 the Fleet Air Arm was, strictly speaking, only a specialized section of the Royal Air Force.

It was still to be some time before Caspar could defeat the opposition of men like Captain Best and achieve his ambition. Released from the confines of Portsmouth, he now joined the Royal Naval College, Greenwich, for the last of the courses to qualify as a Lieutenant. 'Here, we were encouraged to attempt to become broadminded citizens, a tall order in view of our intensive Naval upbringing.' The course covered a wide sweep of subjects including English, French, non-Naval History, and Applied Mathematics, Physics and Chemistry.

He took his exams on crutches. In a game of rugger he had broken an ankle tackling the captain of the English rugger team, W. J. A. Davis. 'Here I lie in mute patience,' he wrote to Grannie Nettleship. 'The surgeon's knife glints in the half-darkness of my nightmares; brightly polished, it flickers 'cross my weary eyes; wringing from me eerie gasps of anticipatory terror. I see it cut, the blood pours out (it is an artery because the blood comes in jerks); and did I budge? Yes, I fetched him one under the left lug and well nigh flaked him out.

'These are the ravings of a tortured soul . . . Thank you so much for the ginger nuts.'

The English paper allowed two hours for an essay on a variety of subjects, ranging from the battleship of the future to London's public monuments, or from Vulgar Errors to the possibility of making emigration attractive. Caspar chose to write on chivalry and presumably knew his subject; at all events he emerged from the Royal Naval College with his promotion to Lieutenant safely assured.

'I had hoped that either at Portsmouth or Greenwich I should have heard something about the Air as friend or foe,' Caspar wrote long afterwards, 'but not a word, though I now had a second chance to apply to be trained to fly as a pilot in the Fleet Air Arm, and thanks to a more broadminded Captain, I was accepted.'

As a first step he was sent to gain some practical experience in an aircraft carrier, and in December 1924, he returned to Malta to join HMS *Hermes*. In the past there had been ships from which aircraft could be launched, but these, like *Furious* and *Argus*, had been converted from other purposes. *Hermes* was the first ship built by the Royal Navy specifically to carry aircraft. It was the ship which Caspar would most have wished to join.

'I hope to be up in London after Christmas,' he wrote to Grannie Nettleship, 'before I finally depart for the Mediterranean, whither I am bound once more to take up my onerous and underpaid duties in the goode shippe *Hermes* – a carrier of airplanes, seaplanes and the like – there to sojourn for about one year prior to my becoming an intrepid birdman.'

Though he was not actively involved with the flying side of the ship, he spent the next eight months learning all about it, and in August 1925, two weeks before his promotion to Lieutenant, he joined the fourth naval flying course at No. 1 Flying Training School, Netheravon. There were at any one time about two dozen young naval sub-lieutenants and lieutenants learning to fly, the upper age limit for the start of naval flying training being twenty-eight (today it is twenty-six).

The aircraft in which they trained were of First World War vintage: the Sopwith Snipe, which had a Bentley rotary engine; the de Havilland 9A, a light bomber; and the Avro 504K, in which the whole engine went round, lubricated with castor oil. Fifty hours solo on each, without accident, qualified the young officers for their wings.

'When I look back to 1925 when *Hermes* started her second commission,' a fellow pilot wrote to Caspar many years later, 'I have the greatest admiration for all those embryo pilots and observers. When we started flying training in the Mediterranean, the casualties were such that one often wondered at breakfast who among the gallant few would be missing a few hours later at dinner.' The demanding nature of the work was recognized by a 'flying duties' allowance' of six shillings a day. The reward may hardly seem princely, but when one remembers that a naval lieutenant in 1925 earned only seventeen shillings a day, the allowance in proportion seems almost generous.

In 1925 pilots were flying machines which were unable to rise above ten thousand feet, and they were usually flying far lower. This meant that they were always 'in weather' – not for them the ability to climb above turbulence as a later generation was able to do. All the aircraft of the late 1920s had open cockpits, and although wireless transmission was in use by then, only the most rudimentary instruments were available to them. The pilot was on his own; his survival depended on his judgement, a good deal of luck, and the 'feel' he had for his machine.

'What were the flying machines – not aircraft – like then?' Caspar wrote in an article twenty-five years later, in which he reflects mischievously on the advantages and disadvantages of the machines' limitations. 'To start with *all* of them had four wings – two each side. Unquestionably a great advantage over modern practice from the pilot's point of view.' Certain types of engine were, from time to time, 'boiled in water – plain water, not coolant', and others kept just below melting point by a natural, rather than a scientific application of air; there were no cowlings or fans.

'Another important feature was that the human content of the flying machine was exposed to the four winds of heaven – notwithstanding that in a flying machine, airborne, there is normally only one wind. This feature was highly prized after a wardroom guest night or some ship's company dances I have known. Full use was made of the valuable cooling properties of free air.' There were no parachutes, so there was no future in baling out, nor were there any dinghies, 'a good thing because without them it was definitely held to be a bad thing to alight in the drink'. This helped to ensure that most pilots returned to the correct flat-iron or aerodrome, although 'this coincidence was less frequent at night'. The absence of wheel brakes was no bad thing since it denied the pilot the means of 'standing his bird on its beak'.

The flying machine of the mid-1920s was popular for its versatility: 'It was only a matter of a few hours to exchange wheels for floats or vice versa. This was an important asset for use in mystifying the higher officials who could never be sure from hour to hour what species of machine they were expected to deal with.' Before radio transmission arrived, there was only 'Da-Di-Da, so there was no need for Air Traffic Control because the Da-Di-Da blokes in the back seats, known as the "TAGs" or "lookers", were not in the habit of telling the pilot anyway.'

Caspar's 1926 Flying Course notebook is filled with simple diagrams and explanations of the internal workings of the machine and such things as R/T procedure, aerial photography and meteorology. Here, under 'Special Phenomena', are listed 'line squalls' – described as lasting only a few minutes 'but are extremely violent, always travel from E – W' – and the three main classes of thunderstorms; a reminder of what the pilot of the 1920s might be up against. 'Reconnaissance' and 'Fleet Spotting' were central to the naval fliers' course. In those days the aircraft might sometimes be referred to simply as flying petrol tanks, but naval aircraft were indeed 'the eyes of the Fleet'.

All the maintenance at Netheravon was carried out by RAF personnel and 'messing' had its own special rules: sergeants messed together and had their own food. Corporals also messed together but ate the same food as airmen. An airman's diet is carefully considered in Caspar's notebook: 'Bacon is a most important article of food and an airman should have at least 12 oz a week . . . Plenty of suet pudding in winter.' The RAF ensured that their personnel afloat got the same rations as the RAF Air Stations ashore.

At the end of the course, 'No less a man than Marshal of the Royal Air Force, Lord Trenchard presented us with our wings,' Caspar remembered. 'Famous protagonist of Air Power and its alleged indivisibility he had a severe distaste for the threat that we naval pilots represented to the RAF's grip on the air. Having presented us with our wings, he addressed us as follows: "I congratulate you on becoming air pilots. I congratulate you on your wings, but I'm damned if I understand the colour of your uniform." We took this good humouredly and continued to absorb much of the RAF's way of life and made many friends in that fine service. To underline the union at our level, we were given dual rank. I became a Lieutenant RN (Flying Officer, RAF).' Until 1937, when dual control of the FAA was ended, all their pilots continued to be given the equivalent RAF rank, which was tagged on in brackets after their names. 'From personal experience, to belong to two Services at once is to mystify both – and in the doing of it one can have the whale of a time,' Caspar once told an audience of RAF officers. For him, this period was to last for eleven years.

From April to December 1926, Caspar was based at the RAF station Leuchars, in Fife, 'a most salubrious spot, the sea a matter of some three miles away and some of the finest Scotch scenery about forty or fifty miles inland,' he wrote to Ethel. 'I play a great deal of the Royal and Ancient Scottish pastime of

Golf at St Andrews' courses. I have not yet fallen into the golf groove!'

His arrival at Leuchars coincided with the General Strike. He told his aunt that he viewed this development with disapproval; whether on political grounds or because of the inconvenience it caused him is unclear. 'Up here we were not really very much affected,' he told her. 'It merely meant flying morning, noon and night with mails and other necessities to various out of the way Scottish towns. We used to have to fly down to Newcastle and pick up mails brought up from London by other aeroplanes. I drove a lorry for about three days full of all types of food to Glasgow!'

At Leuchars Caspar was introduced to the new Fairey IIID reconnaissance plane 'which takes all my powers to control in a safe and orderly fashion, and can be flown either on land or as a seaplane by changing the undercarriage,' he told Ethel. The 450 HP Napier Lion engine made it possible to fly at speeds of up to 120 miles per hour. In freezing weather Caspar flew miles out over the North Sea and across the Scottish Highlands, testing the endurance of the little aeroplane. 'I shall shortly become a second Alan Cobham,' he told Ethel. Cobham was the current hero of the aeronautical world, Britain's finest cross-country pilot and an expert in aerial photography. It was in 1926 that he had made a record-breaking flight from England to Melbourne and back. Caspar could hardly hope to rival his exploits. After performing for the Dominion Premiers gathering at Portsmouth, he flew back solo to Scotland but found it sometimes very hard to navigate, especially between Portsmouth and London, where instead of being able to follow roads and railways, he was continually crossing them. Even so, with one stop for petrol and oil, the flight only took six hours.

His first serious flying mishap occurred not at sea, but when he was flying over the Scottish countryside. The engine suddenly seized at 2000 feet, and he had to force land into a field of summer wheat. The farmer who owned the field happened to witness the accident: he saw the machine fly very low, then reappear from behind some trees with its tail whirling over in the air. Then the nose caught the ground and the aircraft somersaulted through the wheat. Having rushed to the scene, the farmer was amazed to find the pilot standing on his feet beside the upside-down aeroplane, quite unharmed.

Caspar was conducted back to a nearby house where the owner's wife wondered whether it would be the proper thing to offer him a whisky and soda in the hope that it would calm his nerves. Caspar kept saying, 'How awful, £2000 gone west!'

'I don't think you should worry about that,' said his hostess. 'Think how overjoyed your father and mother will be to know you are safe and well.' Some snapshots record the scene: a bashful naval pilot stands among the broken wheat, his aeroplane wheels pointing skywards behind him.

With a little time to spare following a two-day seaplane course – 'the finest sport – you can just alight anywhere you feel when in need of a rest!' – Caspar dashed up to London to see Augustus's current exhibition at the New Chenil Galleries in the summer of 1926. This was a joint show with Caspar's aunt, Gwen.

Forty-four oil paintings and watercolours, with four albums of drawings, were exhibited by Gwen in a separate room. It was at this show that her 'Dorelia in a Black Dress' (painted in Toulouse in the year Caspar was born) was acquired by the Duveen Fund and later presented to the Tate Gallery. Gwen's work never appealed to Caspar, her colours too much on the dull side for his taste: he preferred his father's more dashing style. Included in his exhibition were paintings from a recent stay in Ischia and some Provençal landscapes, his first flower paintings and the faces of Eve Balfour, Rowley Smart, Sean O'Casey, Roy Campbell and Princess Bibesco; thirty-five figure drawings were hung separately. Caspar came to love his father's line drawings – gracefulness always appealed to him – and the portraits interested him as much for their subjects as for their technique. But he had reservations about the so-called society portraits, and later told his father that he thought he was pot-boiling. 'I may well have been right,' Caspar remarked, 'but I was certainly very wrong to say so. There was a loud – near atomic – explosion, and I was excommunicated for several months.'

He met several of the most celebrated sitters and once or twice he was present in the studio while a portrait was being painted.

He almost always painted alone with the sitter; very seldom I think were outsiders allowed into the studio. There was one personal exception when, in about 1937, he was painting one of his portraits of the Welsh poet, Dylan Thomas, at Fryern Court. I was commissioned to keep Dylan supplied with beer. This meant access to the front of the picture, and from a suitable position to watch Dylan's glass. But I was dazzled by the intense concentration of the painter, not only on the general position of the sitter, but on the precise poise of the head and look on the face. Background and light also took their share of critical appraisal.

Once happy with all this Augustus would take up his palette and brushes and squeeze out the colours he wanted. There followed a concentrated look from his piercing eyes, with minor adjustments to the sitter with the paintbrush stem. The time was now ripe for a pipe of tobacco. There followed a quick outline in a weak neutral colour of the general contours of the sitter . . . a deep sigh . . . and the first application of colour. He would not normally require another sitting unless very reluctant to allow what he regarded an indifferent work to see the light of day.

During the war, when Augustus was painting Field Marshal Montgomery in London, Caspar had a different role to play. Monty so disliked the painter that it was discreetly arranged for Caspar, by now a Captain, and George Bernard Shaw to be present to ease the atmosphere.

*   *   *

At the end of the first year of intensive flying training, Caspar faced the greatest challenge: to master the art of landing on the deck of an aircraft carrier. This he did in the Firth of Forth, on one of the earliest converted aircraft carriers, HMS *Furious*. She had been completed in 1916 as a cruiser, converted the following year to carry thirty-two planes, and was known as the hardest worked ship in the Fleet.

When Caspar made his first deck landings, not a single facility existed on the ship's deck – or on the aeroplane – to aid the notoriously difficult and frightening process of 'landing on'. There were neither arrester wires nor crash barriers, no angled deck or mirror landing sight on the carrier, and no hook, wheelbrakes or tricycle undercarriage on the aircraft. There was nothing, save the wind, an empty deck and the skill of the pilot. 'Those men who pioneered deck landing had to *feel* their way back down on to the carrier,' Caspar wrote, 'added to which the aircraft we were flying were out of date and weren't designed for the accuracy needed for deck landing.'

The pilot had to be especially accurate in terms of forward speed; having to land slowly was always dangerous because one could stall, and if that happened one would spin in to the sea, from which there was no recovery at 500 feet. The difficulty was that the deck pilot had to land on a surface that was nearly always rising and falling. The really good pilot learnt to judge the pitch of the deck so that he came in over the round down (stern end of the flight deck) as it was ascending, otherwise he would have to overshoot for another circuit, and that required a split-second decision. In rough weather, the deck could 'scend' fifty or sixty feet, and in such conditions flying would only take place in an emergency. 'One had to have a very fine sense of balance and timing to make a good deck-lander, and like a pianist who suddenly discovers he can play the notes, or a jockey and his horse who can win the Grand National, the technique came to me, and I clung to it. I was confident that whatever I did was right and I felt master of my own destiny.'

After completing half a dozen successful deck landings in a Blackburn Dart, Caspar and his fellow aviators were considered ready to be sent to operational aircraft carriers. At the end of 1926, which was also the end of eighteen months of flying training, he was told to stand by to go to China.

4

China

Augustus threw an all-night party at Gennaro's to celebrate, or at least mark, Caspar's departure for the China Station. It was not known how long he would be away; the situation in China in 1927 was anything but predictable. First he had to rejoin the carrier *Hermes*, already stationed off the China coast, and to reach her he had to chase her out in a P & O liner, SS *Kashgar*.

The sea journey, which began that December, lasted six weeks. 'We have reached half-way between Aden and Ceylon,' Caspar reported to Ethel on 5 January 1927. 'The North-East monsoon is blowing a hot, sticky and wet wind, which keeps one in a perpetually damp condition . . . The first day or two everyone was somewhat stuffy and dreary – very "English Railway Carriagey". However, I soon got to know one or two of the brighter members – some excellent creatures with whom to converse and exercise. There are about ten nurses on board who are going out to the hospitals at Singapore, Hong Kong and Shanghai – they constitute the youth and beauty of the ship.' Life on board was soon reduced to a ceaseless effort to counter boredom with little to do but read, eat and sleep. 'We have managed to brighten things up the last few days by organizing deck sports in which all and sundry compete with great joviality,' Caspar reported. 'I established myself completely undefeated in a pillow fight – in which two persons sit facing each other astride a horizontal bar

Sub-Lieutenant, aged twenty-one, on the Gunnery Course, Whale Island.

The mechanisms on the wheel axle were designed for aircraft carrier wires, not for cornfields! Caspar's first crash, Scotland, 1926.

Heat and damp. China, 1927-9.

Dodo and Vivien in the pond garden, Fryern Court, mid-1930s.

Mary.

Member of the Government
Air Mission to USA, 1938.
Strolling on the deck of
the *Queen Mary* with James
(later Lord) Weir.

across a canvas bath, and endeavour to knock each other off the bar into the water. For some reason I was immovable and was able to deal my opponents the shrewdest of blows.'

At Port Said the ship stopped for four hours to coal; it was 'a horrible hole', Caspar told Ethel, retaining memories of the lash used in the days of coaling the *Iron Duke*. In the Suez Canal they claimed priority as a mail boat, and were given the right of way; after only twelve hours they had entered the Red Sea. 'The coasts of Arabia and Africa were most impressive, though very forbidding mountains and desert, and just before turning the corner for Aden, the days were *decidedly* hot. We arrived at Aden on New Year's Day. A most extraordinary spot – rather like Gibraltar externally – a great rock sticking out into the sea. Hardly a speck of greenery – just a mass of Arabs and camels all mixed up together in sand and dust and a very dry heat. Again we only remained four hours to coal and then sailed for Colombo and Ceylon – and are still doing so. We should get to Shanghai where I expect to find the *Hermes* about 30 Jan which I am afraid feels a very long way off. The China news, which we receive by wireless, appears to grow worse daily – though I daresay it's misleading.'

*   *   *

The warlord period in China was nearing its end. Hundreds of warlords – ex-bandits, generals, Confucian scholars – had held power over certain territories since 1916, their competitive regimes exacerbating the troubles that were already rampant around and inside China; pirates at sea, riots ashore and fighting armies. Caspar's arrival in China coincided with the establishment of the First Nationalist Government by Chiang Kai-shek in April 1927, signalling the end of warlord rule but sparking a decade of warring between the Communists and the Nationalist armies and the Kuomintang.

In the spring of 1927, Chiang Kai-shek's armies threw the Communists out of Shanghai, who then set up their new headquarters six hundred miles inland up the Yang-tse River at

Hankow, a city already crowded with foreigners engaged in trade with China. The British and other foreign residents in Hankow and Shanghai – where the port was under British administration – found themselves living in a frightening environment where murder, looting and mass beheadings occurred almost daily.

Caspar did not know what form his Eastern activities were to take. The Navy was there principally to protect the interests of the British population and to do what it could to prevent any major blood-letting. There was a strong anti-British feeling among the Chinese, and the Navy's presence was regarded with suspicion. The British Government, fully aware of this, ordered the ships to remain at a tactful distance and to respect Chinese sensibilities. *Hermes* did not get involved in any fighting during the time that Caspar served in her, and for her first eight months on the China Station she remained stuck at Hong Kong. Here the chief enemy was boredom, in a situation where they were not even standing by, but only standing by to stand by. 'Hong Kong is a model of what a peaceful colony should be,' Caspar wrote to Ethel in March 1927. 'They refuse to send us away from here. If we appear in the Yang-tse, Mr McDonald will have forty fits and say that we are bullying the Chinese.' Any action that might involve the Navy was likely to occur in and around Shanghai, the Headquarters of the international settlements, or inland at Hankow, where there was constant unrest. 'The people who came out last with the troops were given the best jobs up at Shanghai and Hankow, which annoyed us quite a lot.'

*   *   *

There were altogether fifteen pilots in *Hermes*, ten RN and five RAF. In those days the whole ship, apart from the purely naval side, was run by the RAF. The naval pilots wanted to make the relationship work, so they conformed to the administration, which was in the hands of a Wing Commander, supported by a Squadron Leader who ran the flight deck – all in RAF uniform. But the influx of naval pilots was beginning to show until, after a year, there were 70 per cent FAA pilots and 30 per cent RAF. Some of the latter did not appreciate the FAA, but those who did said: 'This is a damn sight better than the RAF!' Caspar's description of the FAA at that time explains why: 'It was a more amicable, happy-go-lucky show, than the more strictly disciplined RAF.'

While *Hermes* remained in the south, she was under instructions to keep an eye on the activities of the Cantonese Bolsheviks and to look out for pirates in Bias Bay, north of Hong Kong, an activity the British Navy had been engaged in since the early 1800s. The main purpose was to intercept opium running.

'We had a little entertainment at Bias Bay the other day,' Caspar recorded. 'I discovered and reported a Chinese army straggling towards a burning village, whereat our men beat a hasty retreat to their ships in case they should make a war! I also discovered and photographed what I think was a "Robber's Retreat" or "Pirate's Lair".'

Caspar was determined to do as much flying as possible. He and his fellow pilots used as a landing ground a small piece of reclaimed land on the Kowloon side of Hong Kong – Kai Tak airfield – which today is the international airport, and here they would sometimes stay, sleeping in mat sheds made out of broad palm leaves.

Caspar was on a routine flight one day in a Fairey IIIF when suddenly the entire structure of the aeroplane started to vibrate. 'My passenger tapped me on the shoulder and said down the voice tube, "Your tail is falling off!" The actions of the elevator and rudder became spasmodic, confusing my control, and I was faced with two alternatives: to ditch in Hong Kong harbour, or risk a lame flight over the heavily populated Kowloon area. I chose the latter, and fluttered back to Kai Tak using only ailerons and tail trimmer. On landing, an examination showed that all four longerons – the main structure of the fuselage – had fractured towards the tail. We were lucky to be alive.' Caspar's action was considered by his peers to be a remarkable piece of piloting, which saved the lives of three people and is still remembered today by those who witnessed it.

Sports continued to occupy the afternoons, which helped to alleviate the boredom: a few games of golf at Fanling, until it was turned into an army camp; a great deal of sailing, using the facilities of the yacht club; hockey and tennis – but no rugger, at least while the ground remained rock hard prior to the rainy season.

'I have only seen the sun twice,' Caspar wrote in March to a girlfriend, Victoria, sister of his friend Peter Reid, 'both times when I was flying above the clouds. A thick and solid cloud hangs over the place at about a thousand feet day and night ... sometimes the S.W. monsoon blows for a day, in which case we are all temporarily suffocated.' By April the rains had gathered force: 'I have never seen such rain – it is quite unbelievable, accompanied by the most terrific thunder and lightning. They are the only things which cool the air.' By May the ship had become almost uninhabitable, due to the 'foully muggy' heat, and was having extra large fans installed.

The climate was impossible; nor was Caspar enamoured of the food – 'one of the wonders of the world', he bemoaned in a letter to an old schoolfriend. 'Some of the foulest and filthiest muck I have ever seen, and most of it gangrene! They carry small morsels of "guts" from the market tied up in nothing but a piece of string. A fish is not considered in order for consumption until the smell it emits ranks with the most nauseating of stinks in the world. I went to a Chinese tavern, rather a high-class one, and took the precaution of filling myself up with sausages before going so that I was hardly hungry when it came to probing about in a dish for the least repulsive-looking piece of food.' He was soon reduced to a wraith, 'a mere shadow' he reported to Grannie Nettleship.

By far the most exciting event for Caspar in China that year was his meeting with Peter Reid. They met by the barest of margins, when Peter descended from Shanghai just in time to catch Caspar before he went away, and they sat up until 4 a.m. talking: 'It was magnificent to see him and cheered me more than anything else,' Caspar told Ethel. Aunt Ursula turned up in March in the P & O liner SS *Devanka*. 'What am I to do with her?' Caspar demanded in alarm. 'She'll be like a great tigress, filled with an energy surpassing everything. Just think of the way she'll be making *plans*, and getting everything absolutely to time (except herself!). I shall have to take her to the top of Tam O Shan to start off with, and then walk her round the island.'

On the P & O voyage between Singapore and Hong Kong, Caspar had sent an urgent request to Ethel to try and obtain a long list of books. He had evidently been in conversation with a fellow passenger, Arthur Ransome, who was also on his way to China: his little book *The Chinese Puzzle* was published ten months later. Ransome had recently returned from Russia where he had been correspondent for the Manchester *Guardian*, and Caspar's list was headed by five of his books, including *The Crisis in Russia* and *Six Weeks in Russia*. Other authors on the list were T. F. Powys, Ronald Firbank, Gissing, Dostoyevsky (specifying that he wanted *The Possessed* in French), Gogol, Gorky, Jack London and, significantly, H. G. Wells – whose predictions of aerial warfare fascinated Caspar.

It was planned that *Hermes* would return home in October to refit, leaving part of her crew behind, including Caspar. 'We shall be put ashore here while she is away, so I am afraid we shall not see England the Beautiful (and cool) for some two years,' he wrote regretfully. 'I shall return surrounded by a bevy of Chinese beauty.' However, there was a change of plan, and Caspar after all accompanied *Hermes* back to England that September.

'We have reached Colombo on our homeward crawl,' he wrote to Grannie Nettleship. 'I will bear in mind your last letter about the place – I am not thinking just yet of becoming a planter of teas – wait until I am no longer required by my Lords of the Admiralty!'

In 1930, sixty members of Hawke Term were still in the

Navy, the forty who had left pursuing careers as varied as their whereabouts. Among the old boys were to be found a Foreign Office official, a stock jobber, an officer in the Grenadier Guards, a Cambridge don, a night club king, a brace of barristers, a detective and a manager at Fortnum and Mason. Caspar was from time to time to consider the idea of quitting the Navy for some civil job. But flying was a growing passion, and whatever it was would certainly have to do with aeroplanes. Later he was to ask his father if he knew of any millionaire who wanted a private pilot. If he did leave the Navy, or was turned out, he knew that his skills would enable him to find a flying job in Canada or the colonies. The image he retained of Canada seemed still to linger in his imagination; having once dreamt of becoming an animal trapper there, he now could see that the aeroplane had a vital role to play in a country where unimaginably vast empty spaces defeated most forms of transport. For the time being he was content, and certainly not likely to be seduced by the idea of becoming a tea planter in Ceylon.

Hermes docked in home waters in October for her refit, and in December Caspar set about securing an international driving pass so that he could motor through France in a green and cream Wyllis Knight to join Augustus at Martigues for Christmas.

Meanwhile, everything had suddenly been speeded up for the return voyage to China in January 1928. A few jobs in *Hermes* were left uncompleted, but the aeroplanes were on board, which in Caspar's view was the main thing. During her absence the situation in China had deteriorated, and it was felt that her reassuring presence was urgently required. *The Times* had reported mass beheadings of non-Communists and, as if that were not enough, the heads were pickled in brine, stuck on poles and paraded through the streets. The hearts of some of the victims were cut out, cooked and eaten. British subjects would clearly sleep more easily if they knew that the Navy was at hand.

During the second outward voyage, Caspar did a great deal of flying in a variety of roles, beginning in the Red Sea, then over Ceylon, Malaya, Singapore, Bangkok, on up the China coast to Shanghai, and north to Chefoo, and Wei-Hai-Wei on the northeast coast of China. 'It was grand in the Red Sea as we were baking,' he told Ethel. 'I took some papers to a lighthouse called Daedalus – a tiny reef only – the keepers were staggered!' They were then to have photographed a leper settlement, Mimicoi, but the air was too rough for the steady flying needed for aerial photography. On arrival off Malaya they were based for a while at Penang Island, where Caspar's main task was to take photographs of likely air bases and seaplane bases at which the civilian Imperial Airways could land their flying boats along the Malay Peninsula. Civilian aerial transport was at this time being developed all over the British Empire. Soon flying boats from Southampton would be flying passengers down on to the African lakes, across the Indian Ocean to the Malayan creeks, and so on to Australia.

Aerial photography demanded the most skilled flying, as the aircraft had to fly absolutely straight and level; if the nose of the plane went up, the camera tilted, frustrating the attempt to make a series of continuous photographs. Caspar was usually entrusted with the task of taking up the photographic observer – a man weighing seventeen stone – in a Fairey IIIF, an exceptionally fragile machine, and remain hovering at 10,000 feet. 'It was tricky enough to keep level without the additional weight of seventeen stone behind me, so I told him not to move!'

There was time to take some aerial shots of the naval base and aerodrome at Singapore before *Hermes* proceeded into the Bay of Bangkok in early March. Here she dropped anchor for five days and mounted an aerial display for the delectation of the Siamese royal family. Various members of the family, which, in 1928, was headed by King Prajadhipok, were received on board and taken up by Caspar and his fellow pilots.

Caspar wrote to Augustus on Trafalgar Day, 1928:

87

Dear Daddy,

I am told that you are back in America – why not go round the world and return home via China? We've had a much better time in China this year, and seen a good deal more of it. We had six weeks at Shanghai – they were terrific, after the sober life of the North; to be plunged in to that dissipated vortex brought a great strain on the frame internally and externally. A most enjoyable and hectic time.

With its clubs, sporting facilities and international community, Shanghai provided the only opportunity for a Western-style leave in mainland China. A few objects remain in the family from this period in China: a silver spoon engraved with the words, 'Water Polo, Shanghai, 1928'; a handful of Tiger's Head beer labels and some straw hats; a yellow quatrefoil dish. The silks Caspar brought back from China he gave to Dorelia and his sisters, together with some pieces of jewellery. An album of snapshots contains views of eastern China from the air and sea as well as on land: prominent among these as a record of the times are a group of young men with very long queues at *Fan Tan* gambling and a Shanghai corn thief chained to a tree by the ankle. There are some shots of the Ming Way and other rural scenes: women washing clothes in a river; children playing in the dust. There are many studies of junks and sampans afloat on rivers and the open sea, and from the air, views of the Shanghai Bund and famous racecourse as well as Fairey IIIFs formation flying over the lovely island of Wei-Hai-Wei.

*   *   *

The main part of China had become more or less settled, but trouble still simmered around the city of Hankow. The Yang-tse flotilla, with its flagship HMS *Bee*, maintained a British naval force on the river to protect the property and lives of British subjects, such as those working in the Hong Kong and Shanghai Banking Corporation, or individuals practising as doctors or lawyers.

'I remember steaming 600 miles inland up the Yang-tse river to Hankow to lend assistance to whichever side the British Government was backing at the time,' Caspar wrote. *Hermes* only sailed as far as Nanking and must have been one of the biggest ships ever seen on the Yang-tse river. Thereafter it is not known how he continued the journey – possibly he had been detailed to escort the Yang-tse flotilla – but whatever ship he was in, it was not an easy voyage to undertake. Although very wide in parts, the navigable channel of the river was notorious for mudbanks, and crowded with Chinese river traffic. 'A slow moving sampan is sometimes deceptive and on reaching it one finds that on the further side two water buffaloes are secured alongside, swimming very hard,' wrote a contemporary in his diary. 'Very big rafts are sometimes met with and the way they are manoeuvred round corners by means of a sort of sea anchor and windlass is astonishing ... bigger rafts carry a complete village with a main street, chickens, babies and so on ' Even with such hazards, the Lower River bore none of the dangers of the Middle River, which stretched between Hankow and Ichang, a further 354 miles. Pirates would sometimes attack British ships and it was not unknown for a ship to end up in the middle of a paddy field during flooding. The waters of the Yang-tse could in places rise and fall by as much as ninety feet.

Caspar had spent part of the journey flying up in his Fairey IIIF showing the flag and spotting mudbanks; depending on the swiftness of the currents and changing patterns on the surface of the water, it was possible to detect shallow waters at a height of 5000 feet. At Hankow, where a European quarter had been established, the crew enjoyed the facilities of the naval canteen to be found in a wing of the Hong Kong and Shanghai Bank. It was a better developed city than Nanking, which in 1928 Chiang Kai-shek had declared his Government's new capital. Nanking was filthy, with no waterworks or proper roads. During the few days that *Hermes* had anchored there, Caspar took time off to visit the colossal memorial to Sun Yat Sen, father of nationalist

China, which was then being built and was opened the following year.

'We are on our way down to Hong Kong after the summer up north,' Caspar wrote to Augustus, 'then down to Borneo and the Philippines before Christmas which should be interesting. But one never gets to know these places we visit – there is no time or liberty.

'They will not let us go to Japan – too secret perhaps . . . Manchuria is the next scene of action and I think Japan will deal with it. I think another year will see me back in England for a bit. We are running into a typhoon and shall probably spend a bloody night.'

Caspar was beginning to feel that he was losing touch with the frontline Navy in the Atlantic and Mediterranean Fleets, and asked to be transferred. On receiving the news that his request had been granted, the other FAA pilots in *Hermes* got together to give him a farewell dinner at a small club in the middle of Wei Hai Wei – Harry Smallwood, a fellow pilot in *Hermes*, described it as 'a lovely place . . . a small island with a huge bay on the far side of which ran the north coast of China, which provided some excellent duck shooting facilities.' He remembered well what happened:

> It was a jolly party, and at about midnight we decided it was time we got back on board so set off for the beach about three quarters of a mile away. There were no duty boats to catch – each ship had its own party of sampans and you only had to shout the party's nickname, which in our case was 'dog-face', and a sampan would appear. This we did loud and clear and about three sampans appeared out of the darkness. We started climbing in when we noticed that the Guest of Honour was absent. We retraced our steps, heard sounds of singing in the distance and discovered it came from Caspar and Andrew Usher, singing their hearts out from the top of the dockyard chimney! We persuaded them to come

down, returned to our sampans, but again no Caspar. So we gave up. He spent the rest of the night sleeping under a bush and came to the ship by the faithful sampan in the early hours of the morning.

Caspar left China in August 1929, making the long homeward crawl in the SS *Kashgar*, the same P&O Liner which had first taken him out to the East.

5

Air, sea and the desk

In the spring of 1927, coinciding with Caspar's first arrival in China, Augustus and Dodo had moved from Alderney Manor to Fryern Court, near Fordingbridge in Hampshire. It remained their home for the rest of their lives; after Augustus's death in 1961, Dodo continued to live there until her own death in 1969. Here they kept a room for Caspar whenever he needed it throughout the 1930s; an ideal arrangement since he did not keep a *pied-à-terre* for periods of shore leave and Fryern was conveniently close to naval bases such as Gosport and Portsmouth. Ethel always kept an open door for her restless nephew whenever he appeared in London.

Situated in flat countryside between the New Forest and the Wiltshire Downs, Fryern had originally been a friary. It had been turned into a farm, and finally a manor house. The kitchen dated back to the fourteenth century. It had a grey slate floor, a stone sink, and an Aga, and since Dodo refused ever to have refrigeration, food was stored in a couple of cold dark larders. A long rope attached to a bell above the kitchen roof was pulled to signal lunch, tea and supper; breakfasters were called with a cowbell which used to be rung furiously by Mrs Cake at the bottom of the old winding staircase which led up to the bedrooms from the kitchen.

Upstairs, there were seven or eight bedrooms, each with its

own size and character and a couple of four-poster beds so tall that a child had to leap high to reach the mattress. Everywhere floors, walls and ceilings sloped, floorboards squeaked and in the bathrooms the water-pipes would thump and clang when a tap was turned on.

The front of the house had a pale Georgian façade with long sash windows, behind which, on the ground floor, lay the living room where everyone ate at a long oak refectory table. On the other side of the entrance hall was a room which later accommodated a Steinway grand piano, and beyond was Augustus's library and study. Paintings by different artists hung on the walls; works by Carrington, Eve Kirk, Matthew Smith, Alvaro Guevara, Boudin and Gwen John changed places with Augustus's canvasses over the years.

Caspar would descend on Fryern from the sky, and land in the field behind the house. 'Just as well you were not there or you might have screamed,' he once told Ethel after running slap into the fence, which put an abrupt stop to his journey.

He had decided to buy his own aeroplane in 1928 while he was still on the China Station, and had written to his father to tell him. 'I am intent on buying a light aeroplane if possible. I feel sure you would (perhaps you have) enjoy flying immensely, quite different from crossing the Channel. I cannot remember whether Fryern has a suitable landing ground.' Then, on 14 April 1930, following a few months of carrier flying from *Argus*, he wrote again to Augustus to confirm his decision and borrow the necessary money.

> Dear Daddy,
>   I have come to the conclusion that flying is not only very much more interesting and amusing than motoring, but also considerably safer, and I have therefore decided to buy a light aeroplane. I hope to gain some useful experience which should help considerably in securing a civil job when we get turned out of the Navy by Mr MacDonald.

I have the aeroplane in my eye, a two-seater, so I hope you will make use of it whenever possible. It costs £460; I am selling my car and will be just about solvent with £200 war loan as your security.

I have landed a couple of times [at Fryern Court] in the field across the lane with perfect ease in a similar machine.

Is the cause good? If so, I shall be extremely grateful to you.

His father, who was on a rest-cure from excess living, reacted favourably, and Caspar soon wrote again on 22 April:

Thank you very much indeed for your encouraging letter. I'm glad you think the cause is good. I am quite certain of it, mainly from the point of view of something in the future, as I am becoming distinctly bored with the Navy. There is no sailoring nowadays, and I am tired of living boxed up like a sardine.

I shall do as much flying as possible now, and I think I shall be able to get quite enough as I am in England until the end of the year; and if I get sent out to the Mediterranean then I shall fly the aeroplane out to Malta, where there is an aerodrome.

I shall be on the lookout for a flying job ashore meanwhile either in England or the Colonies – I have my eye on Canada as being a very likely spot; perhaps Sir James [Dunn – the Canadian financier and a friend of Augustus] will need some aviation later.

I am fetching the aeroplane this weekend and shall fly it down to Gosport (where I am at present stationed) to start with. I have been keeping my eyes skinned for suitable fields everywhere and I am striking off my visiting list anyone who has no suitable patch of grass for me to land on!

Perhaps when you have finished with the Deanery [where Augustus was recuperating], I may be able to fly up and recapture you – or do you loathe the things?

I will let you know how the aeroplane flies. With repeated thanks.

Finally, a few days later, from Gosport:

I have now got *the* finest aeroplane in the world. Today I flew it from London to Fryern and on to Gosport at Sunset. It is the only method of transport. I'm selling my car and buying a push-bike.
It is rather difficult to get into, so do a little thinning and practise forcing yourself into small spaces!
Buck up and get back – Caspar.

The aeroplane he bought was an Avro Avian, designed by the great inventor and aircraft designer A. V. Roe. Roe had started experimenting in aerodynamics in 1900 using a handmade wooden albatross on the deck of a Merchant Navy ship, and had been responsible for the first ever British flight in July 1909. By 1930, there were 295 privately owned machines listed by the Royal Aeronautical Club, of which 174 were de Havilland Moths, and, second in popularity, twenty-one Avro Avians. Caspar's was fitted with a Cirrus II engine which was capable of 90 m.p.h. – about twice as fast as the contemporary motorcar's top speed. The petrol tank had enough fuel for four hours' worth of flying, and it had two seats with room for a suitcase. A favourable Hong Kong Dollar exchange and the proceeds from the sale of his car paid for most of it; the rest was lent to him by his father.

*   *   *

In August 1930 Caspar had been in the Fleet Air Arm for five years. He was twenty-seven. Throughout the decade his 'flimsies' – certificates of conduct signed by the Captain at the end of a period of service on board a ship – were monotonously favourable. It is only fair to say that the average flimsy is not a particularly revealing document, and many captains were content with a superficial assessment of the subject's character, but the consistency of Caspar's reports cannot fail to impress. 'Reliable', 'efficient', 'trustworthy' are words that recur again and again, but with tributes too to his zeal and extraordinary energy. Resilience, and a capacity to keep going under stress; the ability to cram more into the day than others could manage in a week and still to emerge ready for more; these are the attributes without which success in any competitive career is impossible. Caspar had inherited them from Augustus, and subjected them to a control and discipline which his father never sought for. It was clear to a succession of commanding officers that he was a man destined to go far in the Royal Navy, if not right to the top.

But some of them would have been happier to see him more convivial, 'one of the crowd'. Caspar was a loner, reticent, withdrawn. 'The uprising but dourly silent Caspar John' was how Harald Penrose described him in 1930, at the time of the King's Cup Air Race, in surroundings when, if ever, he might have been expected to relax among his peers. He made a handful of close friends and was capable at times of an almost manic jollity, but by most of his contemporaries he was celebrated for his self-confidence, clear-headedness and an almost monastic remoteness from the social hurly-burly of the mess. 'Must have done a lot of thinking,' concluded a fellow officer who was in China with him. Above all, Caspar was silent. Silence characterized all the sons of Augustus, who had, from childhood, endured his sudden changes of temper and became afflicted at an early age with the John 'glooms'.

Yet he was not chilly or unsympathetic to his fellow men. His younger brother Henry was quick to recognize this. For a long time the two brothers had not been able to get to know each other; Caspar was always away and Henry had been brought up separately by a maternal aunt, following Ida's death when he was only a few days old. 'I am so glad to hear Caspar is back and that you gave him a dance from 5–3,' Henry wrote to Augustus after Caspar's return from China. 'What is he like? It must be fine to be in the Navy and also to fly.' Henry was the only other brother to

have opted for a life of discipline. He had been raised as a Roman
Catholic and, while preparing himself for entry into the Jesuit
Priesthood, had chosen to read philosophy at Campion Hall,
Oxford. He evidently had met Caspar during the latter's period
of foreign service leave. 'What a uniquely rare *combination* of
qualities in C,' he wrote from Campion Hall. 'Very straightforward, terrifically loyal, and dependable,' he told his sister
Vivien, 'with strong standards, and powerfully fond of you and
of Daddie.'

Father Martindale, who had recommended Henry for the
Jesuit Priesthood, thought 'Caspar, Kaspar or (I rather hope)
Q'Aspar enormously likeable', and 'so much believed in
Q.' Beneath 'Q's' carapace of composed good looks, Father
Martindale also saw a sensitive soul capable of strong affections.

To his sisters, Poppet and Vivien, nine and twelve years
younger, he was something of a hero; they adored him. Poppet,
so named when Caspar, aged nine, looked into her cradle and
declared, 'What a little poppet', remembers *her* first vision of
him from her mother's four-poster bed at Alderney Manor. 'I
looked out of the window and saw standing on the grass a *very*
handsome boy in naval uniform and said to myself, 'That's the
chap I will marry!' They would see him periodically while on
home leave at Alderney in the years following the First World
War, and after 1928 at Fryern Court, when he might take them
on a flying trip, tremendously exciting at the time, or accompany
them on long horse rides in the New Forest and over the Wiltshire
Downs.

Caspar went to Osborne when his eldest sister was only four
and so saw little of her and Vivien, but he became quite concerned
about their futures. Augustus had not allowed his daughters any
schooling for the same reasons that he was reluctant to let his
sons go to school. Caspar admired and valued independence in
women (Ethel and Ursula, and Dorelia in her way, were all strong
personalities who followed their own course), and he did not
want his sisters to lead a useless life. 'Why don't you do some-

thing useful like running the railways?' he once asked Poppet. 'Can you imagine!' she recalled, 'at a time when girls were not expected to work and only learn to cook and look pretty – perhaps do a watercolour or two!' He sometimes had some hard words for her which would reduce her to tears. He thought Vivien would make a good racing driver, and did not think going in for painting was wise, the extent of the competition so close at hand being too daunting. He feared for a life going to waste – sometimes as a result of marriage – and encouraged education and training so that even if she became a wife, a woman would not have to sink into the undignified role of 'little woman at home', a concept that saddened and appalled him. While his fellow officers were either yearning or waiting to get married, Caspar showed no interest in the idea. He was not hostile to women, on the contrary he enjoyed their company, but other things came first; he did not have the time for matrimony.

Caspar was not the sort of man who indulged in hobbies; his work was his life. His solitary passion was flying, and he was fortunate not only to have coincided with the 'golden age' of flying – the early 1930s – but also to have been able to enjoy it as a professional activity as well as in his spare time. On duty or on leave, it was his first preoccupation.

His confidence was total; he did not so much believe that he was lucky as fail to contemplate the possibility of disaster. He knew that he was indulging in the most dangerous form of what was then an extremely precarious pursuit, but he knew too that his technical competence was of the highest order, sufficient to overcome anything except the most outrageous whims of fortune. Carrier flying was a risky business. To take off from the deck of a carrier, climb through 10,000 feet of air over the ocean with only a limited amount of fuel in the tank, and land accurately on what had in the meantime receded to a tiny speck in the watery blue, was at the very least a frightening experience – even in the later days of improved aircraft and sophisticated deck equipment. There were plenty of accidents – he himself once went overboard in his aeroplane and his lungs had to be pumped of sea water – but he remained undeterred. Caspar never doubted either that he would survive or that there was great potential in the future of naval aviation.

* * *

By 1930, aviation was big news and becoming big business. Every aspect of flight, military or civilian, public or private, was being researched and developed. It was an age in which aircraft pioneers hankered after record-breaking long-distance solo flights. Women were also flying: Amy Johnson, the Duchess of Bedford, Beryl Markham and Winifred Brown all contributed their experiences to the early history of flight. The thirties – the great sporting decade – were tremendously exciting years for the enthusiastic individual. Private flights abroad were unhampered by the later restrictions. The RAeC (Royal Aero Club) provided large-scale maps and flight carnets to eliminate foreign customs dues on the aircraft used; the pilot merely needed to fill up, take off, and trust to his skill to get him through. In 1926 there were thirty seven privately owned aircraft; by 1930 there were between three hundred and four hundred.

For Caspar, the 1930s was a decade of intense flying activity of every form, from private pleasure trips and racing, to testing new designs of naval aircraft, surveying, demonstrating, night flying, deck landing, not to mention increasing involvement in the design and production of aircraft.

Freed from the relative restrictions of carrier flying, he flew several times in Europe, took part three years running in the King's Cup Air Race, and flew friends and members of the family on innumerable trips. During his periods of leave in 1930, it seems he kept up a ceaseless round of plane-hopping, riding, and dashing from party to party by fast car. 'L/F [Lea Francis sports car] to Fryern,' reads a typical diary entry. 'Then flew to Ilford – gliding – Tickeridge and back. Huge party – slight tipsy. No sleep. Filled up 0300 by carlight. To Gosport 0530 – late!' Activities like this hardly support the view of the joyless ascetic seen by some of his contemporaries, and yet this side of his character was always there beneath the surface.

'We had an excellent party the other night as a farewell to John Macnamara who is off to China,' he had written to Augustus in April. 'We've also had some marvellous rides, about a dozen at a time, in the forest and on the Downs.' John Macnamara had three sisters, Brigit, Nicolette and Caitlin, who had spent much of their childhood with the John family. They lived close by at Blashford, and on rare occasions Caspar would ride with them in the New Forest, and join in picnics and paperchases. The horses were kept in stables at the back of Fryern, where Dodo also kept goats. Goat produce would regularly turn up on the dining table at Fryern. This horrified Caspar, who could not stand the smell; he couldn't stand fish, for that matter, either.

The following month he flew from London to Dublin and on towards Galway, where he was to rendezvous with Augustus at the Renvyle Hotel and attend the Galway races. Augustus was staying on a two-month visit, painting the Connemara landscape and engaged on a second portrait of W. B. Yeats, 'now a silver-haired old man, much mellowed and humanized,' as he described him. Oliver St John Gogarty, a Senator of the Irish Republic, had first met Augustus in 1912. Gogarty revered Augustus, who had become known in Ireland, having painted G. B. Shaw in 1915 and W. B. Yeats as long ago as 1907. On hearing that Augustus's son planned to fly solo to Dublin, Gogarty arranged a cheering reception at Baldonnel aerodrome, and commemorated the event with some dubious doggerel:

> Here is the son of A. John
> Who flew in the upper air
> Causing all Ireland to stir
> As his father before him had done!

After refuelling and the usual customs formalities, Caspar
flew due west towards Galway with the intention of landing on
an old disused aerodrome at Oranmore. He landed instead on the
seashore at Clifden, astonishing a local farmer, who nervously
walked around the machine and exclaimed: 'My God! My God!
Will I jump on the tail of your aeroplane and fly the broad
Atlantic?' Was it safe to leave the Avian overnight in a field of
cows? The farmer thought it would be, but Caspar returned the
next day to find that the cows, overcome with curiosity at the
strange fragile object sitting in their field, had prodded it with
their horns, damaging the bodywork. It was not all that serious;
the aircraft of those days were made out of wood and canvas and
Caspar was able to patch up the holes with sticking plaster. It was
not until the mid-1930s that some grew metal wings, and it was
still later that the first all-metal aircraft, the Skua, was designed.
The wood used was nearly always spruce or ash, the latter being
stronger but also heavier. Propellers were made from walnut, and
walnut or mahogany panels needed to be fitted into the spruce
bodywork, which was too soft to hold a screw.

After a week flying all over the beautiful landscape of western
Ireland – while Augustus was painting it at ground level – Caspar
returned to London, this time accompanied by his sister Vivien,
who clearly remembers climbing into a flying jacket and cap to
protect her from the raw air of an open cockpit. They flew into a
storm and there was much thunder and lightning, but 'I wasn't
frightened because he was so confident,' she recalled.

Whenever the chance came Caspar would offer to act as aerial
chauffeur to members of his family. Next he hopped Ethel to
Hamburg. She was by now working seriously at her lace and
wanted to promote the art in Denmark. The flight to Hamburg
(from where a train would take her to Copenhagen) involved a
stop for fuel at Amsterdam. Rather absurdly, but not unreason-
ably for that time, Caspar was suspected of espionage. No doubt
the presence of Ethel and her lace-making equipment helped
alleviate the suspicion. But it was a real risk for flyers. A later,

more serious incident aroused similar suspicion – this time in the Alps.

Caspar had arranged with his great friend and fellow naval aviator, Dick Pugh, to make a trip to Basle. Caspar and Pugh had joined the Navy in 1916 and had served together in the *Iron Duke* and on the China station; indeed they were never far apart for long in the sixty years or so after the time they first met at Osborne. Too young to have fought in the First World War, they were in at the birth of the Fleet Air Arm, and, when on leave, led a life that was exciting and carefree. In the 'Hawke Term' magazine Pugh was said to move very fast and to extract the last ounce of fun out of life in all circumstances. They had their misadventures, however, which abounded on this trip to Switzerland.

Flying in separate aeroplanes, they encountered bad weather over France. Dick, who was flying with another great friend, Jimmie Buckley, had a heavier load and was approaching the Alps. It soon became necessary to lighten the plane in order to gain a few feet: a heated argument broke out over whose suitcase was to be jettisoned. Buckley had just bought some rather smart pale blue celanese vests and pants and was very loathe to part with his luggage. In the end, the skis, ski boots and both suitcases were jettisoned, and the plane scraped over the top of the mountains, and landed on the lake at St Moritz.

Meanwhile, Caspar had run into thick fog and torrential rain as he neared the French-Swiss border west of Berne, and had no choice but to force-land in a muddy field in the Alps, near the Swiss village of Bonfol. Soon a number of villagers gathered round to stare: like the cows on the West coast of Ireland, they had probably never seen an aeroplane close to – they were usually distant dots in the sky. More worrying to them, however, were the identity and intentions of this dark stranger, who had dropped inexplicably from the stormy sky. Not surprisingly, he came under suspicion; while the Avian was searched, he was interrogated by police, accused of being a spy, and held overnight in the local jail. The next day, he was permitted to contact the nearest

British Consul at Berne, whereupon the Commandant de Police was advised to release him. To celebrate his innocence, the villagers gave him an enormous meal with quantities of beer at the local café-bar. Then, armed with a certificate, headed 'Commune de Bonfol' and signed by the mayor, he was free to continue the flight to Basle. From there he headed south, landed on the sand at Nice – close to where the present international airport now stands – tucked the Avian away in a handy shed and joined his father and sister Poppet who were staying at the villa belonging to Sir James Dunn.

*   *   *

'I have told Trelawney that until he hands over his firearms, I shall come nowhere near Parley,' Caspar had told Augustus soon after purchasing his aeroplane. Infuriated by the noise of low-flying aircraft from a nearby aerodrome, Trelawney Dayrell-Reed had been driven to shooting at the infernal machines with a double-barrelled gun – fortunately without serious result. He was tried and subsequently acquitted in court by a jury composed mainly of local farmers. In spite of this reasonable disapproval of passing aircraft, he was anxious for some aerial photographs of his prehistoric discoveries in Dorset, and Caspar was quite as keen to obtain them for him. This, after all, was the country which Caspar loved and in which he had spent much of his youth: Dorset, Wiltshire and west Hampshire – Thomas Hardy's Wessex – and he had learnt to fly over the prehistoric wilderness of Salisbury Plain. Augustus too was fascinated by the remains of a lost civilization; Caspar took him up to see the great earthworks of Badbury Rings and Maiden Castle. This thrilled him; viewing the archaeological sites of Dorset from the air was for him like reading a book of history. After his flight he declared, 'I have seen more history in an hour than I was ever taught at school.'

To the north of Salisbury Plain in Berkshire lived another Englishman of delicate sensibility, the historian and biographer,

Lytton Strachey. Strachey nursed a very real dread of the flying machine; and in a letter to a friend he explained how he had come perilously close to physical contact with the nasty thing: 'Yesterday there was an event though – 2 visitors by aeroplane – viz. Dorelia and Kaspar John. The latter took C. [Carrington] up for a turn – she adored it: but *I* refrained – the attraction, somehow or other, was not sufficient.' In Michael Holroyd's biography of Strachey, he relates how, after her flight, Carrington again tried to coax Lytton into going up, but he seemed not at all keen, and Caspar John felt that he must be cursing him under his breath. He recoiled from Carrington's entreaties to 'have a go'. 'No,' he said. 'It is too violent – too alarming – too positive – too demanding an experience for me to contemplate.' Carrington replied that she knew him well enough to tell him that it would be none of these things, and Caspar chipped in to say that he would certainly deal gently with one of so refined a nature. Dorelia then asked him how, in future, he would be able to discipline Carrington if he refused a hurdle that she had triumphantly cleared, and the argument continued until they had reached what was for Strachey the safety of the house. The dreaded aeroplane was now out of sight beyond the trees, and with renewed confidence Strachey rounded on his tormentors, and declared that he was the wrong *shape* for flying and that his beard presented a hazard likely to foul the controls. 'Exhausted, he coiled himself down into an armchair. There was no more to be said, and so ended the story of his non-flight with a future Admiral of the Fleet.'

*　　*　　*

Caspar's naval activities throughout 1930 centred around three of the larger aircraft carriers in the Atlantic Fleet; at every opportunity he practised the art of take-off and landing on the decks of HMSs *Argus*, *Furious* and *Courageous*. He even managed a landing on *Courageous* in his own Avian, an escapade that was not warmly received by the powers that be. It was one of the earliest civil aircraft landings at sea.

It all depended on the wind. Diary entries during visits to Gibraltar, Barcelona, Palma and Pollensa in the spring of 1930 reveal to what extent his day-to-day satisfaction could be enhanced or dashed by the wind:

Gale all night.
4 shots to get on – ship pitching.
Too much pitch and wind for flying. Gale.
Heavy swell – 17° roll and great pitch.
Flying! 5 Landings OK.
6 D. L's AM. Flew p.m.
No wind – no fly! Felt mouldy.
Gales.
Swell.
Gales.
Flew.
Blow.
Flew 5½ hours!!

He was in the carrier *Argus*, 'a strange ship and not very thrilling,' he had told Ethel in 1929. She had been designed as a passenger liner, the *Conte Rosso*, for Italy, but was commissioned instead as the first flush-deck aircraft carrier just before the end of the First World War.

Up until the mid-1930s carrier flying was being developed separately in America and England. Thereafter the two navies cooperated and adopted each other's inventions to improve the conditions of landing and take-off. As far as landing was concerned, it was not until the early 1930s that aircraft with faster landing speeds were fitted with footbrakes; shortly afterwards the British Navy adopted the US Navy's arrester wire system. Wires were stretched across the deck, and the aircraft fitted with a hook which would catch the wires on landing. The British had been experimenting with fore and aft wires, but when, in 1925, these were abandoned the pilot had to rely on the strong head wind created by the carrier steaming 'into wind' to abet the slow landing-on process. The US arrester wire system had for a time been classified, and Dennis Cambell, who was later to invent the 'angled deck' (subsequently adopted by the US Navy), remembers that in the 1930 film *Hell's Angels*, 'whenever Clark Gable and his fellow pilots landed on the deck, a sort of black screen on the film came up to blank out the bottom of the picture, concealing the actual mechanism at work'.

After the American arrester wire system was adopted, the safety barrier was introduced, another US Navy invention. This meant that an aircraft that missed the wires could head into the barrier, which also served a useful purpose in protecting parked aircraft. Accidents were mostly sideways ones, and palisades were fitted along the deck edge to help prevent aircraft falling into the sea. It was not until after the Second World War that new types of arrester wires, the steam catapult, the angled deck and mirror landing sight were introduced; for the time being, it was up to the pioneers to experiment their way towards these improvements.

On 17 November 1930, Caspar received a letter from the RAF Base Gosport, stating that he was to revert to General Service and that he had been appointed to HMS *Malaya* as from 2 January 1931. His attachment to the Royal Air Force would cease on the same day and the requisite notification would appear in the London *Gazette*. This reversion to General Service – 'Fish-head time' as aviators called their seagoing periods – was a move designed to remind Caspar of the proper Navy: 'I was regarded with some suspicion by my brother officers, but managed to calm their fears, and behave as well as any of them.'

Possibly a brief appearance by Augustus on board *Malaya* aroused further suspicion. Only on two occasions did Caspar receive his father on board the ship in which he was serving. A little later he conducted Augustus around the aircraft carrier *Courageous*. 'He bravely survived the ordeal,' Caspar later recounted, 'called for a large brandy in the ward room, and publicly declared that he had always suspected me of needing three doctors to pronounce me insane, and now he knew that he was right.' Despite his father's mockery, Caspar drove him back to Fryern Court and gave him 'a good hiding at shove-ha'penny, a game he really enjoyed, and at which he had an astonishing mixture of skill and luck.'

The battleship *Malaya* was a veteran of Jutland. She had been built in 1912 at a cost of £3 million, which was provided by the Federal Malay States, and as a gesture of recognition the ship was named after the donating colony. This was common practice in the days of Empire. She was held in great pride and showered with gifts following her part in the Battle of Jutland, and during her visit to the Malay States in 1920. Among these were a suit of silk ensigns which had been made by the European ladies, gold and silver plates, an elephant's tusk which needed two men to carry it, and carved tigers and elephants in wood and ivory.

In June 1931 the annual rowing regatta was held at Scapa Flow. This was a most important event, kindling an intense rivalry between ships' companies and boats' crews. The results could influence the promotion or passing over of officers in critical posts. Commanding Officers, Commanders and First Lieutenants were the most affected, and their anxieties were made very evident to their subordinates. Caspar himself had little enthusiasm for this kind of competition, especially when it was given such exaggerated importance, but he rowed in the ward room crew and probably trained one of the others. Out of six competing ships, *Malaya* came second.

There followed a programme of visits to various British ports. Life on board remained strictly routine, but broken for Caspar when he was released to race in the King's Cup Air Race, which that year was held on 25 July. This was a far more attractive competition, and in his hurry to get there, he carried away the telegraph wires at Gosport aerodrome.

*   *   *

After the Schneider, the King's Cup was probably the most exciting event of the flying calendar. Sponsored by the Royal

Aero Club and open to pilots from all professions flying any type of British civil aircraft, it attracted a colourful list of entrants, some rich and titled, many more known only to their peers. Prince George and Marshal of the RAF Lord Trenchard were among those who entered their aircraft, but did not pilot them. The names of the planes were as delicate as their construction: Swift, Tomtit, Bluebird, Puss Moth, Widgeon, which were powered by engines named Cirrus, Gypsy, Hermes, Panther, Mongoose and Pobjoy – some of which were capable of speeds exceeding 128 m.p.h.

The greatest challenge of the race was to be able to navigate the course which varied between 750 and 1000 miles and zig-zagged all over England. The 1931 race, for example, encompassed Shoreham on the Sussex coast, Norwich, Leeds, Liverpool and Bristol, with turning points at Leicester, Nottingham, Hull, Birmingham, Manchester and Southampton. The race that year was bedevilled by rain and mist. The Club's regulations dwelt anxiously on the technical problems of avoiding possible collision – with so many machines landing and taking off in a restricted area, the risk was a very real one. Supplementary regulation no. 9 stressed the need for competitors to 'pursue a straight course forward, i.e., at right angles to the starting line' after take-off, while regulation 12 warned, 'When approaching and crossing finishing lines, competitors should keep a sharp lookout for other competitors taking off from the same aerodrome.' Pilots unfamiliar with the course were advised to study carefully beforehand contour maps showing the altitude of the various hills *en route*, as serious accidents had occurred through pilots flying into hills during periods of bad visibility. Weather reports were available at certain control points (compulsory stops), where pilots were free to decide whether to continue in the race.

In 1930, 1931 and 1932, the three years that Caspar joined the race, the entrants numbered between forty-one and eighty-six. Not all those who started reached the finish – navigating the route was something of a triumph in itself; the weather *might* be on the pilot's side, but what if your co-pilot dozed off and slumped forward on to the engine switch, cutting it off in mid-air? Caspar's friends Dick Pugh and James Buckley were in the lead on one occasion when the engine cut out, and Pugh had to force-land in a field, bursting both tyres. Furious, as the other planes roared past overhead, they tried to find out why the engine had stopped. At last they tracked down the cause and, with the help of some men working in the fields who pushed the plane across the field, took off on the bare rims of the wheels, completed the race, and still contrived to come in seventh.

The best finishing position Caspar ever achieved was twelfth. After he flew for the third time he decided that enough was enough. Private flying of this kind was too expensive and he never competed again.

It was customary during the annual sailing races at Cowes for the Navy to provide a battleship as 'guardship' to the Royal Yacht *Victoria & Albert*, with Their Majesties on board. In 1931, the *Malaya* was selected. 'This meant a wholehearted effort to make the ship as smartly presentable as possible,' Caspar wrote. 'This in turn involved a stay in Devonport Dockyard whilst the ship was *enamelled*, which took years off her appearance. The Commander, a fellow called Pegram, was quite a wealthy bloke, and paid for this enamel out of his own pocket! We applied it with our own brushes on the ship's sides, turrets and upper-works. We were beautiful! When we reached Cowes, one of our duties was to provide a steam picket boat with a Lieutenant in charge to follow the 12-metre racing yacht *Britannia* at a discreet distance throughout the races. I had been selected as the officer responsible in case some royal body needed to be fished out of the sea, and had to don a long frock coat, sword and cocked hat — which was considered a suitable rescue uniform! However, His Majesty was too good a seaman to fall overboard, and at the end of the races I was thanked by Sir Philip Hunloke, *Britannia*'s helmsman, and sent for by the King, who said, "I want to congratulate myself on not having to congratulate you for having to haul me out of the water!"'

After recommissioning at Devonport, *Malaya* put to sea on 7 September to join the Atlantic Fleet at Invergordon, and was present at the so-called 'Mutiny'. Whitehall politicians had announced fierce pay cuts which, in the case of the Navy, seemed expressly tailored to penalize those least able to bear them. The Mutiny, wrote Caspar, 'turned out to be an expression of contempt and disapproval by some of the men of a minority of ships for what was rightly considered to be a gross misjudgement in Whitehall of the lowly paid seagoing man's family responsibilities. The able seaman lived on four bob a day and an ordinary seaman on 2/9d. Since there were no married quarters they had to pay for their own rent and rates, buy food and support a wife and children. It was just too little, and too much loyalty was expected from a large number of men.

'We thought the Admiralty was extremely weak at the time in not resisting this tooth and nail, and the Mutiny of Invergordon demonstrated ill-feeling towards the Government (not, as is suggested by 'mutiny', bad relationships between officers and ratings). Certainly there were incidents of disobeying orders, not in *Malaya*, but in *Hood*, which was one of the worst, and the *Norfolk*, *Rodney* and *Adventure*.'

Malaya's new crew had not had time to organize itself to participate in the Mutiny and on the Monday following the rioting in the naval canteen, she steamed out to sea for working-up exercises and remained well clear of the trouble that continued to rumble through the assembled Fleet. Not surprisingly, she was booed by the other ships as she re-entered harbour twenty-four hours later. Caspar himself found no problem in keeping up a good relationship with the seamen, though he did not always get on so well with the junior officers. A contemporary midshipman recalls: 'In his early days in the *Malaya*, we found it wiser to treat him with considerable caution, and never to deviate from complete formality. Even so, he was hard to please (if not impossible, for I do not think he had a high opinion of midshipmen) and words of praise were few and far between.'

After twelve months in the *Malaya*, he was transferred to the cruiser *Exeter* on 31 December 1931. She carried two seaplanes, mounted on catapults. The aircraft, held in place by the cradle, was wound back to one end of the catapult; the pilot then gave full power to the engine, and signalled to the torpedo officer, who dropped a flag. The cordite charge which followed threw the machine into the air with tremendous force just above stalling speed. If the charge failed, the aircraft tumbled into the sea. At the end of a flight, the seaplane was hoisted on board by a crane.

'I was soon used to being flung into the air at the behest of a cordite charge,' Caspar wrote. 'The ship was as happy and understanding a community as one could wish, thanks to the characters of both officers and ratings. We all knew each other's problems from the Captain downwards.' They led a varied life, geographically as well as professionally. The year began with a Caribbean cruise. After crossing the Atlantic by way of Tenerife, where Caspar circled the Pico surveying for a possible flying-boat base, *Exeter* arrived off Trinidad in early February 1932, and spent the rest of the month cruising among the Caribbean Islands, showing the flag and entertaining local dignitaries. They visited St Lucia and Barbados: 'Had I been less devoted to the Navy, I think I might well have deserted to that idyllic scene, but I was brought to my senses by an ugly aerial view of Pitch Lake, Trinidad.'

Near the end of her homeward journey – the Atlantic had been at its worst, causing the ship to roll and leak – *Exeter* anchored in Vigo Bay in northern Spain. A group of British warships was assembled there. 'It was here that my fellow pilot made the most spectacular crash I had seen,' Caspar remembered. 'I had been launched a few minutes previously and from two thousand feet overhead watched him launched in turn. Instead of climbing to join me, he flew straight and low towards a destroyer, struck her foremast between his floats, then somersaulted into the water. I quickly glided down to land close to where he had ditched, hoping that he and/or his passenger might have surfaced, but nothing. I was left to ponder the inexplicable nature of the pilot's action as I taxied back to my ship.'

In August, Caspar was among those sent to take part in the first naval officers' Parachute Course at the RAF Station, Halton in Buckinghamshire. Parachutes had only recently been introduced. With him were Dick Pugh and another life-long friend, John Henry Wood. Here they learnt the intricacies of packing parachutes so that the ripcord was bound to release them. 'An RAF Corporal was our instructor, a fine fellow who introduced us to the routine, "Tuesdays to Fridays we learns to pack, on Mondays we does Manual,"' Caspar wrote. This was the official book of instruction, covering every aspect of parachuting.

'The great day came when I was word and hand perfect, and was told that the following day I would be one of the first to "jump", having personally packed my parachute.

'This process consisted of strapping on the pack and stepping up to the front of an interplane strut between the wings of a Vicker Vimy biplane bomber. We were told to hold tight to the front of the strut and watch for the signal from the pilot to rotate to the rear. The next signal was the order to pull the ripcord and be rudely pulled off the wing.

'The parachute canopy having opened fully, my first reaction was to congratulate myself that I had done the packing accurately. Then followed silence as I floated earthward from some 3000 feet above the airfield. Soon it was time to decide how to twist myself on to the correct heading to prepare for landing; all went well. I collected the parachute, packed it again strictly according to the "Manual" and returned to my ship at Plymouth.'

There followed a tour of Scandinavia demonstrating catapult launching to each navy they found interested and hospitable. The Danish Navy was evidently both. 'Whilst berthing abreast the Langellini Gardens in Copenhagen, we were invited by the

Carlsberg and Tuborg Breweries to visit their factories. After a thirst-provoking tour, half a dozen of us were shown into the boardroom where a beer-drinking contest had been arranged. On the table in front of each of us was a pyramid of bottles. The base, which consisted of six bottles, contained the strongest brew, the peak of the pyramid held the lightest, and between came the intermediary strengths. I got through my pyramid, but had some difficulty closing my sword-belt that evening; there was a dance on the quarterdeck, and I happened to be the officer on duty.' As the winner of the contest, he was awarded the medal of the Tuborg Brewery, 'his only decoration so far, and much prized', recorded the annual news magazine of Hawke Term.

In October 1933 Caspar was promoted Lieutenant-Commander and ordered by Rear-Admiral Maitland Boucher to make the Service trials of the new Amphibian Supermarine 'Walrus', soon to be known throughout the Fleet as the 'Shagbat'. Unlike its predecessor, the Seagull III, which was made entirely of wood, Walrus had a metal hull and wings of wood and fabric. It had an enclosed cockpit and eighteen open exhausts: its top speed was 135 m.p.h.

In order to take it through its trials, Caspar had first to pass a short course of instruction in flying boats before flying the machine to Sheerness, there to be hoisted aboard the battle cruiser *Renown*, and transported to Gibraltar.

Here, Caspar spent some weeks putting the amphibian through her paces. 'My lasting impressions are those of noise and confidence and affection,' he later wrote in the foreword to a book on the Walrus. 'Noise from the open exhaust and the tremendous water clatter on the metal hull; confidence from the Bristol Pegasus engine and the physically robust character of the whole machine; affection because it seemed to possess a most friendly nature.'

Terence Horsley is one of the pilots who have described what it was like to fly this amphibian: 'On a rough day the Walrus behaves more like a cow than a bus – a friendly cow however,' he wrote. 'She wallows in the trough of the rough airs as a heifer knee deep in boggy meadow.' Seven hundred were built, and the plane proved invaluable in its wartime service with the Fleet.

After a brief sojourn in Paris in January 1934 to brush up his French and to study Russian – 'a quaint conceit but likely to be useful' commented the Hawke Term magazine – Caspar went back to flying. He had by now sold his Avian and bought a motorbike. It was a painful sacrifice, but the aeroplane had become too expensive, costing nearly £300 a year to operate. The Rudge TT which he bought in its place offered its prospects of adventure, even if earthbound. Augustus applauded 'this tendency to action' and bemoaned the fact that his other sons were less energetic. On hearing that his son Henry wanted to travel to Syria he wrote to him fiercely: 'most of your brothers are like slugs. Caspar alone moves, and your half-brother Romilly has been known to walk to Rome.'

His work on the Walrus had given Caspar a reputation as a good man to test new aircraft. The first half of 1934 was spent with HMS *Repulse* assessing the merits of three different aircraft which had been designed for operation from carriers: the Fairey Swordfish, the Blackburn Shark and the Gloster TSR. In the end the Swordfish was chosen; it did much valiant work for the Navy and, known as the 'Stringbag', rivalled the 'Shagbat' in the affection of those who flew it. This task behind him, he joined HMS *Courageous* and found himself in the Home Fleet. Neither he nor his ship were to stay there for long.

* * *

'I have had a day off here and there but lately not much on account of Abyssinia,' Caspar reported to Ethel in August 1935. Mussolini, greedy for land, had massed 100,000 troops in preparation for an invasion of Abyssinia, a territory so far untouched by the colonizing nations Britain and France, who had found the problems of settlement too daunting. The invasion did not begin until October, but when the alarm had been sounded in August, a series of anxious discussions was held between the Service Chiefs and the Cabinet as to what, if any, precautionary military measures should be taken in the event of having to go to the help of Abyssinia. Should the Navy send reinforcements from the Home Fleet to strengthen the Mediterranean Fleet? How should sea manoeuvres be carried out without seeming to threaten the Italians? Should Malta be used as a main base, seeing how vulnerable it was to air attack? How willing was France to cooperate in the event of war with Italy?

'Eventually things started to move fast,' John Shepherd, an RAF officer in *Courageous*, remembered. 'Summer leave was cancelled and ships' companies recalled. The Home Fleet formed up and steamed through the Straits of Gibraltar at night. Unobserved by the Italians, it sailed through the Mediterranean to join up with the Mediterranean Fleet by night and emerge at dawn, a combined Fleet in battle order, three aircraft carriers to windward, steaming off Alexandria, where, later in the day, the ships entered and moored.'

'The news of the British naval concentration in the Mediterranean, which convulsed Europe, made little impression in Addis,' Evelyn Waugh wrote drily in *Waugh in Abyssinia*. It should have made a considerable impression on the Italians. Arthur Marder, in *The Royal Navy and the Ethiopian Crisis of 1935–6*, explained the advantages of Alexandria: 'It controlled the Suez Canal, lay on the Italian line of communication to Ethiopia, and was an easily defended harbor.'

In the event, none of this mattered; throughout the crisis the Admiralty were determined to avoid war with Italy. They also opposed the threatened oil sanctions against Italy, on the grounds that this would exacerbate the crisis and delay a return to normal Fleet routine; already the autumn and spring cruises had been cancelled and many men were going to miss Christmas and Easter leave. 'The efficiency and wellbeing of the Mediterranean Fleet, on a war-footing since August, was bound to suffer as the weather turned hot and the terrible strain on personnel continued indefinitely,' Marder wrote.

Caspar was partly relieved by the Admiralty's attitude, partly disappointed. In August 1934 he had joined the staff of Rear-Admiral A. M. R. Ramsey, who was the coordinating authority for the operation and movement of all aircraft carriers – of which there were then six. Caspar liked and admired him, and was not deterred by the fact that Ramsey was said to be the rudest man in the Navy. Indeed, he was rather pleased to hear of this; he would always rather deal with rude straightforwardness than courteous dishonesty. He was happy to work for Ramsey and sorry to leave him: 'He did more than most to prepare the Fleet Air Arm to play a major part in the forthcoming world war.'

As Admiral Ramsey's Staff Officer Operations, Caspar was directly involved in planning what would have been the Fleet Air Arm's first offensive action, had Britain gone to war with Italy – a night attack on the Italian fleet in Taranto Harbour. The germ of the plan remained in existence and eventually bore fruit in the Second World War in November 1940. Caspar was actually to see the aircraft taking off on the operation which he had conceived more than five years before.

In 1935, however, it was not to be. By December the crisis, so far as the British were concerned at least, had passed, and in the New Year *Courageous* and Rear-Admiral Ramsay sailed for home. Caspar, to his delight, was left behind. He was appointed to the carrier *Glorious*, but remained based ashore in tents at Amrhya, an RAF airfield situated on the edge of the Western Desert, some twenty miles west of Alexandria. Here he stayed for the next nine months, a member of 825 Squadron and the long-windedly named 'Fleet Air Arm Reserve of Pilots' Pool'. He did a great deal of flying – mostly at night – including operations from the *Glorious*, which was steaming back and forth between Alexandria Harbour and Malta.

While serving in *Courageous*, Caspar had become friends with John Shepherd, 'through having a repertoire of scurrilous and other songs much in demand on jovial occasions around the wardroom piano. Caspar loved a singsong and, with eyes closed, delighted in singing a song about One Eyed Riley.' The FAA's own repertoire grew over the years until it was collected together and published in book form. One of these, the A.25 Song, is regarded as the FAA 'hymn', and is worth reproducing here in its shortest form of thirteen verses.

The A.25 Song

They say in the RAF the landing's OK
If the pilot can step out and still walk away.
But in the FAA the prospect's more grim,
The landing's PP if the pilot can't swim.

    Cracking Show! I'm alive!
    But I still have to render my A.25 *

As I roll down the deck in my Wildcat Mk IV,
Loud in my earholes the cyclones sweet roar,
Chuff, clank, clank, chuff clank clank, chuff clank clank, chink,
Away wing on Pom-Pom; away life in drink.

    Cracking Show etc. . . .

I sat on the squirter awaiting the kick,
Passing the time by rotating the stick,
Down came the green flag, the cat gave a cough
Coo . . . me cried Wings, he has fallen right off

    Cracking Show etc. . . .

I thought I was coming in much too low, but
I was fifty feet up when the batsman gave cut,
Loud in my ear-holes, the Sweet Angels sang,
Float, float, float, float, float, float, float, float, float,
                            PRANG!

    Cracking Show etc. . . .

* A form that had to be filled in after an aircraft accident.

When the batsman gives lower, I always go higher,
I drift off to starboard and prang a Seafire,
The boys in the goofers all think I am green,
But I draw my commission from Supermarine.

    Cracking Show etc. . . .

When you float all the wires and see Wings frown,
You can safely deduce that your hook isn't down,
When a . . . great barrier looms up in front
Then you hear Wings shout, 'Switch off your engine you. . . .'

    Cracking Show etc. . . .

They gave me a Wildcat to beat up the fleet,
I beat up old Rodney and Nelson a treat
But forgot all the masts that stuck up from Formid,
And a seat in the goofers was worth fifty quid.

    Cracking Show etc. . . .

I came in to land, a cold Arctic night
Bats gave me lower, and lower – alright,
When I saw the flight deck, I . . .
But I soon felt the bump as my undercart splat.

    Cracking Show etc. . . .

I fly for enjoyment, I fly just for fun,
And I'm awfully anxious to shoot down a Hun,
But as for deck landings at night in the dark,
As I told Wings this morning, stuff that for a lark.

    Cracking Show etc. . . .

We'll be over the convoy in five minutes' time.
Said Val in his ignorance sweetly sublime,
But the next ninety miles were a pain in the neck
And with half a pint left they arrived on the deck.

    Cracking Show etc. . . .

Able was night-flying miles from his base
When a look of amazement came over Bob's face
Petrol read zero and Bob had to ditch
Coo! Sink me! said Drip, fifteen miles from the witch.

Cracking Show etc. . . .

Now in the Luftwaffe they do not complain,
Since Goering invented the pilotless 'plane,
They sit in the crewroom and zizz all the day,
And this is the song that they sing, so they say.

Cracking Show! Seig Heil, Vivos Alive! Seig Heil
'Cos we don't have to render our A.25
Cracking Show! I'm alive!
And there's no bunch of guys just like 825!

John Shepherd had also been left behind at Amrhya, and remembers vividly their life in the desert.

The aerodrome was a limitless stretch of hard-baked, fine-grained sand from which billowing clouds rose as soon as a propeller turned. The engines of the aircraft, lacking dust filters, lasted very few flying hours before losing all compression and having to be changed. Everything and everybody at Amrhya was covered in this fine dust, which penetrated the tents in which we lived and the food we ate. We drank water which was chlorinated to the maximum permissible for human consumption. Soap would not lather and food cooked in it tasted horrible. Scorpions abounded and had a nasty habit of creeping into slippers left by our camp beds at night.

Caspar arrived at this awful place in, even for that day, an elderly Oldsmobile (in which, for reasons I cannot remember, I bought a share). This vehicle opened up new horizons for us not only of, perhaps, getting to Alexandria some thirty miles away along a frightful road, but we had spotted on oasis some five or six miles off this track which was reputed to have been developed into a small holiday centre by the Alexandria Greek community, with a bistro selling cold beer. Caspar had no difficulty in filling the Oldsmobile for frequent sorties to this fabulous spot where we were served with cold Asahi beer by a smiling young Egyptian girl called Sunyeem, which we pronounced Sunbeam.

One night, as he drove the Oldsmobile up the slope from the small depression in which our Greek oasis was situated, Caspar noticed a very bright light on the horizon and hastily concluded that this was the one above the sentry box at Amrhya. Why, he argued, be bothered with what apologized for a road when a direct course across the desert would be shorter and no worse for the springs. We headed for the light which, after some minutes bouncing away over the not so smooth desert, appeared to get no nearer. Only after we had pursued our course towards the light for some time did we begin to suspect that although it was rising slowly over the horizon, no camp came in sight, and perhaps we were being misled. From this it was but a small effort of diagnosis for us to realize we had been homing on Venus rising. To make some small excuse, in the desert Venus rising is brighter by far than any sentry's illumination and by it we were able to back-track to the oasis and re-route ourselves more conventionally.

Despite the discomfort of life at Amrhya – there was a lot of thieving as well; almost the only thing that was safe was the aeroplane – the young officers were glad to be freed of the stifling formality of life on board. Almost every evening they would go into Alexandria to visit the bars and restaurants. A favourite was an expensive French restaurant, Chez Pastroudis, 'underground, small, splendid cooking, and with interesting clientele,' remembered Charles Coke, who was also serving in the desert. 'Late at night and filled with his own wine, Monsieur Pastroudis used to imagine himself as Louis XV, and this condition inclined him to pour large glasses of excellent brandy as gifts to favoured clients, an act much appreciated by penniless young officers.'

The Egyptian administration of Alexandria was supervised by the British, and there were many British residents among the cosmopolitan population. One who was particularly hospitable to visiting servicemen was Dick Abdy, an immensely rich, retired banker. Abdy lived in great style, entertained lavishly and was renowned for the elegance and international interests of his salon. Caspar was not immune to such delights but it was not his scene. He would be found more often at the Union Bar or Smouha, where they cooked quails and served Simmond's Reading ale – a favourite with Caspar. Or there was Chatby-les-Bains on a pier off the Corniche, serving delicious Aboukir Bay prawns.

John Shepherd found him formidable but by no means cold or unapproachable. 'He did indeed expect and extract the best from his subordinates but he never did so by fear,' he recalled. 'He was, in fact, of a most tolerant and forgiving nature, particularly where the peccadilloes of the young were concerned. When Scotty Pride, an ebullient RAF officer in his flight – in his determination to discover the aerobatic limits to which his newly acquired Swordfish could be pushed – spread his confidential documents out of the back he knew not where, despite having been counselled by Caspar specifically to avoid such a disaster, it was Caspar who saved Scotty from court martial.'

Italy's war with Abyssinia ended when Italian troops marched into Addis Ababa on 5 May 1936; the lifting of sanctions followed two months later, and that autumn, Caspar sailed for home in *Glorious*. The Oldsmobile travelled with him; when later that year John Shepherd was married, Caspar gave him his half of it as a wedding present.

*   *   *

That December, a telegram arrived at Fryern Court confirming his promotion to Commander. This rank corresponded with entry into 'the Zone'; if he was not promoted to Captain within six years, his naval career was effectively over. In the New Year of 1937 he was appointed to the Admiralty's Naval Air Division, the centre of Fleet Air Arm thought, and the repository of all its hopes for the future.

Here, for the next two and a half years, he worked hard on the practical side of the design and development of naval aircraft, during which time he made many friends and more acquaintances in the aircraft industry. It may well have been at this time that he got to know the scientist Henry Tizard, who did so much to foster understanding between science and the Services. Tizard was to become a great friend and supporter of Caspar; the two men coincided briefly under the roof of the Ministry of Aircraft Production in 1941/2.

The main preoccupation of the Naval Air Division was above all to contrive that the Fleet Air Arm should escape the shackles of the Royal Air Force. The system of dual control did no particular harm in far-flung places, where the pilots had everything in common and got on perfectly well together, but it caused endless mischief in Whitehall, where Admiralty and Air Ministry were apt to consider each other to be the leading enemy and the Germans and Italians an irritating irrelevance. Lord Louis Mountbatten, who was also in the Division at the time, believed that he was in the forefront of the battle, indeed that he was conducting it almost single-handed. Caspar took a rather different view. 'There were just seven of us in the Division, including for a time Lord Louis Mountbatten – as a Commander, RN Film Corps,' he remarked. 'Our Director was very interested in music and the arts. This left five of us to carry the fight to the enemy's camp.'

Seven or five, they proved enough for the task. Within six months of Caspar's appointment to the Naval Air Division, and after long and detailed consideration, the Minister for the Coordination of Defence, Sir Thomas Inskip, recommended to the Government that the Admiralty be given sole control of the Fleet Air Arm. The Inskip Award was made on 30 July 1937.

A great surge of enthusiasm swept through the FAA after this award, which was a major stimulus in overcoming the years of neglect. It immediately created a tremendous amount of work, for the Navy had to build up the Fleet Air Arm almost from scratch against the background of the great rearmament drive. Yet, at the same time, the RAF was expanding, and it required the same men, material and skills. Inevitably the FAA came second to the RAF in priority for resources, a situation which persisted throughout the war.

Caspar recalled this period in a speech he gave in the 1950s: 'We now felt lonelier than ever, in a sea of Jack Tars and battleships. We needed a lot of their men and money. Whereas the weapons were reasonably effective, the parent aircraft were all too slow and deficient in range and load-carrying ability; and the carriers were obsolete.'

It was obvious that the British forces would not be sufficiently well armed without help from the United States, and in the spring of 1938, Caspar was selected to represent the FAA in a Government Air Mission to the States, headed by the industrialist James Weir, son of William Weir who had been prominent among those who tried to keep the Fleet Air Arm with the Royal Air Force. Representing the RAF was Air Commodore 'Bomber' Harris. The object of the Mission was to study what could be procured from the USA aircraft manufacturing industry. It prepared the way for the massive help Britain was to receive from the United States during the Second World War – now only fifteen months away.

They sailed in the liner *Queen Mary* to New York. It was Caspar's first visit to the United States; his father had preceded him on three occasions in the 1920s, leaving something of a reputation. Augustus had again crossed the Atlantic shortly before Caspar was to make the crossing in the other direction. He had been staying in Jamaica and returned in a banana boat with many portraits of 'young African belles' which were exhibited at Dudley Tooth's Gallery and sold like hot cakes throughout the early summer of 1938.

Caspar had no time for belles – African or otherwise. His time in America was spent rushing round the leading aircraft manufacturers – Grunmans, Boeing, Douglas – explaining Britain's needs and asking them 'with a begging bowl' to back up British industry. With Harris jealously looking over his shoulder to make sure he did not poach on the preserves of the RAF, he was limited to studying deck-landing aircraft and flying boats. It was easy enough to identify the types he needed, sometimes harder to persuade Weir that they were essential for the Navy, and markedly better than anything British manufacturers could supply. From this visit came aircraft such as the Hellcat, the Avenger, the Corsair, and the Wildcat.

The journey was justified for this achievement alone, but in the course of his travels Caspar made many contacts and a few firm friendships that were later to prove invaluable. He always got on well with Americans – he liked their dynamism, their energy, their straightforwardness – and they seem to have liked him too. Before very long this fact was to prove of considerable importance both to him, and to his country.

6

<hr>

War: HMS *York*,
London and Washington

At the outbreak of war in September, Caspar was at sea between
Bermuda and Nova Scotia as second-in-command of the *York*,
'an improbable looking cruiser. We used to call her the Ugly
Duckling – she had raked funnels and very tall radio masts.'
York's captain, Reggie Portal, had been Deputy Director in the
Naval Air Division and it seems probable that he had been
sufficiently impressed to ask for Caspar's services again. Almost
immediately they were detailed as ocean escort for the first East-
West convoy from Halifax, Nova Scotia, named HX1. 'The
assembly of the convoy in Bedford Basin, the pre-sailing briefing
conference, the conduct of the convoy forming up and on passage
were first-class performance, as though all concerned had been
practising for years,' Caspar told Arthur Marder. After a more or
less trouble-free passage across the Atlantic – 'we knew that the
Deutschland, a German pocket battleship, was at sea which kept
us on our toes – the ship was ordered to join the Northern
Patrol, in one of the foulest weather areas of water in the
world.'

The winter of 1939/40 was freezing. In spite of severe gales,
Sam Hall, the pilot on board *York*, flew the Walrus from dawn to
dusk on a continuous anti-submarine patrol. *York*'s principal
job was to detect and intercept enemy merchant ships returning
to German ports with valuable cargoes of strategic materials.

'After a while we did find what we were looking for,' Caspar recorded, 'a ship with a cargo which included mercury. It was not long before she stopped and began to settle in the high seas. We rescued from the water as many of the men as we could – we learnt that the sea-water cocks had been opened so there was no hope for her – and watched her founder. Several of the men we saved from drowning, at some risk to ourselves, gave the "Heil Hitler" arm salute as soon as they were dragged over the rails, which did not endear them to us.'

After some months in this foul climate, the ship was ordered to Rosyth to take on board an Army detachment destined for Norway. Following Hitler's invasion in April 1940, one of the Royal Navy's tasks was to rush army detachments to her aid at selected points along the Norwegian coast. *York* disembarked troops at Andalsnes, and before leaving Caspar begged the Commanding Officer to disperse their boxes of ammunition ashore. German Junker 88s were known to overfly likely targets from 5 a.m., and here would be such a target, as long as it remained concentrated. Caspar's words were unheeded; the Junker duly came and, 'with a loud bang', he remembered, the ammunition went for a burton. HMS *York* had fortunately already departed the scene on antisubmarine patrol, and with the Walrus being catapulted from the ship's deck, made countless searches in and out of the many fjords – beautiful but deadly hiding places for submarines.

At the end of April the Navy was ordered to evacuate the troops they had so recently disembarked. HMS *York* proceeded to Namsos, a cluster of coloured wooden houses clinging between the mountains and the water, where it had been decided that the evacuation of both French and British troops should be carried out during the three hours of darkness which the northern spring provided. The officer commanding, the one-eyed, one-armed General Adrian Carton de Wiat, had judged the task impossible, but the ships, creeping in through a dense sea mist, accomplished it. He was embarked in *York*, together with his

ADC, Major Peter Fleming, an author whom Caspar much admired, and with whom he shared a half-sister, Amaryllis Fleming, fourteen years old at the time and destined to become a distinguished cellist. Augustus was her father.

'The Army turned out to be mostly French Chasseur Alpins,' Caspar recorded, 'fine men who burnt their heavy and brand new mountain equipment before embarking. Not so their rations, which turned out to be heavily impregnated with garlic. After transferring them to French troopships at Scapa Flow, the ship's company turned to with a will to rid the mess-decks of the smell of the back streets of Marseilles.'

From the icy waters of the North Sea, the ship was now ordered to make for the sweltering heat of the African continent. Her task was to escort the liner *Duchess of Bedford* and two large New Zealand shipping line cargo ships round the Cape of Good Hope to Port Said in Egypt. On board were valuable supplies of equipment, particularly tanks, destined for the British Army in North Africa. To avoid the war zones in the Mediterranean, these had to be laboriously carried the whole way round Africa. The journey involved calls at, among other places, Freetown, the capital of Sierra Leone, where the ship anchored for forty-eight hours. The Walrus was catapulted off and flown ashore for flying exercises. It landed in a small field where there was a contingent of Fleet Air Arm personnel.

Sam Hall recorded what happened in Freetown:

> We hired a taxi, which was an open vehicle of doubtful parentage. The black driver, clothed in a sarong and driving bare-footed, chatted away in pidgin English. I remember after we had gone some distance, we saw a large house, standing on a hill overlooking Freetown. We asked the driver who lived there, and he replied, 'That Sah, is where Number One Jesus Christ, boss man lives,' from which we deduced it was the Bishop of Freetown's residence.
>
> In Freetown harbour there was one character who

always paddled, wearing a black top hat and loin cloth. He was not only a character, but a mimic. He could, and did, imitate a bo'sun's pipe, and then call near the starboard side, 'Away Captain's motor boat.' Invariably the crew of the Captain's motor boat manned the boat and brought it alongside, asking instructions from the Officer of the Watch. The bo'sun would deny that the pipe had been made. Whilst this contretemps was going on by the starboard gangway, Joe in his black top hat would paddle his boat round the stern, innocently grinning.

When the ship's crew fell in for Sunday Divisions and the padre appeared in his flowing robes, Black Joe from his bum boat, alongside the quarterdeck, immediately doffed his top hat and in his loud booming voice called: 'Good morning your reverence.' The padre glanced over his shoulder with a disdainful look on his face, ignoring Joe, who immediately returned his top hat to his head and called out: 'Very good reverence, no black vimen for you tonight.'

Other calls included Simonstown and Aden for fresh water. The monotony was also broken by the almost daily receipt of a message from Winston Churchill urging the ships to proceed faster. Since the convoy was already going at full speed, this served little purpose, and on arrival at Port Said no time was wasted in unloading the valuable cargoes for Wavell's North African campaign.

The next few months were taken up with duties in the Mediterranean and Aegean Seas; 'we were a kind of policeman on the beat,' as Caspar described it, 'checking the German and Italian infiltration into the Aegean Islands and North Africa.' By the latter half of 1940, a year after the outbreak of the war, Britain's Navy, Army and Air Force, and her civilian population, were at full stretch. Most of Europe was in enemy hands and Italy had recently joined Germany; England was virtually fighting alone.

Hawker Osprey two-seater fighter/recce, C.J. in
the cockpit, HMS *Eagle* below.

Talking to the Commanding Officer of French troops rescued
from Namsos, Norway. HMS *York*, mid-North Sea, 1940.

Home from sea. Caspar with
Caroline, Rebecca (centre)
and Phineas, Cornwall, 1951.

On holiday in 1960: (left) Caroline and Mary;
(below) Rebecca, Phineas and Caspar. Caspar's
tattoo of a snake was paired on his left arm
with a sea eagle.

The Mediterranean sea route was still open to ships, but they had to be heavily escorted. The odds against Britain were daily increasing, with the French fleet largely neutralized or out of action and enemy air power established on the northern shores of the Mediterranean. The Royal Air Force was fully committed in Northern Europe and in the Battle of Britain, and had no resources to spare to reinforce the Mediterranean. Thus, almost the only available air striking power in the Mediterranean came from aircraft carriers. The decision was made that the Fleet Air Arm should attack the Italian Fleet at Taranto. On the night of 11 November 1940, twenty swordfish aircraft operating from the aircraft carrier *Illustrious* torpedoed and bombed ships and installations. The attack was well planned, and caused sufficient damage to restore the balance of naval power in Britain's favour in the Mediterranean and release badly needed ships to fight the impending battle of the Atlantic. It was the Fleet Air Arm's greatest victory. Caspar watched the aircraft take off, rejoiced at their success, and regretted that he was no longer a pilot like the others who could take part in such an operation.

With the Germans occupying Greece, *York* was ordered to embark anti-aircraft guns and as many soldiers as they could manage, and transport them from Port Said to Piraeus. 'It seemed to us like Norway all over again, too little too late. It was doubtless a difficult decision to switch the Army from success in North Africa to face the Germans in Greece, but to us it seemed like a big letdown.' It was to be a Caspar's last direct involvement with the war at sea.

Early in 1941 he received orders that he was to return to England immediately for some special duty. He was put ashore at Alexandria. He was lucky; not long after *York* was sunk in Suda Bay off Crete. Reggie Portal reported in glowing terms on his second-in-command. Caspar had performed 'entirely to my satisfaction in all his duties. A very able Executive Officer with outstanding qualities of leadership, devotion to duty and loyalty. These qualities combined with a quick and active brain and all the attributes of a first-class staff officer fit him well for the higher ranks of the Service.'

How he was to get back to England, avoiding the war zones between Alexandria and London, was a problem that exercised Caspar greatly. He had circumnavigated Africa on the outward journey; travelling alone, it might be possible to cross Africa by air, although Sunderland Flying Boats had ceased flying along the North African coast due to the fighting. Imperial Airways, pioneer of civilian trans-African air routes, had been taken over by the newly formed British Overseas Airways Corporation the previous year. They had an office in Alexandria, and from there Caspar was able to organize the first stage of his journey home. With petrol still in supply, BOAC was operating a twin-engined de Havilland biplane, *Rapide*, between East and West Africa with five overnight stops across the Sudan and Nigeria. It was much in demand. 'The airlines along the trans-African route constantly found themselves in charge of some important personage in a mad hurry,' reported Eve Curie, a journalist on a mission across Africa in 1941. 'American Generals passed in a flash, then repassed . . . The hospitable residents of remote Sudanese districts could not tell who might drop in unexpectedly for dinner – an American Ambassador, the King of Yugoslavia, a Greek General, or a Soviet expert.'

First Caspar had to fly south to Khartoum; from there the aeroplane headed due west to El Obeid and El Fasher, still in the Sudan. It flew over the swamps of Chad into Nigeria, where it stopped first at Maiduguri and then at the ancient walled city of Kano set in scrubby desert. Finally, the plane landed at Lagos, 'the home of delay', as Peter Fleming described it.

Caspar was in a hurry; it was not in his nature to stay still, yet here he was stuck, with no transport immediately or even remotely available to cross the several thousand miles of sea water between West Africa and Britain. The local naval officer in charge told him that he would be able to get as far as Freetown by cruiser, but only after a three-week wait. Some people would have gratefully accepted three weeks unsolicited holiday. Caspar found employment. The campaign in the Western Desert depended on war material having to be ferried almost daily from depots on the West African coast. Caspar contacted Takoradi, an RAF station not far from Lagos, and offered his services as a pilot. He made six trips across Africa, ferrying Blenheims and Beaufighters from Takoradi to Aboukir in Egypt, an RAF depot he had known when stationed in the desert in 1936.

The British cruiser *Dragon* eventually arrived on her journey from the Cape, and Caspar was able to get to Freetown, 'hot as hell, and at that time a big naval enclave for Atlantic convoys'. Here he managed to secure a berth in a Dutch liner, part of a convoy heading for England.

'I spent most of the time up on the Bridge advising the Dutch Captain how to avoid German submarines, of which I knew quite a lot, having been in Atlantic convoys, and of which he knew little, having come from the East Indies.' This entailed a wide diversion into the Western Atlantic, zig-zagging and altering course so as to remain elusive and exploit the difficulties of any lurking U-boat.

The convoy finally arrived in one piece at Glasgow, and Caspar was now faced with what he mockingly described as 'the hazardous 400-mile rail journey' to London. Surviving this, he reported for duty at the Admiralty, where an old FAA friend happened to be the Commander responsible for individual appointments. 'You're wanted across the way,' he said.

'What's that mean, across the way?' Caspar asked. 'France?'

'Oh no; at the MAP.'

The Ministry of Aircraft Production, situated on Millbank, had been created in 1940 to help relieve the Air Ministry of the responsibility of procuring supplies, and to initiate the research and development of a large range of equipment, including up-to-date radar which was required principally by the RAF. Caspar was appointed Chief Naval Representative (CNR) and Director General Naval Aircraft Development and Production

(DGNADP). Now more urgent than ever, his work was once again concerned with the design and production of aircraft for the Navy. With the new appointment he was promoted Captain in May 1941, having served four years as Commander.

His immediate task was to obtain more aircraft for the Navy from the British Aircraft Industry. This meant convincing Lord Beaverbrook, the Minister of Aircraft Production, that he should adjust his priorities to give the Navy a larger slice of the cake. Beaverbrook was notoriously not an easy man to convince. What was the sense in giving priority to bombing Germany when much of what was needed was being sunk by German submarines in the Atlantic? Caspar argued. Beaverbrook accepted that he had a point. 'Sailor, you have a good case,' he replied, 'but it is inopportune for me to change course.' Caspar's chief concern – that the Fleet Air Arm was so inadequately equipped that it was unable to play an effective role in the Atlantic – did not sway Beaverbrook; his mind was fixed on the paramount need to continue the bombing of Germany. Caspar saw only one possibility; to try to obtain from the USA what was needed for the Fleet Air Arm. He duly reported this to the First Lord of the Admiralty.

*   *   *

The Admiralty had been represented in Washington since 1940 by the British Admiralty Delegation. Unhappily, there was no qualified naval aviator on the BAD staff; but a British Air Commission staffed exclusively by Air Ministry civil servants and RAF officers was already at work in Washington when, in the early summer of 1941, a very junior naval officer, Acting Lieutenant-Commander John Millar, was sent out by the Fifth Sea Lord, Vice Admiral Sir Arthur Lyster, to find out why the Admiralty was not getting the aircraft which it had on order for the FAA. The Commission, whose instructions were to carry out a Cabinet decision that the FAA was to have bottom priority, did not welcome Millar's arrival.

'When I arrived,' wrote Millar, 'I asked for copies of all orders for naval aircraft on order with American manufacturers and the delivery status of each. This information was a long time coming and my position was made as uncomfortable as possible. I was allocated what was not much more than a broom closet to work in and Air Vice-Marshal Jones so resented my presence that he sent a signal to the Ministry of Aircraft Production that I should be withdrawn.' This signal was referred to the Admiralty who promptly signalled back that Millar was to remain as an assistant to Richard Smeeton.

Smeeton, another junior Lieutenant-Commander, had been installed in Washington as the Admiralty's sole Air representative barely one month before Millar's arrival, and until the spring of 1943 was single-handedly responsible for the ordering of naval aircraft, while at the same time he was expected to deal with the complex technical and production side of the differing American system.

Shortly before America entered the war in December 1941, the respective heads of American and British naval aviation, Vice Admiral Jack Towers and Vice Admiral Sir Arthur Lyster, met in Washington. The two men got on extremely well. 'The upshot of the meeting between the two Admirals was very interesting,' Millar wrote. 'First of all the deck landing signals for the two Navies were standardized – the "batsman" signals had been exactly the opposite – so that at least from then on British aircraft could land on American carriers without confusion and vice versa.' Towers, whose attitude to the Admiralty delegation was one of sympathy, decided to give the FAA decent representation on Constitution Avenue. 'We dark blues must stick together,' he told Millar and Smeeton. 'I'm not at all happy at the way your Royal Air Force and our US Army Air Corps are cosying up together. You two boys come down to my Bureau of Aeronautics on Monday morning at a quarter of eight and I'll give you an office next to mine and all the aeroplanes you want.'

'That was a wonderful offer which of course we accepted,'

133

Millar wrote, and they set up the Fleet Air Arm Representation in the Bureau of Aeronautics on Constitution Avenue. Towers made it plain that they must always be at their desks by a quarter to eight each morning as the Chief of Naval Operations (USN equivalent of First Sea Lord) arrived then and did not like to see anyone coming in after him. Although America was not at war, while England was fighting for her life, the Americans were unable to speak on the telephone with any of the British Missions for an hour every morning because no one in the British Missions came in before 9 a.m.

Prior to the attack on Pearl Harbor in December 1941, Dick Smeeton had been carrying out lengthy discussions on requirements with Lt-Com. George Anderson USN (who was later to become Chief of Naval Operations in 1962). 'Progress was slow,' Smeeton wrote, 'chiefly because there was no money voted by Congress to start the physical construction of new factory space in which to build the aircraft. The attack on Pearl Harbor changed all that and the US Navy asked me how many aircraft were required by the RN for the duration of the war.' The estimate, although complicated, resulted in an order for 2500 aircraft from the USN. This was gladly received because they could now expect a larger sum from Congress to expand the factories producing naval aircraft. Without the British requirements they would have had to make do with smaller factories, and British orders would have suffered accordingly.

But the Admiralty was consistently slow in agreeing to Smeeton's requests for authorization to order the required number of aircraft. Time and again he could only assume that the authorization would eventually come, and had to sign on his own responsibility for millions of dollars' worth of aircraft. When Smeeton and a colleague from the British Air Commission were preparing to sign the programme requiring 2500 aircraft – and an increase in the number of 'Woolworth carriers' – nothing had been heard from the Admiralty until the morning they were due to sign. Then, just as they were leaving the BAC building, a signal was handed to Smeeton, the gist of which said that the Admiralty was anxious to avoid any responsibility for the Programme unless a certain number of the aircraft could be delivered by the end of 1942. It also implied that after that date, British production would take care of the RN's needs. Exasperated by the late arrival of this signal and its contents, Smeeton ignored it, and went ahead to the US Navy department and signed the requisition forms on behalf of HMG. He was later ordered to England to explain to their lordships why he had acted as he had done. 'They seemed to find it difficult to accept that in order to build aircraft in large numbers it is first necessary to spend millions of dollars on building the factories.' The point was that had he ducked out at the eleventh hour, Britain's share would have been removed from the Bill before it went up the Hill for Congressional approval.

After America had joined the war, it became obvious that a close integration of the requirements of the two navies would be necessary rather than a continual placing of separate contracts. Dick Smeeton had been doing extraordinarily well, but it was obvious that activity at an altogether higher level would be necessary if the Air side of the British Admiralty Delegation was to be placed on a proper footing. The Admiralty was now disposed to do this, and they recognized that no one was better qualified to find out exactly what the Americans could provide, and to secure it quickly, than Caspar John. He was selected to represent the Admiralty in a high-powered joint Air Ministry-Admiralty Mission despatched to Washington in October 1942 under the leadership of Oliver Lyttleton, who had now replaced Beaverbrook as Minister of Aircraft Production. Caspar welcomed the task because he knew that it was something of supreme importance which he was more than able to cope with, but left to himself he would have far preferred to be back at sea in command of an aircraft carrier.

They left on 28 October: 'Up at 0600. Spam and cold tomato breakfast. Luggage muddles,' Caspar scribbled in his diary. From

Shannon, the Mission flew south to Lisbon, Dutch Guinea and Liberia before crossing the Atlantic to Belem on the Amazon. From there they flew north to San Juan, Puerto Rica, and landed at New York on 1 November. Caspar stayed in the United States for only one month on this visit, investigating the means of procuring aircraft which were being built at a far greater rate and in larger numbers than in the UK at highly efficient factories all over the States.

The immediate result of this Mission was the signing of an agreement which established firm allocations of aircraft for the first six months of 1943, and tentative arrangements for the second half of the year. This gave the Admiralty a much better idea of the quantity of aircraft it could expect from the USA. It also became evident that the number of aircraft required from the USA would continue to grow throughout the war and that their production and supply would call for constant review and negotiation. Problems of shipping and distributing the aircraft, for example, were becoming more and more complex, as also were the modifications needed to meet special British requirements. The small Naval Air Representation in Washington was severely overtaxed, carrying responsibilities far greater than those the junior officers concerned could reasonably be asked to shoulder. The obvious solution was to strengthen the NAR so that it could deal efficiently with the flow of some 250–300 aircraft a month from US factories. In March 1943 Caspar returned to Washington and was appointed Naval Air Representative in the British Admiralty Delegation; he was also the Fifth Sea Lord's representative and was made Naval Air Attaché at the British Embassy.

He sailed in the liner *Queen Elizabeth*, celebrating his fortieth birthday somewhere in mid-Atlantic. With him was Commander Dennis Cambell, who after a spell as test pilot with the Blackburn company had deck-landed their new aircraft on the *Illustrious* in the Clyde. 'Caspar beckoned to me across the flight deck after my last landing and said he was forming a team for Washington to take over the jobs which Richard Smeeton had been doing single-handed.' Caspar wanted to place someone in the British Air Commission who could monitor and report on all aspects of USN aircraft design and development and hold his own with the Bureau of Aeronautics officers in charge of such work. Dennis Cambell, a former Skua Squadron CO, who had recently had experience testing aircraft, was an obvious choice. Another member of the team was Commander Frank Hopkins, fresh from earning his DSO at Malta.

The *Queen Elizabeth* docked at Halifax on 25 March. Caspar was met by John Millar in the twin-engined 'Beechcraft', a transport plane allocated to the RN by the US Munitions Assignment Committee and reserved for the exclusive use of naval members of the British Air Commission, who used it to fly all over North America on their separate missions. On this occasion, they flew almost immediately into a snowstorm, but once through it Millar let Caspar take over the controls so as to get used to the machine. This was to prove useful later.

From his experience with the Lyttelton Mission and his earlier contacts with the US naval authorities, it was obvious to Caspar that close personal touch would have to be kept with the various departments of the Bureau of Aeronautics if satisfactory co-ordination was to be achieved. His predecessors had never been given a proper chance, and the Admiralty had done little to support them. By the time of his arrival, however, the staff of the Bureau of Aeronautics fully understood and sympathized with the Admiralty's problem of rapidly building up the Fleet Air Arm, given the very small numbers of naval air personnel who were available – a legacy from the interwar years of dual control. Individual US Navy officers were very friendly and, as far as they were able, extremely helpful. But the US Navy was a vast organization, and it was often difficult to know to whom to turn for information or a decision. 'I think the term "rat race" probably derived from those days in Washington,' Caspar said later. There was also a background of misgiving among the

Americans as to whether the Admiralty was sufficiently determined or experienced in air matters to be able to carry out its expansion programme. Some sceptics asked whether the US Navy was justified in assigning to this doubtful cause a substantial quantity of aircraft which it badly needed itself. This attitude persisted to a greater or lesser degree throughout the period of Caspar's appointment in Washington and coloured all discussions and negotiations.

There was also the fact that different types of war were being fought by the British and the Americans. The latter were mainly concerned – as far as its carriers were involved in particular – with the war in the Pacific, whereas the former were operating, or about to operate, carriers in the Atlantic, Mediterranean and Indian Ocean. The war never meant the same thing in Washington as it did in London. Caspar remembered that what really brought home to his friends in Washington the immediacy of the war was a shortage of whisky. 'They said, there's something really serious going on in the Atlantic and in Europe, we're running short of Scotch!' Pearl Harbor was the event by which all their calendars were regulated, not Dunkirk or the Battle of the Atlantic.

The language difference was no less of a problem. It prompted Dennis Cambell to write a short comedy sketch called 'After all, We Both Speak the Same Language', with the subtitle, 'A good-humoured angle on Lease-Lend from the British Air Commission in Washington'. It started with a hypothetical signal received from the UK:

'*Corsair*. 1. Trouble has been experienced with elongated tail-wheel yoke during deck landings. Cases have been reported of wrinkling and damage to fuselage.

2. Please discuss with Bureau. Are any remedial measures proposed?'

The ensuing dialogue between the USN Commander and a RN Commander demonstrated the total failure of the American officer to grasp what the British officer was trying to get across, not only because of differing emphasis in speech patterns, but because the two people looked at technical problems in a different way. 'One USN aircraft type used to lose its wings if handled too ham-handedly. They brought in a modification to strengthen the wings, and when such incidents fell to only one a month (!) they reckoned this was OK,' Dennis Cambell recalled.

Whereas the frugal British relied on spare parts, the Americans were unconcerned with them. This had a marked effect on the manufacturer, whose chief concern was to beat the target with production of complete aircraft: 'In the final analysis, it was no satisfaction to the manufacturer to produce "X" items of spares when with the same effort he could produce "Y" completed aircraft,' Caspar reported.

It was all highly efficient: 'on engines, it takes 2.5 man-hours to produce one Horse Power,' someone worked out, and emergency crews would arrive on Sundays to sort out bottlenecks. To Caspar and his FAA colleagues it felt as if they were working round the clock. 'It was extremely hard work, immensely interesting, and I felt and thought and knew that I was doing a really constructive job.' There was very little time off, but when the chance arose they might attend a baseball match – a Wren working in Washington at the time remembers Caspar dispensing hot dogs and popcorn, saying, 'Who are you rooting for?' – and there were official cocktail parties to attend and other social functions, such as John Millar's wedding in New York at which Caspar was best man. 'It was almost impossible in wartime America to get on the train or a commercial airline or to get enough petrol for a car,' John Millar remembered. 'We were going to go to Ponte Vedra in Florida for our honeymoon, so Caspar said to me about two weeks before the wedding, "I'd like you to fly me to Jacksonville in Florida to pay a call on the American Admiral in charge," and added that he thought we should have a flight nurse in attendance. That was all that was said.' The flight nurse was, of course, to be John Millar's new wife who had been working for the American Red Cross. On the day after the wedding, she put on her Red Cross uniform and accompanied her husband on their honeymoon flight as the flight nurse.

* * *

'From my first contact with the US Navy,' Caspar recalled, 'I had nothing but help and cooperation, for which the Royal Navy owes a major debt of gratitude. We immediately established an organization for procuring and distributing what was mutually agreed were our requirements surplus to the US Navy's needs. This involved organizing the training of air and ground crews to fly and maintain the quite new and different types of US Navy aircraft.'

The interests of the BAC were spread over a vast geographical area – from Chicago to St Louis, from Maine to Florida. Roosevelt Field on Long Island was the centre for the reception, packing and shipping of aircraft to scenes of war around the world by vessels waiting at the New York waterside. 'From this complex organization we were able to re-equip the Royal Navy in the air worldwide, fully capable of taking its place alongside the US Navy in the Pacific, enabling aircraft carriers to fight and live another day,' wrote Caspar, referring in particular to the armoured decks of British carriers which enabled them to withstand direct hits from Japanese kamikaze bombers.

During Caspar's first visit to Washington in 1942 he and Dick Smeeton had flown in the Beechcraft to Connecticut to pay a visit to the Vought Sikorski plant at Stratford. The purpose of the visit was to meet Igor Sikorski and see how his helicopter programme was progressing. Sikorski was an ex-Russian naval officer who had fled Russia after the Revolution and formed a company in the USA to continue his work as an aircraft designer, but his personal interest centred on helicopters which hitherto had not been put into military use. His first experiments in flight had begun in Russia in the 1900s (contemporary with the Wright Brothers in America and Louis Blériot in France), and were aimed at vertical lift-off. The machine he built jumped rather than flew, and it was nicknamed 'the Hopper'. He subsequently became famous for his 'giants' – aeroplanes with a wing span of 30-odd metres. In the USA the Royal Navy had been following his helicopter developments but failed to convince the Bureau of Aeronautics that there was any future for them at sea. During his visit to Sikorski's plant, Caspar tackled the subject directly with him: 'I was strolling with Igor Sikorski one day,' Caspar subsequently wrote, 'and I mentioned to him the problem of the antisubmarine war in the Atlantic. He had been an ardent supporter of the large flying boat, and I asked him if he could bring his talents to bear on rotary winged aircraft in the antisubmarine role. He seemed more interested in photography at the time, but replied, "Yes, there are obvious advantages in stationary flight; you shall have one of my YR4A helicopters tomorrow for whatever tests you wish."'

The machine was of very limited capability at that time but it was still a great deal better than nothing. Caspar secured the services of a merchant ship, the *Daghestan*, which was fitted with a stern platform from which the helicopter could operate, and made a series of trials in Long Island Sound. These seemed promising. It was the true beginning of the helicopter as a practical aircraft, and the Admiralty ordered 250, 'a remarkable act of faith not supported by the US Navy, but heavily backed by the US Army Air Corps, and by the US Coastguard, on whose airfield, Floyd Bennett, we established an international Helicopter Training School, with the White Ensign proudly flying.' When, later, the US Navy and Army Airforce began to clamour for them Sikorski had to tell them that the British were his first customers and that they would get the first few hundred built. However, by the time the first helicopters were coming off the assembly line, Germany was defeated and the Admiralty lost interest. They cancelled the contract, but Dennis Cambell persuaded them to retain just twelve so that the Navy could keep a foothold in this entirely new branch of aviation.

Hence Westlands, and it was not until 1952 that the Navy got them in any numbers.

Almost as important as the provision of military aircraft was the programme for the training of British pilots in the United States. Caspar had become involved in this operation, which had been set up in 1941 by Vice Admirals Lyster and Towers and was known as the 'Towers scheme'. From his headquarters adjoining that of the Chief of Operations in Washington, he was given the responsibility of controlling the progress of the trainee pilots from the beginnings in Michigan, to an advanced course in Pensacola, Florida, and finally specialization in either dive-bombing, torpedo or fighter planes. In this way one third of the FAA pilots and maintenance crews who took part in the Second World War were trained by American instructors in American planes.

*   *   *

In August 1944, Caspar was recalled to England. The machinery of procurement and pilot-training had been successfully set up and only routine maintenance was needed to keep it going. He sailed from New York on 11 August and arrived at Liverpool ten days later. He was to spend the last twelve months of the war in command of two aircraft carriers in home waters – HMS *Pretoria Castle*, a former Union Castle liner converted in Belfast, and HMS *Ocean*, a brand new light carrier. In the *Pretoria Castle*, working closely with the Royal Aircraft Establishment, Farnborough, and the aircraft industry, a variety of experiments and tests were carried out to improve the practical operation of aircraft at sea by day and night.

'A highlight was the operation of the US Army Airforce fighter Airacobra,' Caspar wrote, 'with a tricycle nose-wheel undercarriage, an innovation at the time and destined to simplify deck landing in a big way. I had to pull some private and friendly strings to have an arrester hook installed. We were at sea most flying days and nights, largely because the "Tail of the Bank" anchorage off Greenock was overfull with convoy ships, and finding a spare berth there in blackout and rain was a dicey business.'

*   *   *

It was during the war that Caspar met his future wife, Mary Vanderpump. They had met in 1941 when Mary was an ambulance driver based at the Old Bailey. She had gone for a drink at a pub in Swiss Cottage with her fellow driver, Dorrie John, wife of Caspar's elder brother David. David and Caspar joined the two girls, together with the painter Matthew Smith. 'I tried to ride a bicycle afterwards with my hands crossed on the handlebars, which made it rather complicated to steer,' Mary remembered, 'so it was all very jolly and larky. I was rather smitten by his lovely warm brown eyes.' Physically she was his opposite, with fair hair and blue eyes. Caspar had a small house in Canning Place in Kensington and Mary used to visit him there and darn his socks. When, later, he moved to Elm Place in Chelsea to stay with his sister Poppet, they continued seeing each other whenever their wartime work permitted. While Mary was in the Ambulance Service, Caspar had undertaken fire-watching duties on the roof of Westminster Abbey as well as working at the Ministry of Aircraft Production.

'We had bicycles,' Mary recalled. 'He had a large, heavy bike, and I more a racing type – rather like a bomber and a Spitfire, I used to think. London was empty of traffic and with nothing in the way one could *whizz* around Hyde Park Corner. We used sometimes to put them on the train and go to Suffolk, or on Saturday nights to Hampton Wick to play shove ha'penny in a pub and drink pints of beer with his brother David and friends.'

Mary had been born in New Zealand in January 1916. Her father, Stuart Vanderpump, was of Dutch descent and had emigrated to New Zealand before the First World War. Her mother, Margaret Cullen, was the eldest of twelve children and had sailed from Britain in 1912 to decide whether she and other members of the family should settle there permanently. Her marriage to Stuart Vanderpump was not a success and as soon as the First World War was over, she returned to England with Mary. For twelve years they lived with Margaret's mother and her sisters and brothers in a large house in Finsbury Park. Mrs V. de P. – as she was sometimes known – was an ambitious woman. She not only had to but wanted to work hard. She wasted no time in setting about earning her living and eventually became a partner in a successful clothes business off Bond Street which specialized in designing handmade blouses and camisoles, in silk and lace. Her attitude to life, always very proper, and the pride she took in her work, seems reminiscent of Caspar's grandmother, Ada Nettleship: both of them strict Victorian women, but in Margaret's case having a sense of humour which sometimes brought tears to her eyes.

In order that her mother could work, Mary endured a succession of bleak boarding schools and at the age of fourteen was sent to a convent in Belgium to become fluent in French. She grew up a tough and spirited girl, without airs and graces, but with an energy and spontaneity that Caspar found immediately appealing. Mary had, at an early age, rebelled against her mother's disciplined way of life and domineering concern over the way one should dress; she reacted by treating clothes as something to which the minimum of attention should be paid.

By the time Caspar got back from Washington in August 1944 Mary had left the ambulances and was now working on the Grand Union Canal. She had had enough of sitting in garages in different parts of London waiting to drive to an emergency – first at the Barbican, then at the Old Bailey, and bleakest of all, Moon's Garage in Bloomsbury. Canal work was considered a worthy alternative to the Land Army or the women's services. Together with the other girls her job was to load steel and aluminium at Limehouse and transport it by barge along the Grand Union Canal to the factories at Birmingham, a three-week round trip. Caspar would sometimes join them and help out with the more difficult jobs. 'He used to come down to Limehouse and help us cloth up, a beastly job. He only ran the boat on the mud *twice*, steering it in the Jackdaw Pound, a notoriously bad, winding and muddy stretch.' The girls worked the barges in trios and on one occasion when Caspar was there, one of them, Emma Smith, fell into a deep lock in front of an oncoming boat. 'With great presence of mind,' Mary remembers, 'Caspar leapt across the boats and saved her life by pulling her heavy weight clear with one arm.' On another occasion when Caspar was with them, they tied up at Marsworth, near an airfield. Some American airmen saw them and asked Caspar to pose with the girls for a photograph of a family of typical boatmen. Regular boat people, who helped the girls splice ropes and repair fenders, formed the sound opinion that he was 'An 'andy man on the Cut!'

In wartime, weddings tended to follow very shortly after an engagement. Caspar and Mary's was no exception. Since neither of them were interested in religious ritual, the couple settled for a registry office. The ceremony was performed so rapidly that Mary's Aunt Luli, who needed to go to the lavatory on arrival, emerged to find that it was all over. It was, Caspar wrote, 'The greatest experiment of all, which stood the test of time.' His verdict on the marriage was that he had married his opposite. 'Uncertainty is the life-blood of Mary,' he once observed; something which a man as regulated as he was found in many ways admirable but sometimes difficult to live with. She provided a background not unlike his own childhood; something which he appreciated and yet, since he had joined the Navy to escape from it, he did not always welcome it in later life.

Mary was initially daunted by Augustus. When Caspar first took her to Fryern Court to meet her future father-in-law, she found it 'rather an alarming experience; he had darting eyes which were quite frightening.' And it was very difficult to talk to him. His increasing deafness meant that any conversation had to be conducted at a shout; but in spite of this drawback he kept a sharp ear out for any word wrongly used, something which so incensed him that he'd pounce on the offending word and roar it back. But things improved. When, in the 1950s, Mary began to sculpt terracotta heads of her children and friends, Augustus encouraged her and asked her if she had studied Etruscan sculpture.

Dodo she found more sympathetic, and later would often remark on how difficult Augustus must have been to live with. She herself had to endure the John 'cafards' – the glooms – that afflicted the sons of Augustus.

7

HMS *Ocean*
and worldwide thoughts

HMS *Ocean* had been built during the war on the Clyde, launched in July 1944 by Lady Willis, wife of the Commander-in-Chief of the Mediterranean Fleet, and finally commissioned on 30 June 1945. Destined to be the first night-fighter aircraft carrier in the Navy, she was just ready to join the war in the Far East when peace was declared, first in Europe in May and then with Japan in August 1945. Caspar had been sent to take command of this carrier from the moment of her commissioning, with eight hundred officers and ratings to man her and 'make from a metal shell a liveable happy community with a sense of purpose'. Yet at the same time he had to face the fact of demobilization. With the war ended, many men longed to get back to their families and found it hard to believe that the strains of night-flying operations were necessary or justifiable. Caspar thought they were, but his task was made far more difficult by the constant coming and going of individuals in the ship's company. 'I like to think that I influenced the waverers on board to stick it out,' he wrote. 'We retained a hard core of dedicated men who gave us the spine to continue.' Not one of the aircrews ever asked for a less demanding life; 'He worked the ship like mad,' recalled his second-in-command, Nigel Henderson.

Caspar was always a strict disciplinarian, and he insisted on the ship's flying routine being meticulously followed. He would never condone the unnecessary taking of a risk. The pilots were said to be more alarmed by the prospect of their Captain's wrath than they were by the physical dangers involved in crashing their aircraft. But his main priority was to keep up the morale of the ship's company, and the welfare and conduct of his men were always at the forefront of his thinking. If, for instance, there was a choice between cinema in the hangar and preparing aircraft for flying, he always put cinema first; and every Sunday he would chat with the assembled sailors on the flight deck, an occasion they all looked forward to because he was always 'whimsical, and modest, and down to earth,' Nigel Henderson remembers, who believes these chats did more to keep people happy than almost anything else.

After the completion of some months of flying practice conducted off Liverpool and Glasgow, *Ocean* was preparing for further trials in the Mediterranean. While steaming off the Isle of Wight, an historical event took place: the first ever jet landing at sea. The 540 m.p.h. jet, a de Havilland Sea Vampire – the latest British jet-propelled fighter, believed then to be the fastest aeroplane in the world and still very much on the secret list – was piloted by the Navy's chief test pilot, twenty-four-year-old Lt-Commander Eric Brown, known as 'Winkle' to his Fleet Air Arm friends. In wintry weather, and despite the heavy swell that was causing *Ocean* to pitch and roll, and a loud-speaker announcement that the pilot had been ordered to remain at Ford airfield, Sussex, the Vampire, reported the *Daily Sketch*, 'screamed over the flight deck, made a roll and streaked away to circle the ship. The carrier's decks were immediately cleared and she turned into wind. Brown brought his plane directly astern and came in at 95 m.p.h. to make a perfect landing, picking up the first arrester wire and stopping in a hundred feet. Taking off, the pilot was airborne in half the length of the flight deck.'

On the passage out from the Clyde to the Mediterranean, it was agreed to spend a weekend anchored off Bangor, Co. Down, which was tranquil, unbombed, and more or less free from the worst of the food rationing. Here, perhaps, was a chance to get some Christmas shopping done, and accordingly, a few hundred turkeys were taken on board and stowed in *Ocean*'s hold ready for Christmas feasting at Gibraltar. But a still more unusual consignment took passage in *Ocean* when she later returned to England from Malta: seven Wrens. Living aft in the Captain's quarters, these were the first girls ever to have lived and travelled in one of HM ships. They had been specially selected for the honour and were known on board as the 'Top Flight Honeys'.

One of the Wrens who took passage, Sheena Weston, recalls that there were no troopships to take them home, due probably to the fact that they were fully occupied in the Far East collecting ex-prisoners of war. The Wrens were lucky to have been offered a lift in *Ocean* as many other Captains would have regarded having women on board as a possible great nuisance. 'It also meant giving up his day cabin to us. I thought him a wonderfully mannered and courtly gentleman. We didn't see him during the sea voyage at all; he was in his sea cabin on the Bridge. There were active flying exercises taking place all the time, particularly night landing practice. We slept on mattresses in the Captain's day cabin aft, and the noise when the aircraft landed at night was truly terrific. Night landings were a new thing in those days and some of the young pilots due to be demobbed did seem to wonder if their luck would hold out. We ate in the Mess, and the paymaster commander made a point of sitting as far away as possible from us and glaring at us. Obviously women on board was anathema to him.'

The challenge of keeping up the morale of the ship's company was inevitably compounded by the teething troubles which affect a carrier starting from scratch.

At the end of the first four months of HMS *Ocean*'s work-up on the Mediterranean Station, from January to April 1946, the Captain had to submit a report to the Commander-in-Chief, Mediterranean. This consisted of eight appendices with headings such as 'Diary of Events', 'Ship's Features' and, wordiest of all, 'Radar'. Because of its special role as a carrier for night-fighter aircraft, *Ocean* had been given what was supposed to be the last word in radar equipment. Caspar, who never minced his words, commented harshly on the deficiencies of the device. His comments may have caused irritation in Whitehall but in the end the inadequacies were corrected.

Ocean had been designed as a light fleet carrier, and her steadiness at sea – or lack of it – caused some concern, and interfered with aircraft maintenance. 'The ship is very lively indeed for her size,' Caspar reported, 'and would not be suitable for operating aircraft in areas where rough weather was prevalent. Her motion is quick and jerky, and a head sea causes the stern to shake vigorously.' At such times it was difficult to move weighty equipment such as propellers and radio sets.

Accommodation posed something of a problem, because in a night carrier a proportion of the ship's company needed to sleep while others were working, and noise from the flight deck, where there was always something happening by day – oiling at sea, fuelling aircraft, engine tests or men taking exercise – was bad enough to disturb the sleep of those who had worked throughout the night.

In December 1945 the ship had embarked one squadron of Fairey Fireflies and one squadron of Hellcat Night Fighter aircraft, and during her period of service in the Mediterranean, Caspar conducted three months of day- and night-flying operations including 1100 deck landings by day and 250 by night. All this was done without serious accident, an astonishing record, considering the hazards of pioneering night flying from a carrier. As usual Caspar was concerned with finding improvements in the design of these aircraft which would make for easier deck landings. He decided that neither of the aircraft was fast enough to be effective as a modern night fighter, and that it was better on the whole to have two-seater rather than single-seater aircraft, particularly on dark nights. 'Flying a high-performance aircraft at night is almost a full-time job in itself, and leaves no time for efficient radar watch-keeping or dead-reckoning navigation. Apart from the increase in morale caused by presence of a companion, the added scope and efficiency given by a second human brain in all night-flying aircraft is considered to be well worth the weight expended in its installation.'

An additional complication about life on board a night-fighting carrier was the need for aircrews to carry out tests on their own aircraft during the day so that any defects discovered could be put right by nightfall. This caused a considerable strain on all concerned, since it meant long working hours in conditions which were never less than hazardous. When to this was added the fact that the majority of the men were more concerned about getting demobilized and finding a new job than chasing mythical enemies, it was clear that the problems of sustaining morale were considerable. However, the men at least had the satisfaction of knowing that they were pioneers in the new art of carrier night-fighting. They took pride in their rare skill and found in it some consolation for the discomfort, tedium and danger it involved.

Correcting defects in aircraft by night in overcrowded hangars was made more difficult still by the rules about lighting, which stipulated that all lights be dimmed to a faint red glow while the hangar lifts were down. While the lights were on at their full power, maintenance ratings were made to wear dark goggles so that their vision would already have adjusted to working in the dark when the lights were dimmed.

Caspar himself gained some relief from the gruelling demands of maintaining discipline and boosting morale when *Ocean* paid a five-day visit to Cyprus. He got to know the Mayor of Limassol, who was an ardent communist and had played an active part at the time of the recent civil war in Greece. He and Caspar 'got on like a house on fire', Nigel Henderson recalled, 'with a lot of leg-pulling and exchanges of hospitality. By the end of the visit they were real buddies, and we all felt sure that the mayor, if he really had any communist sympathies at the beginning of our visit, had none by the end of it.' One wonders whether the Mayor's staff felt the converse to be true of their distinguished visitor. But the incident was typical of Caspar, who enjoyed befriending unlikely characters and would always have preferred conversation over a drink in a bar to dancing attendance on the mighty in the corridors of Whitehall.

Later that year *Ocean* was engaged in flying exercises to the west of Corfu when, on 22 October 1946, Caspar received a signal that the British destroyer *Saumarez* had been mined in the North Corfu Channel off the coast of Albania, where mines had been illegally laid by the Albanians against the Greeks. All aircraft were recalled, but while they were still landing a second signal reported that the destroyer *Volage* had in her turn been mined while towing the *Saumarez* to safety. Caspar at once decided to go to their rescue via the South Channel. 'It became a pitch-black night with not much sea room. However, we found what we were looking for, and after stopping the *Ocean*, I went in a motor boat to visit the two ships, badly damaged and steaming slowly stern first.' Rear-Admiral Selby, then Captain of *Saumarez*, remembers that just half an hour after having his red-hot side hosed down by HMS *Raider*, the boats from *Ocean* and others were seen coming to the rescue with all their navigation lights showing in the darkness – 'a wonderful cheering sight after six and a half hours struggle'. Caspar did what he could to lift their spirits, and returned to *Ocean* with many badly wounded men to be cared for in the sick bay. The hospital ship *Maine* was due in Corfu harbour to take the wounded and dying to Bighi Hospital, Malta. Ten of the dead were buried in the British cemetery on Corfu; the bodies of thirty-one from both ships were never recovered from the wreckage.

After a few weeks an operation began to send minesweepers through the Channel, supported by destroyers and cruisers of the Fleet, while *Ocean* maintained constant fighter patrols overhead. 'We had only about two dozen assorted fighters on board,' James

Stewart Moore, an officer in *Ocean*, recalled, 'but we made the best impression of strength we could. We were only able to keep eight aircraft in the air at a time, and these had to change round every two hours or so. We made sure that the eight flew around well within sight of the Albanians every twenty minutes or so; then, when the time for changing around came along, we flew off the new patrol and they and the old both flaunted themselves in front of the Albanians for a few minutes. Then the old lot came back and landed, while the new lot disappeared from sight for fifteen or twenty minutes and returned from a different direction. We hoped to give the impression that we had at least sixteen fighters in the sky all the time, and more when needed.' Whether the Albanians were indeed fooled by this device is open to question, but at least they never made any attempt to interfere.

The 'Corfu Incident' had a profound effect on Caspar, and when, in 1966, I visited the island, he asked me to be sure to find the cemetery and report on its condition. I found it beautifully kept, blooming with native Mediterranean flowers and sheltered by olive trees.

*   *   *

At the end of 1946, *Ocean* was ordered to Malta; Caspar's time in command was up. 'I returned to England to learn my fate. I was loath to leave the *Ocean*, but I had no redress. I knew she would give a good account of herself if mixed up in a war.'

Back in England he was told by the Admiralty that he had been selected as a student for the Imperial Defence College 1947 Course. This college, which was attended by officers from all three Services and civilian officials, together with their counterparts from Commonwealth and allied countries, was designed to give officers of Naval Captain's rank, or its equivalent, a broad outline of world affairs. In Caspar's year were Indian and Pakistani officers, civil servants of comparable rank, British Army and RAF officers, diplomats, and United States officers and civilians. The course gave officers what was probably a unique opportunity to think over a long period about issues which did not immediately relate to their daily work. One of the tasks was to write a thesis on a general subject. Caspar made his a wide-ranging review of the present and future state of the world, and entitled it 'Worldwide Thoughts of mid-1947'. It is of considerable interest, being his most sustained statement on his political views and the proper priorities of British foreign policy. His argument begins with the familiar proposition that in an ideal world there would be no individual national sovereignties. In present circumstances this would be wholly unrealistic; therefore some way should be found to adjust national differences while averting war. Internal stability, prosperity and absence of deep ideological differences are prerequisites which do not exist – on the contrary the recent war had exacerbated them. 'A plan for recovery is necessary, and not one plan but a hundred, each one of them interdependent, and requiring for its execution a high level of ability and understanding.' This was equally true of Russia as of the West, but the West must never forget that Russian policy is founded on the belief that the capitalist order must finally collapse.

He believed Russian hostility to be a fact. 'Politically, we in the Western world are uncertain of the future. The Russians are quite sure of it; the world will ripen towards Communism.' However, there was no reason to believe Russia to be aggressive in the military sense. The West must counter Communism by adopting the best features of it. 'It is, I believe, a mistake – a mistake which the Americans are now making and which we often make ourselves – to suppose that this new religion is something altogether evil and unholy.' And he felt that the bourgeois had lost confidence in the order they had themselves created: 'there has been no confident affirmation of the idealist value of bourgeois society, nothing to set against the positive, hard, totalitarian materialism of the Marxist faith.' A US/British Commonwealth combination was the best hope for the West,

Caspar thought, and in the long run, the East-West confrontation presented the worst threat for the future.

The emphasis would of course be different if the thesis were written today. The German nihilism that Caspar feared has conspicuously failed to develop; the Anglo-American partnership has not matured as it seemed reasonable to hope in 1947. Caspar, no more than anybody else, did not foresee the speed of the collapse of British power. His analysis reveals a surprising liberalism for a generally conservative member of a notably conservative profession. He saw nothing to deplore in the existence of a socialist Britain: 'The last General Election in this country showed the extent to which the English people expected something more from the War than the overthrow of Hitler.' He respected, even welcomed those aspirations:

> This period of revolution will not end, in Europe or in our own country, until the establishment of something like the Russians – even the first Bolsheviks – intended their own state to be; a state without the old class distinctions, with much greater equality of incomes and much more social security, with much fewer opportunities for private enterprise than we have known in the past; in other words a state in which the political structure mirrors the economic interests of the working class. Unless this revolution is accepted, there is little chance of internal stability. If it is accepted by the governing class, as the old English governing class accepted the Reform Bill of 1832 and the social changes which this Bill stood for, there is a very considerable chance of stability.

Such was the profession of faith of a humanist who respected the rights of every section of humanity to share in the nation's prosperity, and did not begrudge the sacrifices which his class would need to make to bring it about.

8

From action to influence

The end of Caspar's time at the Imperial Defence College ushered in his last four years of ten as a Captain, and also signalled his changing role in the Navy from man-of-action to man-of-influence. With the exception of some months of flying and one last year at sea, his work from now on was largely desk-bound. But he was far from settled.

In January 1948 he was appointed to command HMS *Fulmar*, the Royal Naval Air Station at Lossiemouth in Morayshire. Soon he turned it into what was known as a master airfield – able to provide assistance to aircraft in difficulty, twenty-four hours a day all the year round.

'Prowling round the hangars one day, I spotted a US Navy single seater Hellcat, apparently in need of a flight,' Caspar wrote, 'so I had the machine put into working order, and commandeered it as my personal hack.' He spent many productive and enjoyable hours flying the machine in order to test the Station's emergency landing organization.

Lossiemouth was a main training ground for Fleet fighter pilots, which created some formidable aircraft noise. Gordonstoun School, situated on the western edge of the aerodrome, was among the neighbours that suffered. Caspar got on well with the headmaster, Kurt Hahn, and made a pact that whenever the school had a special 'do', such as a play or a prize-giving, he would do his best to keep the aircraft away. Another, trickier neighbour was a Scot known as the Laird of Pitgaveney, a local landowner and fisherman who resented the intrusion of aircraft over his land. 'He telephoned me one evening to ask where he could purchase barrage balloons. I put him on to the right source, and asked him against whom had he in mind to protect himself. "Against your damned aeroplanes," came the reply. So it cost me some of the local brew to smooth his ruffled feathers. He became a good, if violent friend.'

At the end of the summer of 1948, after only nine months in Scotland, Caspar received orders that he was required to work at the Admiralty. 'I felt rather like a rolling stone . . . pushed about from pillar to post.' What was worse the new job, entitled 'Deputy Chief of Naval Air Equipment' turned out to be 'thoroughly non-worthwhile'. What he had to do was quite interesting, important even, but there was not nearly enough of it to satisfy his insatiable appetite for work. He complained to the appropriate quarters, who for once were in a flexible mood, and he was appointed instead to be Director of Air Organization and Training (DAOT) at the Admiralty. The job involved keeping the Fleet Air Arm in step with and trained to do what the rest of the Navy required of it. 'This was right up my street, a key post in the conduct of the Navy.'

Still obsessed with the desire to improve the operation of aircraft to and from the carrier's deck, Caspar now felt he needed to bring himself up to date on the practical side of flying. In the autumn of 1949 he arranged to join a refresher course at the Naval Air Station in Yeovilton, Somerset, and a course of instrument flying at Culdrose in Cornwall. This latter course gave him the ability to fly 'blind' in all weathers and to respond to ground controlled approach, a system of radio/radar to guide one down to the runway in low visibility. 'I now felt fully confident that I was well equipped to make a success of my new responsibilities.'

The development of Caspar's active flying career had become

wholly bound up with the improvement of aircraft and carrier facilities. He now realized that the British and Americans would have to achieve some important breakthrough if disaster was to be avoided. Aircraft were getting larger and heavier with increased landing speeds and longer take-off runs. Either the aeroplanes used by the FAA were going to be unable to compete with enemy land-based aircraft, or they would become too big and too fast for the ships which provided their base. It was therefore necessary to give the ships the facilities to provide greatly increased power for take-off and a more powerful system for braking upon landing.

The short-term solution came from a number of devices which were introduced at intervals throughout the postwar years and into the mid-1950s: ever more powerful steam catapults, driven by the ship's boilers; rocket-assisted take-off; improved types of arrester wires; the angled deck – invented by Dennis Cambell who had worked with Caspar in Washington during the war; and the mirror landing sight – a system of mirrors and lights which gave the pilot an accurate flight path which would bring him down on the right spot on the deck. All these helped, and Caspar worked indefatigably to encourage their development, but they could never provide a complete answer. 'When all is said and done,' Caspar remarked in a lecture he gave in December 1952, 'what we really would give our shirts for would be a vertical landing and take-off, and, according to the degree of faith in such forms of levitation, it would completely solve our problem.'

Although it was not his direct responsibility, Caspar played a very active part in persuading the aircraft industry to spend money and effort in the design and production of up-to-date aircraft for the Fleet Air Arm. These were urgently needed to replace the worn-out veterans of the war and to match the modernity of the carriers.

'I felt the need for new blood,' Caspar wrote. 'Our efforts resulted in aircraft such as the Hornet, Mosquito, Venom,

Hawker Sea Hawk, the de Havilland Sea Vixen, and the Blackburn Buccaneer, this from a brand new design team. Westlands, at Yeovil in Somerset, tackled the problem of helicopter operation. All these in their time were as good, if not better, than maritime aircraft available elsewhere in the world. Gone were the days of second-class aircraft for the Navy.' If Caspar had anything to do with it they were gone, never to return.

*   *   *

One day towards the end of 1950 Caspar met Charles Lambe in an Admiralty corridor. Lambe stopped him and asked whether he had heard who was going to take his place as Rear-Admiral commanding the Third Aircraft Carrier Squadron in the Home Fleet. Caspar had no idea, but Lambe's manner left him in little doubt that he himself was the chosen man. It was the job he would have wished for above all others. And so it turned out. Caspar was promoted Rear-Admiral on 8 January 1951.

In time Caspar was to take on two more appointments that Lambe had previously held: those of Flag Officer (Air) Home and finally of First Sea Lord. The two men were quite different from each other, though neither corresponded to the popular image of an admiral. Charles Lambe was outwardly gentle, urbane, almost alarmingly cultivated, though he could be as tough as anyone if need arose. Caspar appeared harsh and stern in comparison. Once described as looking like some Oriental prince in his youth and a medieval king in his old age, he was beginning to fiercen in looks. He was still tall and thin, but he was balding and this seemed to accentuate his black eyebrows which stuck out like wings over his dark brown eyes. Lambe was a more than competent landscape artist, who played the piano well, and was enthusiastic about embroidery; apart from helping Mary look after three very small children, Caspar had no occupations outside the Fleet Air Arm and his career. In fact, the differences were not so marked as at first appeared – both men

159

had a quick wit, a strong sense of humour, open and liberal minds – but the styles they affected were very different.

The two grand pianos that Charles Lambe had installed in his flagship, HMS *Vengeance*, were duly removed, and Caspar took over.

For a man like Caspar, who was happiest away from the jungle of Whitehall, this appointment was cause for some celebration; hard work certainly, but not demanding the application and perpetual attention of life at the desk. Admirals tend to fall into two categories: those who make their names at sea and those who excel at bureaucratic in-fighting and manoeuvre. Caspar, through no choice of his own, indeed strongly against his will, found himself in the second category. For the time being, however, he was now in a position to influence the course of naval aviation at sea, and put into practice many of the tactics and much of the equipment which he had introduced throughout his Whitehall appointments. The task was simple: to implement the many changes in operating practices made necessary by the purchase of new aircraft carriers, aeroplanes and weapons.

This transition from old to new required a thorough reappraisal of men and machines, a responsibility which Caspar was uniquely well qualified to undertake. He was to spend twenty months at sea, as Flag Officer, Third Aircraft Carrier Squadron – (HMSs *Theseus*, *Indomitable* and *Vengeance*) – for the first year and as Flag Officer, Heavy Squadron for the other eight months. This change of title arose from the reorganization of the Home Fleet in late 1951 by the Commander-in-Chief, Admiral Sir Philip Vian, an occasion which produced the usual light-hearted greetings from his ships: 'Heavy Father, I salute you. In spite of increasing avoirdupois we hope to continue to defy gravity in your company,' signalled the carrier *Indomitable*. 'Heavy children make difficult berths,' read the message from the elderly, last surviving battleship, HMS *Vanguard*. 'Welcome at the birth of this weighty but buoyant child.' Caspar was clearly much respected and admired, but never feared.

The First Sea Lord arrives at Lossiemouth, 1962.

Taking the Passing Out Parade after opening the
Caspar John Hall at Dartmouth, 27 July 1963.

With Douglas Bader
(left), Dennis White,
Director of the Fleet
Air Arm Museum, and
Rear-Admiral
Ted Anson,
Yeovilton, 1981.

Eighty years old. Arranging a bow-tie for his
granddaughter, Iona. Covent Garden, 1983.

'I feel just like a new boy at school,' he had written to his mother-in-law on taking up the appointment, 'not quite knowing how to behave. Perhaps I shall learn in time. Meanwhile here we are in mid-ocean with salt water all over the place. I must try and enjoy it, but I don't enjoy leaving Mary and the tiddlers.'

Every opportunity was taken to display the Fleet to the British people; many visits were made to ports where the ships were opened to visitors and Caspar and his officers ran the gauntlet of generous hospitality ashore. There were inevitably occasions when he was required to make a speech. He had an unusual command of the English language when speaking in public and soon built up a reputation for wit, cogency and brevity.

Caspar had much to occupy himself in this bridging period between the old and the new; while the Royal Navy was rapidly being run down, the pressing need was to modernize what remained. The Light Fleet Carriers *Triumph*, *Theseus*, *Glory* and *Ocean* were at war in Korean waters with outdated piston-engined aircraft expected to battle with the new menace of Communist jet-engined aircraft. But the new jets were already being manufactured and the Sea Hawk, Sea Venom and Wyvern were just around the corner. Plans continued to be laid throughout the 1950s for a new generation of aircraft which required the new carrier equipment Caspar had spent so much time promoting. Whatever the future held as regards the reduction in size of the Fleet Air Arm, quality was not going to suffer.

The enjoyment Caspar derived from his last appointment at sea was reflected in his ship's high morale. Although a hard taskmaster, he was essentially a realist who was never outrageous in his demands, and he satisfied his men that he did not ask of them anything which he was not ready and able to do himself.

All too soon he was plunged back into the hurly-burly of Whitehall. In 1952 he was appointed Chief of Naval Air Equipment at the Ministry of Supply, situated in that grey no-man's-land between Fitzrovia, Bloomsbury and Covent Garden. His primary responsibility was still to supervise work on the design and production of aircraft and aero-engines but the job carried greater significance than that. It was his function to get relations between the Ministry of Supply and the Admiralty working on a satisfactory basis without upsetting the susceptibilities or arousing the jealousy of the Air Ministry and the War Office. Someone had to make sense of the increasingly complex relationship between the three Services at a time when the soaring cost and elaboration of weapons systems was frightening. For the Admiralty Caspar was that man. In his own words, his task was to take a tentative first step towards 'the latter-day unification of the three Services into the Ministry of Defence'. No work could have equipped him better for the highest command.

The relationship of the Royal Navy and the Royal Air Force preoccupied Caspar increasingly throughout the last ten years of his naval career, and indeed became the theme of several of the lectures he was delivering around the country to RN and RAF establishments at this time.

'At the moment I happen to be a fifth rate aerial ironmonger in the Ministry of Supply, trying desperately to improve the deplorable state of affairs regarding naval aircraft which lag some five years behind the times,' Caspar told an RAF staff college in January 1953. 'Because naval aviation operates afloat and the RAF operates ashore each can perform certain jobs which the other cannot. To my mind the big policy question is not: should the Navy be allowed to run its own private water-borne air force? The question surely is: can the country forego the performance of those tasks which only naval aviation can perform?'

To picture the aircraft carrier of the mid-1950s, Caspar once asked his audience to think of the following:

1. An RAF Station operating sixty to eighty single or small twin-engined aircraft. Add the fuel, stores, fire-fighting equipment and so on which go with it.
2. A couple of batteries of heavy anti-aircraft guns with ammunition and control gear.

3. A minor Battersea Power Station.

4. A big radio transmitting and receiving station.

5. The radar, communications and other ancillaries of an RAF fighter sector controller.

Consider all the men (about two thousand) and accommodation wanted for these functions, then issue them all with three month's provisions.

Now put the whole lot inside a metal box eight hundred feet long by ninety feet wide, by about ninety feet high, make the box self-propelled and operate aircraft from the top of the lid.

There is your Aircraft Carrier.

In the mid-fifties, there were twenty remaining Naval Air Stations in Britain dispersed between Scotland, Sussex, Pembrokeshire, Oxfordshire, Northern Ireland, Shropshire and Lancashire. Each station had a separate function which, when combined, provided comprehensive support for the aviation needs of the Fleet at sea. To find the skilled personnel to man the stations and fly the planes was something with which Caspar found himself increasingly involved.

Candidates for the FAA were subjected to a very stiff training programme. In 1954/5 there had been 817 volunteers from civil life for short service commission. Fifty-five failed the first suitability test. Next, 166 failed the medical examination; 362 were rejected by the Admiralty Interview Board, while a further 129 had by this stage withdrawn for personal reasons. Three hurdles passed, the candidate then went to the Home Fleet Training Squadron for general naval training afloat, where a further nineteen failed. Of the original 817 volunteers for short service, only ninety-six went on for flying training.

A principal factor accounting for the low number of men qualifying for training was that many of those who joined got a low score in the intelligence tests given them in the early stages. This kind of intelligence, Caspar suggested, might have been dispensed with in bygone days when aircraft were little more than canvas and wood. The aeroplane of the day, however, was a 'highly complex and expensive piece of ironmongery'. To illustrate the difference, he compared a Seafire, which cost £5750 and weighed 6000 lbs – 'a pound per pound' – with a modern replacement, which cost a quarter of a million pounds and weighed seventeen tons – 'just on £6 per pound'.

It took approximately eighteen to twenty-four months to equip a pilot or observer with the professional skills needed before he could work in an operational Squadron. On completion of training, the successful men would be qualified to become part of what was known as the Air Group. This comprised a number of squadrons which, when embarked in their parent carrier, provided a balanced operational capability to meet the Fleet's requirements. The number of men and aircraft varied slightly, depending on the size of the carrier and its operational programme. To fulfil the needs of this carrier programme, squadrons were formed, embarked and disbanded, a process known as the Air Group cycle. The carrier itself had a cycle of maintenance, work-up, deployment and refit. Matching the Air Group cycle with the carrier cycle was a demanding and complex problem requiring careful coordination of training, preparation of aircraft, logistics and support. This was the important area over which the Flag Officer (Air) Home presided from the 'Clapham Junction' of all Naval Air Stations, Lee-on-Solent. From June 1955 until March 1957, Caspar, now promoted Vice Admiral, held this important administrative post.

9

Oil and water

While Caspar was at the Imperial Defence College he and Mary lived in one big room in Bolton Studios off the Fulham Road, but after Mary became pregnant in the freezing winter of 1946/7, they left their warm room for a Chelsea flat, No. 1 Rossetti House in Flood Street. A scraggy privet hedge adorned the pavement outside the flat, a magnet for passing dogs.

Their first child, Rebecca, was born in 1947, and was quickly followed by another daughter, Caroline, and a son, Phineas, in 1948 and 1950. Mary gave birth to Phineas at home, and when the moment came had to turn Caspar, who was ill with 'flu, out of bed. 'He went downstairs and got on with some ironing,' Mary remembered. 'He was wonderful when the children were little, quite undemanding for himself. He would always say, "I'll help you, wash the nappies in the bath, take the children out, give them their bottles and walk up and down the room with them."'

On the top floor of Rossetti House lived the writer and critic John Davenport – he and his great friend Dylan Thomas were frequent drinking companions of Caspar and Mary – and for a while Elizabeth Smart, the Canadian writer and poet, stayed in the building. The Antelope pub off Sloane Square was their meeting ground, favoured not only for games of shove ha'penny, but for Benskin's beer, considered the best and available only in some half-dozen pubs in postwar London.

Mary had spotted an old London taxi for sale, quickly decided that it would be suitable for young children – much more space to move around in at the back than in a conventional car – and bought it for £40. It was the model known as the 'tall type': painted a muddy red on the outside, it had a curly roof rack and a hood which could be folded down in fine weather. There was no front passenger seat, just a wooden box to sit on. Nor was there a front passenger door or any form of heating so that in winter the driver had to keep a thick rug wrapped around the legs so as not to freeze at the steering wheel. In summer, the hood would be triumphantly flung back and the children and their friends would scramble for a place on the back seat where they could stand and let the wind fly in their faces. When the leather hood perished, Mary had it replaced with canvas by the sailmakers in Newlyn, Cornwall. Later, the red taxi was swopped for a blue 'low loader type', and a half door was fixed next to the front passenger seat. This was done for safety reasons, but the door seemed to possess a life of its own; without warning it would fly open when the taxi turned sharp right, and out would tumble a child. Fortunately it was a slow vehicle; no one was ever injured.

Coinciding with Caspar's last appointment at sea, the family left Flood Street in October 1950 and moved three hundred miles away to Mousehole, in Cornwall. The cottage, which stood in a row called 'Saltponds', was tiny; it overlooked Mount's Bay and in the distance the Lizard lighthouse could be seen flashing at night. Inland from Mousehole, moors and fields stretch to the north coast, and three miles along the coast road past Newlyn lies Penzance.

In the spring of 1951, Caspar brought his flagship, the aircraft carrier HMS *Vengeance*, into Mount's Bay opposite Penzance and dropped anchor in preparation for the christening of his three children on 6 May. This had been planned at the last moment; an opportunity snatched to repair what Caspar felt to be an omission. 'You know what we are – dilatory and then sudden decisions,' Caspar apologized to Mary's mother, who was unable to attend due to the suddenness of the event. Caspar did not outwardly show that he attached any great importance to the rituals of the established church, but he never forgot the time when, as a young man at Dartmouth, he was going through a religious phase and decided that he wanted to be confirmed. When it was discovered that he had not been baptized, a pre-requisite for confirmation, he felt badly humiliated. It was the memory of this and the fact that the children were now aged 16 months, 2½ and 3½ that precipitated the event.

If asked whether he believed in God, he would probably have replied that he did, but it did not assume any great significance in his life and it is doubtful if considerations of divine approval or disapproval affected any major decision. But he believed that things should be done in a proper and orderly way, and since christening was a generally accepted part of the British way of life, he felt it right that his children should undergo the ritual.

The ceremony was performed on board *Vengeance* by the ship's chaplain. Guests and children were taken out in a motor-launch from Penzance. The christenings were brief and simple: the ship's bell was turned upside down and filled with water, prayers were read and the sign of the cross made on the foreheads of the three children. The few relations attending – Great Aunt Luli, a cousin or two, a sister-in-law and some friends from the village – were photographed by the press and tea was given to the half dozen children attending. One of them decided that this was a perfect opportunity to play 'runny runny Granny all over the hills' with the treacle, not only over a plate of steamed pudding but over the wide open spaces of the white tablecloth as well. For some reason nobody is smiling in the photographs recording the event, and yet no one who attended has ever forgotten the occasion. It was not the first time that an admiral's children had been baptized at sea 'in the Diocese of Canterbury and the High Seas': in 1912, Admiral of the Fleet Lord Chatfield's second child, Mary Katherine Medina, was similarly christened aboard HMS *Medina*, the ship she was named after.

After only two years in Cornwall the family was on the move again. Caspar's new appointment at the Ministry of Supply meant that the family had to move to London. No. 13 Woodlands Road, a Victorian house in Barnes, in southwest London, remained the family home for twenty-four years. (The number was later changed to 25, an illogical and irritating consequence of the construction of two new houses at the end of the road.) Woodlands Road was a cul de sac; a dark brown stream called Beverley Brook slid past the end of the road on a mysterious journey from somewhere in Richmond Park towards the Thames at Barnes Village. Children climbed like monkeys around the wire netting and concrete walls which reached down to its shallow waters; it was littered with rusty ironmongery and was not a very attractive feature. At the other end lay Barnes Common, erratically planted with trees and bushes, its bumps and hollows and soggy patches providing a fabulous setting for games made up by the Woodlands Road gang. The house backed on to an eighty-foot garden, planted at the bottom with a row of tall lime trees which turned into a scented green curtain during the summer months. Inside the house, children and animal chaos won hands down over naval orderliness, and it became one of the most popular houses in the road among neighbouring children. The backdoor key was left in place twenty-four hours a day for the best part of twenty-four years.

Once Caspar had attained Admiral's rank, the press at each promotion could not resist references to his 'Bohemian' father. Constant harping on the contrast between his life and his father's infuriated or bored him; it sometimes seemed to him that he suffered for his name as much as Christopher Robin Milne or a fellow admiral, the unfortunate Sir William James, who had been the sitter for Millais's celebratedly sentimental portrait 'Bubbles', and was never allowed to forget the fact.

Augustus himself would acknowledge his son's promotions by inviting him to help himself to a drawing. On one much earlier occasion – probably his promotion to Lieutenant in 1925 – they celebrated the event together: Caspar found himself emerging from a cell in Vine Street Police Station at 5 a.m. one morning, propping up Augustus who 'had dined well but not too wisely. The Bobbies were good to us – they knew him to be a kindly, generous, warm-hearted man, and they respected my King's Commission.'

When the question was once put to him, 'Your father was an artist, yet you chose a naval career – was there a clash of temperaments in this choice?' Caspar pounced on the word 'yet'. 'Why say yet? Does every artist's son take up art, or every dentist's son dentistry?' But he also conceded that he joined the Navy in part at least to escape the family disorder, as well as his father's violent moods. 'Although poles apart professionally, we made a pact. We agreed that our respective ways of life – though honourable – were not compatible. He once said to me: "You cannot mix oil and water. You stick to the sea and I'll stick to my paints." We agreed not to interfere with each other's preoccupations – neither of which was comprehensible to the other.'

What did influence Caspar was his father's attitude towards professional discipline and orthodoxy: the former was most important – though Caspar sometimes felt that Augustus made his own rules – and the latter should be questioned. 'Thus, in spite of the diverse nature of our interests, we had enough common ground on which to base a close relationship.' Caspar had also inherited from his father an acute ear for the misuse of language, which, coupled with the usual tendency to distort, gave rise to an explosive contempt for journalism. He could not abide deliberate distortion of the truth. In his speech-making he would often take a word and juggle with it so as to underline a point. He was once speaking to a navigation and directional school in Pembrokeshire in the late fifties where academic French studies were part of the course. 'The adjective *propre* used before the noun, as in *mon propre mouchoir*, means my own handkerchief; after the noun, such as *mon mouchoir propre*, it means my clean handkerchief. And by juggling this adjective before and after the noun one can achieve the phrase "my own clean hand-kerchief". So it is with the Navy – one can refer to a proper Navy, and my proper Navy would include a strong air component; or one can refer to a Navy proper – a clean Navy – untarnished by matters aeronautical.'

Augustus and Caspar moved in their separate worlds un-affected by the usual prejudices and emotions generated by the English class system. Caspar was as much at home standing in a public bar with a pint of beer as he was performing ceremony in high places with high people. He avoided the London upper-class swim, preferring to meet friends in a favourite pub or to throw a party at home. His children loved him for calling them honky tonks.

From Augustus, and Trelawney Dayrell-Reed, Caspar had learnt a repertoire of songs and ballads; these he sometimes would sing at home after a crowded lunch, but at Christmas it was custom.

'Later in life,' Caspar wrote, 'Ursula, somewhat crippled physically but mentally alert and active and still teaching singing at her home on Cheyne Walk, came regularly to our Christmas dinner and aftermath. I would fetch her from Chelsea at about noon; on the drive to Barnes we would chat about our latest hopes and achievements – but our conversation always ended with a "Royal Command" from her that I was to *sing* something after lunch from my limited repertoire, such as the ballad "Lord Randal". I always did so and with luck she would say, "That's made my day!" Not being a very competent singer such praise also made *my* day!' 'Lord Randal' tells the moving story of a handsome young man who suffered from an overdose of poisoned eels boiled in broth and was anxious for his mother to 'make my bed soon for I fain would lie down'. In the darkening afternoon, and with candles burning on the table, Caspar would close his eyes and sing out – shout – the chilling tale, bursting into terrific crescendos so that even the dog twitched her ears. There was usually a stunned silence when it was over, so he would quickly start a more lighthearted song like the one about the girl who lost her spotted cow . . . or Newry Town . . . or Botany Bay . . .

Caspar's brothers David and Edwin also had their special songs. 'Spotted Cow' really belonged to David, and 'Clementine', sung by Edwin, was soft and moving. Although pursuing very different lives – David had been an oboist for thirty years and after that a postman, Edwin a middle-weight boxer and skilled watercolourist with a studio in Paris – the brothers knew that these songs symbolized the essence of their childhood together. They had heard their father sing in Welsh, French and English, and never forgot the sound of his voice. Sometimes a word or line would slip from memory so that it became a matter of urgency to write down the lyrics and save them from extinction. The words of the seven-versed French song 'Cric-crac' (the title refers to the creaking of a wooden bed), were written down by Caspar and sent on to his brother David and then to Edwin in Paris for spelling corrections and comments about the correct pronunciation and accentuation of the words. 'Augustus used to sing it with the accent on the first syllable of "*j'entends*", whereas I fancy that the correct pronunciation would accent the second,' Caspar carefully noted to his brothers.

*   *   *

Augustus punctuated his spasmodic letters to Caspar with exclamations of angry alarm at the state of the world. 'Our chief enemies are not the Russians, Chinese or Germans, but the Yankees, who are corrupting the whole world,' he wrote, after congratulating Caspar on the award of a CB in 1952, and added, 'Plankton is going to save the human race.' Augustus was appalled by current developments in weaponry, and urged Caspar to read Bertrand Russell. Caspar wrote to him a few years later:

> I will read Russell, but I fear he is saying what all sensible people already know and feel. We speak in Whitehall of a 'Scientific Break Through' to make a

bigger or more 'sophisticated' explosion – or indeed to explode the opposition's explosion before it explodes us – but what we really lack is a politico/psychological 'break through' the Iron Curtain, propped up as it is by scientists being false to their trade.

A modern Samson with a different purpose – obviously I joined the wrong regiment.

There is a device on the market called a 'deep freeze' – everything inside it is frozen until the electric power is switched off. It seems to me we need just the opposite.

I don't despair but I feel desperate.

In 1960, when Augustus was in his young eighties, he again raised the subject of Bertrand Russell. He was considering the possibility of finishing his portrait of the Queen Mother which had been 'so rudely interrupted by a bomb' during the war, but he told Caspar that he first wanted to undertake a drawing of Russell, 'although you, and probably Her Majesty, may not approve of this old gentleman who considers the depopulation of the world by scientific methods to be immoral. I find myself as an artist largely in agreement with him.'

Caspar found himself as an admiral largely in agreement with him too. He would never have been a unilateralist, or a subscriber to CND, but he would have supported wholeheartedly any efforts to cut down the nuclear armaments of the great powers or to check the proliferation of nuclear weapons.

In 1958, he was invited to attend the annual Royal Academy dinner. This was a huge affair: two hundred male guests, including the Prime Minister, ambassadors, patrons of the arts, Air Marshals, Major-Generals, painters, conductors and members of the press. Caspar, as Vice Chief of Naval Staff, was to stand in for the First Sea Lord, Lord Mountbatten, as the representative of the Armed Forces. This entailed a speech. Augustus, who had declined the invitation to attend – 'I haven't a wedding garment and I am under a vow never to patronize Moss Bros again' – suggested to Caspar that he confine his remarks to the Armed

Forces, 'but you might perhaps let it be suspected to which inevitable end their employment may lead us and our unborn . . . I suppose a joke or two should follow, but I'm buggered if I can think of one.'

Caspar took his father's advice. 'I must confine myself to responding to the toast, "The Armed Forces of the Crown",' he began:

> and at once I ask myself, 'armed with what?' Armed with all manner of lethal weapons, ranging from the crude, impersonal, undiscriminating, all-destructive nuclear explosion to the personal and highly selective fists and bayonets of hand-to-hand combat. This all-embracing and near super-human variety of weapons is relatively recent in the history of armed forces, and tormented as we are by scientific achievement, we cannot stand idly by without reaction.
>
> We would, I am sure, as men of peace and sensibility, gladly call a halt to these potentially catastrophic armaments. We would, I judge, wish to limit scientific explosive endeavour and substitute constructive fusion for destructive fission. But as military men we cannot fail to contemplate the whole wide range, however distastefully, of the modern attack and defence armoury, just as long as our duty lies in trying to preserve the almost equally wide range of life of this United Kingdom. Consequently, I sense we are not amongst the more popular features of society, indeed, armed forces in peacetime never have been readily accepted. We are not dismayed by this, nor are we surprised at such an outlook from a population so closely devoted to the maintenance of law and order by unarmed agents [the Police].
>
> We are, nevertheless, I claim, as good citizens as can be found. We are no more bloodthirsty than any other walk of life, or cross-section of the product of the fathers and mothers of this country. We have a simple

belief that these islands contain a hot-bed of good works and good intentions, worth safe-guarding, and however much the ways of life of the military and the artistic may diverge, and however we may fail to comprehend what makes each other tick, I know personally that the three fighting services, even in their modern guise, retain a strong sense of endeavour to preserve the conditions under which Associates and Royal Academicians – and indeed the whole wide sweep of creative artists – can continue to practise their vocations undisturbed by war, and recurrently alarm, enliven, shock and delight our senses in the doing of it. And as the minutes of our lives tick past, our sense of allegiance and humble duty to the Crown persists undiminished.

*   *   *

Caspar's appointment as Flag Officer (Air) Home in 1955 meant that he and the family embarked on a new form of life. The job was one of some prestige, and carried with it promotion to Vice Admiral and the knighthood which he was awarded the following year. It meant moving into Admiral's House, a redbrick affair situated in spacious grounds on the outskirts of Lee-on-Solent in Hampshire. The house was fully staffed with stewards, a chef, a gardener and a joiner. A vast shining, black Austin Princess was provided with a chauffeur. But the blue taxi was still very much in evidence. 'The Admiral dislikes pomp,' a local newspaper explained, when Caspar turned up in it to take over the Flagship, and was received by the out-going FO, Vice Admiral Sir John Eccles, with a guard and band.

Mary and the children, who did not move permanently into Admiral's House because of the problem of schooling, would travel down to spend weekends and holidays at Lee. There was always competition as to who should travel in the crate – 'so slow' – and who go in the Princess, so sleek and luxurious. Sometimes the taxi would follow the Princess at the outset of the journey from London, but the convoy soon broke up, the taxi unable to compete over 55 m.p.h.

It was a new life. Admiral's House, carpeted throughout in pale green and furnished with chintzy armchairs and a very long shiny dining table, represented a world that was foreign to the family, but nevertheless did not drastically inhibit their life style. The usual dramas that accompany the bringing-up of children were not going to vanish in these new circumstances, and there was much leg-pulling and teasing between the children and staff.

The house faced an immaculate lawn which dropped a couple of feet halfway down to become a croquet lawn. A walnut tree was used as stumps for spontaneous and fiery games of cricket, in which Caspar joined as energetically as anyone. Close by, somebody had planted a yew-hedge maze in a dank corner of the garden. Beyond the flower garden lay the vegetable and kitchen gardens, and new to the house, twenty-odd chickens, introduced by Mary and Caspar.

There was a constant stream of visitors to Admiral's House: friends from London, Augustus, Prince Philip, the children's schoolfriends, as well as the flow of naval personnel and colleagues. On 30 July 1956 the Queen and Prince Philip were received for the Presentation of the Queen's Colour to the RN Barracks.

The presentation – something of an honour for the FAA – was carried out in recognition of the achievements of naval airmen since the Royal Naval Air Service had been formed in 1914. In 1924, the Queen's grandfather, King George V, had approved that eight King's Colours should be given to the Royal Navy to be kept at various stations at home and overseas, and in 1954 the Queen gave her approval to the addition of a further Queen's Colour to be given to the Fleet Air Arm at Lee-on-Solent. Strict rules surround the Colour. A white silk Ensign adorned with various symbols, it is never paraded on board ship or on foreign territory; ashore it is paraded only on certain and particularly grand ceremonial occasions.

On the day preceding the ceremony, the south of England was hit by the worst summer gale in memory. Boats were wrecked, trees uprooted, roofs damaged; tree-lined Manor Way which led to Admiral's House, was 'covered with a green and brown carpet of leaves and branches', reported the *Portsmouth Evening News*, and most of the decorations erected along the royal route ripped from the lampposts. On the morning of the ceremony, the wind was still blowing at 25 knots, and on the runway where the parade was to take place, stands had been blown away. Every sailor in Gosport was called out to help manhandle them back into position. As the officer in command of the parade put it: 'Caspar got more than he asked for . . . As the drums were being stacked – all part of the ceremony – one of the big drums took off and bowled down the runway smack into one of the girls in the WRNS front rank. It was quickly rescued, restored to the pile and the ceremony continued. Caspar later sent this girl a letter of commendation and two pairs of nylons. The Queen, who up to that point had not been at all happy due to the wind and her skirt, enjoyed the event enormously and in the end had more fun out of it than was normal for these Colour ceremonies.'

10

The Vice Squad

Some time in 1956, Caspar received a message that Lord Mountbatten, the First Sea Lord, would like to see him in the Admiralty for a chat.

> I duly presented myself in his office, where the following conversation took place:
>
> MB: I have been thinking of who should relieve William Davis as Vice Chief of Naval Staff, and I conclude that you are the man.
>
> CJ: The VCNS must have a specially close relationship with the First Sea Lord. You and I have never served together for long, and we really only know each other by repute. After all, the VCNS is your right-hand man; do you firmly feel that you could rely on *me*?
>
> MB: Caspar, if I didn't feel strongly that you would do all and more than I wanted, I would not offer you the post.
>
> CJ: Well, we have each had our say. I would only add that I can be a virulent critic of my own, and other peoples' actions; so be it. I accept and will do my damnedest to make a happy and effective partnership.
>
> MB: Thank you, Caspar. I will take your criticisms in

the spirit in which they are made; I do know that I am open to them.

CJ: I know that, like you, I have a reforming zeal, and I discern many ways in which the Navy could do better. I must get back to my air stations, and will await your bidding to relieve Davis.

MB: I must just add a point: Charles Lambe, who is the First Sea Lord designate to relieve me, tells me that nothing could make him happier than your becoming VCNS to him.

CJ: Till then.
And I departed.

At first Caspar was wary of taking up the appointment of VCNS. He was in despair about the state of the Navy which was then at the nadir of its postwar fortunes, a fate due in no small part to the indifference that had been shown to it over the previous decade by that most eminent 'former naval person', Winston Churchill. This would have been an argument in favour of taking on the task, but Caspar doubted whether Mountbatten was the right man to put things on a better footing and – still more – whether, if Mountbatten *was* the right man, he, Caspar, would be the right man to support him. He had seen very little of Mountbatten but what he had seen he did not much like. He deplored the flamboyance, the self-promotion, above all the deviousness of the First Sea Lord. Blunt and totally straightforward himself, he disliked any kind of trickiness, and Mountbatten was known as 'tricky Dicky' throughout Whitehall. In time he grew to respect Mountbatten's immense qualities of courage, energy and open-mindedness, but at the start it was the vices which seemed all important. And yet he would be the First Sea Lord's stand-in on the Chiefs of Staff Committee and responsible for running the Naval Staff and the operational side of the Navy on his behalf. If the two men did not get on well together it would bode badly for the Navy.

Caspar told Mountbatten of his concern about much of the Navy at that time, saying that he would want a fairly free hand to put it right. In other words, he would not want Mountbatten breathing down his neck and upsetting his plans with his indiscretions and grasping nature.

> I don't think he had been spoken to quite so bluntly before – at any rate by a junior. His reaction was immediate and to his credit. He said, 'Caspar, if I had not forecast that this was the kind of way you would speak to me, I should not have offered you the post of VCNS. I need your reforming zeal and I need you to give me six of the best whenever you reckon I deserve it. Now go away and write down your ideas for reforming the Navy, and how you would propose to do it.'

Mountbatten's record of the meeting is somewhat less dramatic, but the two men soon established a sound working relationship. Caspar played a vital role in helping keep his ebullient Chief's feet somewhere near the ground. 'His intellectual honesty and moral strength were never more evident than when he was VCNS to Mountbatten,' wrote Air Chief Marshal Edmund Hudleston, who was his opposite number in the Air Force at the time. 'Without his stabilizing influence, Mountbatten's reputation as First Sea Lord would have been far less noteworthy.'

The announcement that Caspar was to become VCNS was made in October 1956 but he did not take up the appointment until May 1957. Since one of his principal responsibilities would be the strategic deployment of the Navy around the world, he felt it only proper that he should make a global tour, visiting naval stations and meeting the dignitaries of the Commonwealth and allied navies. The Admiralty accepted his proposal with enthusiasm, and on 17 March 1957 Caspar set off for the Far East and a gruelling round of visits. In a little over three weeks he called in on Hong Kong, Singapore, Manila, Honolulu, San Francisco, Washington, New York, and so on to Montreal, Ottawa and home. 'I have at least a reasonable mental picture of the non-aeriel Navy abroad or home-based,' he wrote on his return, 'and I'm sure it's a valuable thing for a VCNS (designate) to possess – if he remembers how dangerous a little knowledge can be. Everywhere I went I was graciously received and most ably indoctrinated in what went on and what the problems were. But what of the state of the Navy around the world?'

This was one of Caspar's chief concerns, and in order to sustain or improve it he had to immerse himself in the world of Whitehall. It was a world which he viewed with mingled disdain and horror. 'Whitehall is just about as mad as ever I have known it,' he wrote to his old friend and fellow Fleet Air Arm pilot John Henry Wood, before taking up his duties as VCNS. 'On second thoughts it is far, far madder – *it* knows it, so I get dragged into spheres in which I should by rights play *no* part, simply because my mind is reasonably clear of Civil Service tosh – at the moment.' His fear that his mind too might become corrupted by 'Civil Service tosh' never left him. 'My life is now quite crackers amid the madness of your rulers in Whitehall,' he told John Henry in July 1957. 'It is a completely crazy existence, and in many ways a bastardization of one's poor talents,'; and then again in the following December: 'All is hideous chaos in Whitehall . . . How can one explain all this to the Jack Tar on board ship?'

The trouble was that Caspar took up his post in the midst of the depression that followed the Suez Crisis, and at the time that Duncan Sandys had been installed as Minister of Defence by Harold Macmillan with a brief to cut the defence budget savagely and impose some degree of integration on the three Services. The first and most ferocious battle was over by the time Caspar returned from his tour. The thirteen so-called 'final' drafts of the Defence White Paper for 1957 had come and gone, and the final result for the Navy, though painful, could have been a great deal worse. But it fell to Caspar to implement the provisions of the Paper: to close the base at Scapa Flow; to reduce the strength of the Reserve from 30,000 to 5000; to condemn all but a single battleship to the scrapheap; unkindest cut of all, to close four out of ten naval air-stations.

And this was only the beginning. No sooner were the provisions of the 1957 White Paper being implemented than the battle was renewed for the following year. By the late autumn of 1957 those near the top of the Admiralty were contemplating suicide or resignation. 'It is a sad job for Chiefs of Staff to have to participate in planning the rundown of their services,' Mountbatten told Nehru, and Caspar found it quite as sad to be a Vice Chief, doing the preliminary work and making the recommendations that were at the basis of the Chief's final assessment. In the event the Navy was generally agreed to have got away more lightly than the other Services: retaining a strength of 88,000 men in exchange for some reduction in the role of its aircraft carriers west of Suez, and buying an extra carrier for the price of another two naval air-stations closed.

When the war was on between the Services as to who should make the greatest sacrifices, meetings in Whitehall were apt to be at the best acrimonious, sometimes explosive. In spite of his denunciations of the bureaucratic jungle, Caspar commanded the respect of his opponents in the 'Vice Squad', as he called it, by his patent honesty and sincerity yet never conceded a point of principle. Air Chief Marshal Sir Edmund Hudleston, who as the Air Force representative on the Vice Chiefs' Committee found himself frequently in disaccord with Caspar, paid a handsome tribute to his performance: 'The harmonious working of the Vice Chiefs of Staff in those competitive days was due in large measure to Caspar John. He was never afraid to take an independent line away from his naval brief if he was convinced the views of his Army or Air Force opposite numbers were more compelling . . . Even in disagreement he never lost his friends.'

*   *   *

The house at Barnes was still a most convenient if not entirely conventional home for a VCNS but the children were growing up. They needed somewhere to go for their school holidays and Caspar could escape from the pressures of his work. In the spring of 1958, the family went to spend two weeks of the Easter holiday in a remote cottage in the Cotswold Hills. Walking through the woods one day, Mary emerged from the trees on the other side and discovered an empty stone cottage standing in a lonely spot at the edge of some fields. It was filled with bales of hay and apparently had not been lived in for some time. But it had potential; 'Needlehole' became the family bolt hole for the next twelve years.

Needlehole – so named because it stood at an old threading point for sheep – was made of Cotswold limestone and dated back three or four centuries. It seemed to be in the middle of nowhere; there was no local village, yet Cheltenham was only five miles away and Cirencester twelve miles in another direction. To reach it, people were advised to travel by Land Rover, but even Land Rovers would get stuck. Stones, sacks, stray logs and human muscle all had to be employed to get the roaring khaki beast out of the mud. It could take up to four hours, while everyone got sprayed with pelting mud and the smell of scorched rubber rose into the air.

The cottage had four rooms, two up, two down, with one cold water tap above an old stone sink in the kitchen. Sometimes the wind-powered water pump would stop turning, and water had to be collected in a milk churn from its echoing tank. In winter, when snow could fall up to six feet deep, supplies bought in Cheltenham had to be pulled on sleighs across two fields. The cottage was heated with paraffin stoves – useful for leaving a stew to cook on – and a wonderful log fire kept everyone cosy, sometimes stupefied, in the living room. This was where Caspar slept, in an old low bed he called his bunk. Most of the room was taken up with a large scrubbed table, bought for 17/6d from a junk yard in Cheltenham. In the evenings, when the combined heat of paraffin lamps, candles and fire had warmed the rooms up at last, Caspar would retire to bed, usually before anyone else, and fall asleep instantly, whatever racket was going on around him. The children slept in sleeping bags in the two dusty bedrooms upstairs — cobwebs were too pretty to sweep away — or in summer, outside under the stars or among the bales of straw in the big black Dutch barn nearby.

After Caspar became First Sea Lord, his work required that he be at the end of a telephone. Needlehole was miles from the nearest telegraph link; fifteen new poles had to be erected over fields before a telephone could be installed, an expensive operation which was paid for by the Admiralty. At first, it seemed incongruous, a joke, that Needlehole should have a telephone, but it proved useful. It was not unknown for someone to trek through the woods or over fields to use it; none of the other neighbouring cottages had one.

Gloucestershire in the early 1960s had not yet become 'Royal Gloucestershire', and the area frequented by Caspar and Mary was free of the kind of society they did not seek. At Needlehole clothes didn't matter, the way a table was laid didn't matter; it was simple, private, and devoid of the silly trappings of 'taste'. Apart from the odd coat of paint, no attempt was made to do it up. Here, it was possible to unwind. Mary believes that for Caspar it was a lifesaver.

11

First Sea Lord

Towards the end of 1959, Charles Lambe, who had earlier that year succeeded Mountbatten as First Sea Lord, told Caspar that he was recommending the First Lord of the Admiralty to offer him the command of the Home Fleet. This would entail a move to Northwood – in suburban Middlesex – an unlikely site for a naval headquarters, but conveniently located near that of RAF Coastal Command.

'I am really pleased to see brains and hard work going to the top, and I hope up to First Sea Lord, in place of advertisement,' Admiral Alexander Ramsay wrote to Caspar. 'The capability was always apparent to me, but I was not sure whether your angles and spikes were as bad as mine, even though you were most patient with me. So keep your claws in as much as possible.'

While not wholly enchanted with having to move with his family into the Commander-in-Chief's mock-Tudor official residence, the prospect of commanding one of the major fleets, and of escaping – at any rate for two years – from Whitehall, was one that pleased Caspar. Charles Lambe had already indicated that he had it in mind to recommend Caspar's name to be his own successor in 1962. Caspar knew, therefore, that his time in command of the Home Fleet would be his last chance for some sea air, and an opportunity to refresh his mind before a likely return to the jungle.

In April 1960, Caspar had been relieved of his appointment as Vice Chief of the Naval Staff by Walter Couchman, a choice about which he had some reservations. In the meantime he had visited the Commander-in-Chief's headquarters at Northwood in preparation for assuming command, settled many of the domestic details for moving into the official house, and had begun to assemble his personal staff – at the same time taking some much needed leave at Sir Philip Dunn's villa in the north of Mallorca, not far from Pollensa Bay where, in 1922, he had anchored in *Iron Duke* and competed in a series of gig races.

Suddenly, in the middle of his leave, he heard the disturbing news that Charles Lambe had suffered a severe heart attack. Within a few days, it was clear that the First Sea Lord's doctors would advise him to resign. Soon afterwards, Lord Carrington, the First Lord of the Admiralty, told Caspar that he would like him to take over right away as First Sea Lord. This he did in May 1960, after only a month's rest from the burdens of his appointment as Vice Chief of the Naval Staff.

The prospect was a daunting one. Caspar was not unambitious and wished to do every job as well as it could be done, but the post of First Sea Lord was not one on which he had especially set his sights. It was the peak of the naval hierarchy, and as such could not be disdained, but there were other things in life to care about and Caspar would willingly have settled for a long tour at sea and then retirement; indeed, those who were closest to him professionally believe that his secret prayer was 'let this cup pass from me, but my country's wish not mine be done'.

'You were – indeed are – very wrong to be pleased for *me*,' he wrote to John Henry Wood, his great old friend from *Exeter* days. 'I view this prospect with very mixed feelings. I just was not bred for six consecutive years in that distasteful Whitehall scene. However, Charles had the last persuasive word from his sick bed, and an over-developed sense of duty and loyalty brought this trouble about me – against all ambition and desire. I feel humbler than ever and very bewildered that life can turn out thus.

185

However I have had all the encouragement I could hope for and I must steel myself to have a bash.'

Each First Sea Lord will take with him to the top his own expert knowledge of the field he specialized in, such as navigation, submarines, gunnery. Caspar became the first – and so far the last – naval aviator to become First Sea Lord. This was something of a triumph in view of the fact that 'big guns' had dominated naval thinking for half a century and that the Fleet Air Arm had been regarded as the 'Cinderella' service.

The first few weeks of office were swallowed up by the initial rush to clear the backlog left over from Charles Lambe's sudden retirement – 'subjects such as Burmese intrigues and complaints from Admirals of the Fleet that they judge the Navy is going – or has gone – to the dogs.' Burmese intrigues involved the activities of Lord Mountbatten of Burma; Mountbatten had been Lambe's closest friend, and Caspar's succession inevitably made the relationship between Chief of Defence Staff – as Mountbatten had now become – and First Sea Lord rather less cosy than it had been previously.

For his personal staff, he was able to inherit Charles Lambe's Naval Assistant Tony Troup, and to bring with him his Secretary from his days as Vice Chief of the Naval Staff, Colin Dunlop. His principle adviser was Walter Couchman, who had so recently replaced him as VCNS. Here arose Caspar's first problem. Walter Couchman was an old friend and colleague and Caspar admired his qualities as a commander and a naval aviator, but he had never felt that Whitehall was Couchman's strong suit; indeed when the proposal that Couchman should replace him as VCNS had been mooted, Caspar had told Charles Lambe that he had doubts whether Walter was the right man for the job.

After assuming his duties as First Sea Lord, Caspar's doubts about Couchman's suitability were renewed. He seemed to have got himself immersed in a not fully thought through reorganization of the whole administration of the Royal Navy, at the expense of his proper role of concentrating on strategy, both in the Fleet and in Whitehall. They discussed the subject together frankly and as friends, and decided to give it a few weeks to see how things worked out. In the event, after two or three months Caspar decided that Couchman would never be able to gain his confidence and felt bound to tell him so. To his great credit, Walter Couchman behaved splendidly and sent Caspar that evening a letter saying that for private reasons he would like to retire from the Royal Navy.

Couchman was succeeded as Vice Chief of the Naval Staff by Vice Admiral Varyl Begg – who was himself six years later to become First Sea Lord. The change was a step for the better; both men, though of differing personalities and holding their own, occasionally differing views of the direction in which the Royal Navy should be headed, held each other in the highest regard and worked in harmony together over the next three years.

Under the political direction of the First Lord of the Admiralty, the First Sea Lord was (and still is) the professional head of the Royal Navy and a member of the Chiefs of Staff Committee. This Committee is chaired by the Chief of the Defence Staff, at that time Mountbatten.

To Carrington and Mountbatten, Caspar had been the obvious choice to succeed Lambe, but when Carrington made his recommendation to the Prime Minister, he later admitted that he 'did not quite realize what an exceptional man John was'. In his role as middleman between the Navy and the Government, the First Lord had a particularly close working relationship with the First Sea Lord; Carrington, who was a much younger man, was to find Caspar one of the most stimulating people he had ever worked with, 'one of the outstanding personalities of his generation, with all the best traditions of the Royal Navy combined with a certain inherited bohemianism which lightened the very serious side of his character. He inspired awe and affection, and for those who were privileged to work with him, admiration as well.' Caspar himself held Carrington in the highest regard, his only fault being, he felt, that the First Lord was perhaps 'too much of a gentleman'.

On the Board of Admiralty in those days there were six naval members, the First Sea Lord being regarded as *primus inter pares*, and as the Government's principal naval adviser. Other naval members were the Second Sea Lord in charge of personnel; the Third Sea Lord and Controller of the Navy in charge of material procurement; the Fourth Sea Lord in charge of Dockyards, Supplies and Transport; the Vice Chief of Naval Staff in charge of plans, operations and intelligence (and a member of the Vice Chiefs of Staff's Committee); and the Deputy Chief of Naval Staff in charge of ship and weapon requirements. The post of Fifth Sea Lord in charge of naval aviation had recently been abolished and his duties transferred to the Deputy Chief of Naval Staff. Other members of the Board were the First Lord himself, who was of course the chairman, the Parliamentary Secretary and the Civil Lord – all three being political appointments; and finally the Permanent Secretary, the senior Civil Servant. It had long been established custom that the First Sea Lord, in his role as the professional head of the Royal Navy, brought together the work of the naval members of the Board whenever coordination was required, and he advised the First Lord on all appointments of Flag Officers and Captains, as well as chairing the promotion boards to Rear Admiral's rank and higher.

When he assumed office, Caspar was happy to find that, apart from his uncertainty about his VCNS, all his fellow naval members of the Board were men who enjoyed his full confidence; one, the Controller – Admiral Sir Peter Reid – was his oldest serving friend in the Royal Navy.

Perhaps, however, the biggest personal load upon any First Sea Lord was (and many will say still is) his position as the naval member of the Chiefs of Staff Committee. This body, the highest military forum in the land, was responsible for advice to the Government on the whole range of military affairs, both strategic and operational, allocation of resources, size and shape of the armed forces and, in conjunction with the Foreign Office, politico-military policy. It involved an immense burden of personal work in formulating ideas on policy, and studying a vast number of complex but vital papers upon which great issues could hang. The post for any First Sea Lord required a most difficult balance of loyalties between trying to determine what was the best and most effective allocation of the nation's resources and fighting the Navy's corner.

The First Sea Lord's Army and RAF colleagues were on the horns of the same dilemma, and each, in good faith, was bound to be influenced to some extent by the needs of his own Service. To each it was of particular importance that he should maintain the morale and sense of purpose of the Service of which he was the professional head. This led from time to time to accusations that Admirals, Generals and Air Marshals were jealously battling it out without reference to the needs of the country. There was some truth in the charge, but Caspar felt it was right that the voices of the individual Services should be heard on high. It was this problem of striking the right balance that he found the most painful, and which led him to view Whitehall as a jungle – nearly, indeed, an impenetrable one.

In this jungle, personalities were particularly important. Caspar found his first Army colleague, Field Marshal Festing, an easy man to work with and, while never on quite such close terms with Festing's successor, Field Marshal Hull, they worked well together. It would be idle to pretend, however, that he found relations with his RAF colleague, Air Chief Marshal Pike, so easy. While they were people of a very different type (despite both having been distinguished aviators), Caspar liked Tom Pike quite well as a man; but professionally he found their relationship difficult, not only because their respective Services were fighting each other for the allocation of limited resources, and were in disagreement about the best way to fulfil certain major operational roles, but because often when, as heads of their two Services, they had agreed some compromise solution together,

Caspar found that Tom Pike would later retreat from it, leaving the two Services in open and public conflict – to their mutual disadvantage. In this turmoil, the 'referee' was the Chief of the Defence Staff, Lord Mountbatten. Caspar's view of Mountbatten as a professional at this period can best be summed up by the words he used to one senior officer when the latter took up an appointment on CDS's staff: '50 per cent genius, 30 per cent dark blue [i.e., narrowly committed to the Navy], and 20 per cent boyish over-enthusiasm.' Such was the basis of Caspar's relationship with the Chief of the Defence Staff.

The problems that Caspar had faced when he was VCNS had not miraculously cleared away now he had become First Sea Lord. It was becoming increasingly clear that the Navy could no longer, within its likely share of the budget, maintain a major presence in the Atlantic, the Mediterranean and East of Suez; the joint strategy for intervention by British forces overseas was the subject of major RN/RAF disagreement; the large aircraft carriers *Eagle*, *Ark Royal* and *Victorious* were soon to reach the end of their useful lives and would need to be replaced, together with their aircraft, if Britain was to be able to deploy air power worldwide; the current airborne nuclear deterrent was rapidly becoming outdated and many thought that a submarine-deployed deterrent would be the most cost-effective replacement; the future role of the Royal Marines was a subject of controversy; and the next generation of conventional weapons, which would be increasingly expensive, needed to be decided upon. All this had to be considered against a background of increasing Soviet maritime expansion.

Moreover, this daunting list omits reference to the many personnel issues facing the Royal Navy; to the difficulties of the naval shipbuilding and weapon production industries; and to the increasing complexity of the dockyard and supply organizations. Although such matters lay in the hands of the Second Sea Lord, the Controller and the Fourth Sea Lord respectively, the First Sea Lord was ultimately responsible for anything that went wrong.

Keeping in close touch with Commonwealth and Allied Navies was a prime concern. It was fortunate that, as the personal staff officer responsible for organizing Caspar's visits to his own and foreign navies and to Staff Colleges, he was joined early in 1961 by David Williams as his Naval Assistant. They formed a close personal friendship which lasted until the end of Caspar's life. Aided in the office in London by Colin Dunlop, they became a team which, despite Caspar's occasionally moody personality, was a happy and united one.

At that time there were three major fleets – the Home Fleet deployed in the Atlantic with its main role the support of the NATO Alliance; the Mediterranean Fleet, based on Malta, with the Naval Commander-in-Chief fulfilling also the role of NATO Commander-in-Chief – CINCAFMED; and the Far Eastern Fleet, based on Singapore, with a smaller Command in the Persian Gulf. The Far Eastern Fleet's role was to protect sea communications from the Suez Canal to Hong Kong, and to give naval and air support to any British military intervention that might be required in this vast area.

To Caspar, it seemed that the Navy's resources in money, manpower and ships were unlikely to be sufficient to support all these three theatres concurrently and in adequate strength. One of the Fleets would have to be run down across the next few years. After long and anxious thought, he concluded that it was the Mediterranean Fleet to which lower priority must be accorded. The Russian presence in the Mediterranean, so familiar nowadays, had not yet built up to the formidable threat it currently poses; the Arab/Israeli conflict, while ever an incipient danger to world peace, had not then assumed its present very dangerous level; the long-established base at Malta was looking increasingly less secure, while the Suez Crisis had made it all too clear that in an emergency in the Far East, the Canal could no longer be used as a waterway for the rapid reinforcement of the British presence east of Suez. Yet that presence seemed more important than ever. The spread of Chinese, Korean and Vietnamese communism, with the threat this posed to Western interests and the residual parts of the Empire and Commonwealth in the East – particularly to the old Commonwealth countries – was an overriding one. Britain's eyes and her horizons were not at that time so firmly focussed upon Europe as they are today.

Caspar, therefore, decided that the advice he would give to the First Lord and the Chiefs of Staff was that the Mediterranean Fleet should be accorded the lower priority for naval resources. Understandably, this policy was not welcomed by the Commanders-in-Chief of the Mediterranean Fleet – Alexander Bingley and then Deric Holland Martin. Though old friends, they both, forcefully and over several years, expressed their strong disagreement with the Admiralty's conclusion.

The policy was, however, fully supported by the Chiefs of Staff and the Government, and it was to the Home Fleet and the forces East of Suez that higher priority was accorded. This led on to two major issues which affected the future shape of the Fleet: the need to replace the ageing carrier force and to determine the shape and size of the next generation of submarines. There were those who believed that, looking well to the future, the Navy would become primarily an underwater one, based on nuclear propulsion, the technique for which had recently been acquired from the Americans. Caspar's view was that a primarily underwater Navy would be too expensive to allow for the deployment of an adequate surface Fleet; and also that, so long as shipping moved across the surface of the ocean, which it seemed likely would be the case for decades to come, the Navy could not disappear wholly under the water. Nevertheless, he strongly supported the submarine service and he fought long and hard to get Government approval for *Warspite* and *Valiant*, the first all-British nuclear propulsion submarines, together with the establishment of bases at Faslane and Chatham to maintain and refit them. Indeed, in Caspar's time, it was decided that all the Navy's future submarines should be nuclear propelled.

Computers were in their infancy when Caspar was First Sea
Lord but their enormous potential importance in every aspect of
naval affairs and the country's defence policy was already becoming apparent. Caspar welcomed anything which would make
the Navy's work more efficient or economical, and he accepted
that properly used a computer would do both these things. But he
had grave misgivings about overdependence on no more than
valuable gadgets. 'In the words of the Duke of Edinburgh,' he
once said, 'Do not make the existence of computers an excuse to
give up thought and the exercise of judgement.' If the question or
problem posed to the machine was a stupid one it would give a
stupid answer which could be disastrously misleading: no
machine could take account of the unpredictability of human
nature. 'The mental processes of those in charge of defence policy
must not be subjected overmuch to what comes out of a
computer.'

But the issue that caused Caspar the greatest concern, and
imposed upon him the most severe emotional strain, was un-
doubtedly the future of the Fleet carrier force and the next
generation of naval aircraft; indeed the whole future of the fixed
wing Fleet Air Arm, to which he had devoted so much of his life. It
was an issue which profoundly affected his relations with Tom
Pike, the Chief of the Air Staff, and those between the Admiralty
and the Air Ministry as a whole. Some critics have suggested that
Caspar's approach to this major issue was influenced by his Fleet
Air Arm background. Those closest to him both in the Naval
Staff and among his personal staff would not accept this as fair.
Throughout the long series of Whitehall battles over this question, Caspar carried with him the Naval Staff – composed of
officers of many different backgrounds. His personal staff –
David Williams and Colin Dunlop – both recall his self-critical
approach, and how in the quiet of his own room, he would ask
himself in front of them whether the course he was setting was
that which was in the best interests overall of the Royal Navy and
of the country. As a man, he always disliked and distrusted vested

interests and sacred cows, and was not by nature likely to establish his own.

The problem in brief, and oversimplified, was this. The Fleet carrier force and its aircraft were ageing and it had to be decided whether to replace these, and if so by what. This decision could no longer be postponed. To be constantly assured of having two Fleet carriers operational, three must be built; it would obviously be a waste of time to build carriers which could not operate the most modern high-performance aircraft; it would equally be absurd to build carriers so restricted in size that they could not operate sufficient numbers of aircraft to form a viable force. But such a new force and its aircraft would inevitably be very costly, at a time when defence resources were, more than ever, stretched. The Air Ministry was determined to oppose going ahead with a new generation of aircraft carriers. They were anxious to order for themselves a new generation of high-performance strike and fighter aircraft, and they feared that there would not be the money available within the defence budget if the carrier force were to be replaced. They argued that the support of the Army outside Europe and the Navy anywhere could be provided more cheaply, and more effectively, from land bases. Land air bases, capable of operating high-performance aircraft, could quickly be constructed if no existing air base was situated in the right place, and would not be as vulnerable to attack as the aircraft carrier. You can't sink an airfield was the Air Force contention.

Caspar disagreed fundamentally with the Air Ministry's arguments. Land air bases were inflexible, and could not necessarily be sited where a threat would develop; they were vulnerable too, at the mercy of any development in the local political scene. The concept of support by air of any operation paid no heed to the massive weight of ammunition, stores and equipment which any modern military force required. Seaborne forces carried their own logistic tail around with them and used the politically free high seas.

To Caspar, one way of effecting large savings stood out as

eminently desirable. The Royal Navy and Royal Air Force should get together, instead of standing apart in their separate corners, and develop jointly agreed requirements for future generations of high-performance aircraft, each making some sacrifice to achieve a common purpose. There would be great savings in development costs, and also, because orders for individual aircraft would be much increased, production costs would be correspondingly reduced.

Regrettably no such compromise could be found, for the Air Ministry would accept no changes to their own requirements which would permit new aircraft to be operable afloat as well as from land. The Air Ministry, for instance, would have nothing to do with the Fleet Air Arm's Buccaneer aircraft, arguing that it was totally unsuitable to their needs; yet in years to come when the Buccaneers were forced on them, they became a much-valued part of the RAF's front line. Caspar felt, to the end of his days, that the underlying Air Ministry motive was a wish to see the Fleet Air Arm wither and die. The Air Force, no doubt, felt equally suspicious about the Navy's motivation.

It was in Caspar's attempts to find an accommodation with the Air Ministry, rather than to allow events to lead on inexorably to a head-on clash, that he found it so difficult to work with Tom Pike. On several occasions, they would reach an understanding as the professional heads of their respective Services. To reach such understandings, Caspar would have to concede on certain points, and sometimes be faced with the unconcealed disapproval of his staff for doing so, but he felt that this was what leadership of his Service was all about. He expected to find in Tom Pike the same readiness to lead, rather than follow, his staff. Yet on all too many occasions, within a day or two, a personal letter would come which showed that the Air Staff had got at Tom Pike, and he could no longer support what had been agreed 'at the summit'; on more than one occasion, such a letter sought to accept the concession Caspar had agreed to make while at the same time withdrawing from its *quid pro quo*.

So, disagreement prevailed between the two Services throughout Caspar's term of office, and indeed long thereafter, and there was public criticism of the inability of the Services, and of the Chiefs of Staff, to agree. Caspar's arguments over the replacement of the fleet carriers prevailed, however, and towards the end of his term of office as First Sea Lord he had the satisfaction of receiving Government approval of the ordering of CVA 01 – the first of a new generation of fleet carriers – and of the ordering of the appropriate number of Buccaneer aircraft.

History records, of course, that two years after Caspar had retired from office, the new carrier programme was cancelled and the plans were to phase out the fixed wing Fleet Air Arm, but that was under another Government and with a dramatically reduced strategic role for Britain's armed forces. History also records that in the event the fixed wing Fleet Air Arm was not to die, but to play a vital role in 1982 in just the sort of unexpected conflict – the Falklands War – that Caspar had always argued must be provided for. There are men who would have been alive today, and ships that would not have been sunk, if governments had stuck to the policy Caspar put forward. It was fitting that he lived to see that day.

Another great issue was the means by which the next generation of the British nuclear deterrent was to be deployed. Unlike today, there was little dispute about whether or not Britain should continue to have a nuclear deterrent; the issue was how it should be deployed.

Throughout the 1950s and early 1960s the nuclear deterrent was deployed by the RAF's V Bombers, but by the end of the 1950s it was obvious that the newest Russian missiles had become so potent that the day of the strategic manned bomber was over. Other possibilities were considered but the only feasible answer, though unpopular with the RAF and causing some consternation in naval circles, was to go underwater. Submarine detection was almost impossible, because of the physical structure of the sea. Sonar either bounced off it or dissipated itself which made it notoriously difficult to detect a silent submarine lying stationary on the ocean bed.

Caspar was not in the least enamoured by the prospect of having to accept the responsibility to deploy Britain's nuclear deterrent. 'A filthy week,' he recorded in December 1962. 'This millstone of Polaris hung round our necks. I've been shying off the damned things for 5½ years. They are potential wreckers of the real Navy and my final months are going to be a battle to preserve some sort of balance in our affairs.' But it was the Government which had to make the final decision, and his advice to Macmillan, with whom he got on well and on whom, Carrington commented, he had made an 'immense impact', was unequivocal: 'If you want to get into the deterrent business, Prime Minister, go underwater.' At the same time, though, he warned that Polaris would skim a lot of cream off the technical talent of the Navy for it was no good putting a second-rate fellow in a Polaris submarine: he would not last the course. And he insisted that the Navy would not support 'these things . . . unless we get an absolute cut-and-dried promise that somebody is going to pay for them', that is, above the normal naval vote.

Following the 1962 Nassau Agreement between President Kennedy and Mr Macmillan that the USA should supply the missiles, the Polaris submarine building programme began and was carried out precisely to the planned time scale. The first Polaris submarine was completed in 1967. Once the decision had been made, Caspar was faced with the problem of finding the right man to take charge of the complexities of creating a Polaris Force from scratch. The Naval Secretary was sent for, having been given barely two and a half hours to draw up a list of candidates for this awesome role. 'I duly presented myself with the only three possibles,' recalled Joc Hayes. 'Eventually Caspar looked up: "Is this the best you can do?"

"In the time, Sir, I don't think I've done too badly."

"Ah well, it's always nice to meet an officer who *thinks* he's done well."'

Another issue at the front of Caspar's mind during his time as First Sea Lord was the spread of Russian maritime strength and the impact that it would have upon the whole position of the Western world. The intelligence establishment in the early 1960s, and indeed for a number of years thereafter, was apt, for reasons that are still not clear, to base their assessments on the premise that Russian naval expansion was related only to the defence of Mother Russia. Caspar was one of the few who saw what is now manifest to all – that the Russians had studied the writings of the nineteenth-century US naval strategist Mahan, and others, and that the massive expansion of their naval forces and merchant marine was designed to give them the capability to use the seas for the spread of Soviet influence throughout the world. Caspar's constant endeavour was to encourage awareness in Government circles of the potential Russian threat at sea; and to encourage throughout the NATO Alliance a maritime strategy which did not confine itself to the Atlantic north of the tropic of Capricorn.

*   *   *

Caspar's life was not wholly dominated by the jungle of Whitehall or by inter-Service strife. He had always attached high priority to the First Sea Lord's role of getting away to the outside world, in order to see and be seen by the Fleet and Allied and Commonwealth Navies – and in the spring of 1962 at last found the time to embark on a round-the-world tour, which he had been planning since he took office as First Sea Lord. This included stopovers at Singapore, Australia, New Zealand, Fiji, Honolulu, Christmas Island, San Francisco and Washington.

Regrettably, it was towards the end of his visit to India – on October 31 1961 – that Caspar received the news of the sudden death of Augustus, and had to fly home. As he said at the time, but with great affection, 'Augustus never did have a sense of timing.'

There had been occasions during the past ten years when Caspar's crowded schedule had been disrupted by unexpected visits from his father. His personal staff recall the first time that

Caspar put his head round their door and said, 'I'm off to lunch now; my old Dad's up in town and I'd better give him half a pint of beer, so I may be a few minutes late back.' The diary for the afternoon was filled from 2.30 onwards with various Sea Lords and other senior officers due to call in, so the staff put everyone back by half an hour. Time passed; excuses such as, 'Sent for by the First Lord', 'Sent for by the Secretary of State for Defence', and even 'Sent for by the Prime Minister', were beginning to wear thin; but it was not until 5 p.m. that Caspar arrived back. It had clearly been a good party, so all the same excuses had to be trotted out to explain why appointments must be put off until the following day. The staff learned fast, and a few months later when 'my old Dad' again visited London and was in need of half a pint of beer, they found out in advance and no appointments at all were made for that afternoon.

After one of Augustus's London appearances, Caspar came back from lunch holding his father's hearing aid which had ceased working (clearly Augustus had stubbed a cigarette through one of the leads from the battery). Somehow it had to be mended and got back to its owner. Fortunately a friendly naval officer of the Electrical Branch serving in the Admiralty repaired the hearing aid in a few minutes, and Colin Dunlop set forth round London to find Augustus. After touring a number of promising pubs without success, he tracked Augustus down to his daughter Poppet's flat, where he lay sleeping it off on a bed. He awoke with a start saying, 'Who the hell are you?' but relaxed when offered the hearing aid and was glad to find that it now worked. Colin explained that he was one of Caspar's staff: to which he got the reply, 'Ah yes, my boy Caspar, he went into the Navy – I saw him today; is he doing well in the Navy?'

After Caspar received the news of Augustus's death in India, the last appointments of the tour were cancelled. 'I was very lucky to have a Comet readily to hand at Bombay,' Caspar wrote, and we made the dash and got to Fryern late at night before the funeral. My brother David and Vivien did marvels and Dodo has been beautifully composed throughout. I am watching carefully for any reaction.' Augustus died with a smile on his face; his last words were: 'Mind you give the doctor a drink.'

One project that died with Augustus was that of painting his son in full uniform. Ever since 1956 he had been trying to find a few hours in which both men might be free. 'It would be a fine thing to record this magnificence,' he said with mingled wistfulness and irony when an old friend, Lettice Ashley-Cooper, described Caspar in all his glory – 'buttons stripes and all'. Somehow, however, there were always stumbling blocks and the portrait was never begun, though he painted Caspar three times in plain clothes when he was a Lieutenant.

Caspar at this time was indeed an impressive figure. His stern air and bushy eyebrows (which were a subject of fun at home with his children) seem to have made an unforgettable impression on those who met him for the first time. He frightened a lot of people in Whitehall, and the fact that he was a man of few words did not help to put people at their ease. When he did speak, he was concise and brusque, sometimes disconcertingly so. On a visit to the Anti-submarine school at Londonderry, he was taken out to sea in a frigate to witness an anti-submarine exercise. 'These can be very dull if the surface ships, with their sonars, cannot find the submarine,' explained John Hamilton (Flag officer, Flotillas, Home). 'Caspar sat huddled in a corner of the bridge saying nothing. He did not ask to go round the ship or visit the ops room, where one could see a bit more of what was going on. From where he sat there was nothing to see except the sea and the other frigates a little distance away. The Commander of the ship thought it best to leave the great man to his thoughts, and got on with his job. The search was unfruitful, and after what seemed an eternity, the figure in the corner spoke: "I'm bored," it said, "Take me home!" – which Commander David Parker proceeded to do at 25 knots. . . .'

*   *   *

At this time, important developments that were profoundly to affect the whole position of the Board of Admiralty, not to mention their opposite numbers in the War Office and the Air Ministry, began to be mooted in London. Mountbatten, as Chief of the Defence Staff, prepared and tabled a paper for the Defence Secretary and the Government, proposing the abolition of the separate single-service Ministries, each with its Minister of Cabinet rank and its own Permanent Secretary at the highest level in the Civil Service. Instead, Mountbatten proposed the creation of a single Defence Ministry, headed by one Secretary of State chairing a Defence Council, which would consist of the Chiefs of Staff, the Chief Scientific Adviser and one Permanent Secretary. Navy, Army and Air Force would continue to exist as separate services but would be administered by less powerful bodies, known as the Admiralty Board, the Army Board and the Air Force Board and subordinate to the Defence Council. The Chief of the Defence Staff would have an enlarged staff operating direct to him and would be recognized as the Government's chief military adviser, although the First Sea Lord, the Chief of the General Staff and the Chief of the Air Staff would, if they considered it essential in the interests of their own services, have direct access to the Secretary of State for Defence and indeed the Prime Minister on matters affecting their morale and fighting efficiency. At the same time as this reorganization took place in Whitehall, the Commands in the field abroad were to be reorganized so that there would be a single Unified Commander in each theatre, responsible to the Chief of the Defence Staff.

Mountbatten had earlier discussed these ideas with Caspar, who had given them his cautious support. He disliked as much as anyone the loss of independence that would be entailed for the Navy, but reluctantly accepted that the sacrifice would be worthwhile if the new organization developed in such a way that the Government was better advised on priorities for the allocation of defence resources, and so avoid the public squabbling that had characterized Defence Policy for so many years. He also believed that the experiences of the Second World War demonstrated clearly the benefits of unified command in the field. Nevertheless he felt considerable anxiety about how the proposed reorganization would work out in practice, not least because it was bound to be affected by Mountbatten's own personality, in which concern for his personal position would have a significant influence.

As events turned out, this reorganization proved only to be the start of a process of centralization of Defence administration at Government level which has continued right up to the present time, and is still developing. Caspar's attitude might best be summed up as being that he saw it as correct in theory but well nigh impossible to develop satisfactorily in practice. So far no one can say that he has been proved wrong.

*   *   *

Towards the second half of 1962, Caspar told Lord Carrington, still the First Lord of the Admiralty, that he felt that he should be replaced as First Sea Lord soon after the middle of 1963, when he would have served three years and three months in the post. Some feelers had been put out as to whether he would be ready to have his name considered for the post of Chief of the Defence Staff, but he emphatically refused, believing that six years on end in the Whitehall scene had been enough. Indeed, towards the end of his period as First Sea Lord, both his family and his personal staff could detect in him unmistakeable signs of the strain which this long period had imposed on a man who had proved himself a conspicuously successful Whitehall warrior, yet hated the battle and everything connected with it.

The formal responsibility for submitting the name of the First Sea Lord's successor for the Queen's approval rested at that time upon the First Lord of the Admiralty. Clearly, before doing so, he wanted to know the views of Caspar himself. There were two likely candidates – Alexander Bingley, formerly Commander-in-Chief in the Mediterranean and then the Commander-in-Chief,

Portsmouth, or David Luce, currently the unified Commander-in-Chief in the Far East. There is no specific record of what advice Caspar gave to the First Lord, but it is an open secret that he felt Bingley would be better fitted for the Whitehall scene, though he did not think the choice would be popular in the Navy as a whole. Mountbatten backed Luce – being delighted by his performance as unified Commander-in-Chief at Singapore where he had practised successfully what Mountbatten had so long preached. The voice of the Chief of Defence Staff proved too powerful and the choice fell upon Luce.

Luce therefore arrived in the Admiralty early in August 1963 to take over as First Sea Lord. On 6 August Caspar took leave of the Admiralty quietly and with the minimum of fuss – sad to be at the end of his career, but delighted to be emerging from the jungle into the fresh air of retirement.

12

Odd jobs

Unlike Admirals, Admirals of the Fleet do not officially 'leave' the Navy – they remain on the active list and are consulted over important issues from time to time, as was Caspar over the defence cuts preceding the Falklands War. There are only some half dozen Admirals of the Fleet at any one time and it is the highest honour the Navy confers on its veteran leaders. Yet those who met Caspar for the first time only after he had left Whitehall found it difficult to believe that he had spent forty-seven years in the Navy and had crowned his career with such distinction.

He was a man of great humility. In his London house and various country quarters, there was no show of his past life as an aviator or naval officer, no framed certificates, no boastful displays of trophies or photographs – and no talk. He did not believe in indulging in nostalgia for the past. He was a man who liked to adapt to his immediate surroundings, and did not stick rigidly to one lifestyle – hence the exaggerated description of him 'turning into a Bohemian' at home.

Here, there was little attempt at formality. Mary, over the years, had bought works from artists which were hung on the walls in a spontaneous manner – high up, low down, big next to little – it didn't matter so long as the result was lively. The 'matching' of furniture, or cups, or glasses was unimportant and as if to prove it, Mary occasionally walked around in odd socks – 'that's how they come out of the machine'.

Even so, some visitors could have a hard time. Caroline remembers: 'There was an unspoken code, practised in the John family, which tested visitors and discovered quickly which were the "goers" and which the "stick-in-the-muds". I used to feel extremely anxious when introducing anyone new, as to whether they'd pass the test or not.'

The test could be rigorous, for Caspar, even at home, could be an intimidating figure, prone to retreating into a brooding silence if he found the company displeasing, or just felt disinclined to contribute to the conversation. Yet many people remember him as a wonderful conversationalist who hated humbug and had the wit to shoot it down. He was quick to see through people and could detect with disconcerting ease the smart, the superficial, the intellectually sloppy or the layabout. He much preferred female company; with women he would flirt and twinkle, but with young men he'd grow thunderous or ignore them altogether. 'Agreeably truculent . . . didn't give in to the soft demon of niceness,' in the words of one young man. But Caspar was genuinely interested to know how people's minds worked and never dismissed another person out of hand because he held views different to his own.

He was quickly able to establish a rapport with children by playing the fool, and he used to arrange tea parties at home for the children of neighbouring friends in Woodlands Road. It was not surprising that he was asked to be godfather to eleven children.

When the children were younger, and he was not working under so much pressure, Caspar would play his own special games with them: 'heads, bodies and tails', 'racing demon' and 'playing horse'. But there was one in particular which he used to play sitting in a squashy armchair by the fire at Barnes. With some swift trick movements of the hands, he'd magic a coin to any-where in the world . . . faster than the speed of light . . . to

Switzerland, the North Pole, the Indian Ocean . . . anywhere the children wanted, until suddenly it was back. 'We stared at it in wonder,' Caroline recalls, 'utterly convinced that the coin lying in the palm of his hand had just returned from some far away country.' It was still just a dull old coin; no dents, no scratches after its 10,000-mile two-minute journey. One of them at least wished to see it covered in dust from the desert, or stuck with snow and pine needles from the Swiss Alps.

'The main thing about Caspar as a father,' Caroline felt, 'was that he said to us children, "I'll support you in anything you choose to do as long as it makes you happy." This allowed us a tremendous amount of freedom. I can remember very little that was expressly forbidden except chewing gum in the house, smoking and quarrelling in his presence.'

The John family were no different from any other, so did this mean that the whole of England consisted of a network of rowing families? 'Staggering weather,' Caspar wrote while holidaying in the spring of 1965, 'alternating between really viciously heavy snow/sleet stuff and strong winds – to bright warm sunshine. Rather like our family relationships? At least to *that* extent natural – rather than supernaturally benign the year round.'

Caspar's worldwide travels instilled in the children a longing to see the world for themselves. Often, at their request, he would reel off the names of all the countries he had visited. 'What countries *haven't* you visited?' someone would eventually ask. What of the sights he had seen – 'the worst' – they wanted to know. 'Seeing a man being beheaded in China,' was the answer that gave the most satisfaction. What of the voyage he was supposed to have made in a four-masted barque to Australia? He'd shake his head and wince at the memory of the pain caused by his fingernails being torn in the rigging. The voyage, unrecorded in his official records, was not something he wished to remember; at any rate it has now been lost in the mists of time.

'I feel just like a dockyard,' Caspar wrote home when all three children in their teens were bent on foreign travel, often returning home at short notice. He accepted it with equanimity, as he did their uncertain moods, 'heights of enthusiasm followed by depths of dejection.' Caspar insisted that there was nothing new about that. 'I always deny that those problems of living are confined to adolescence,' he remarked. 'Far from it; they persist through life.'

Throughout the mid-1960s, when the children were immersed in 'O' and 'A' levels, home life was livened up by impromptu parties. There was always a mixture of ages, very good food cooked by Mary, plenty to drink and a huge pile of 45s. Caspar would often start the dancing – he'd roll back the rugs, raise his arms, spin on one foot, take someone by the hand and off they'd go, just missing the fireplace. The whole point of those parties was to dance, and it wasn't long before it felt as if the floor would collapse. Party or no party, Caroline remembers the welcome Mary and Caspar gave visitors: 'Fires burning, drinks flowing, lots to eat and then song and dance. I thought that was the way of the world till I was about fourteen, when I went visiting and was very shocked at the absence of that sort of welcome.'

Rear Admiral Colin Dunlop recalls the first visit he and his wife Pat made to the house at Barnes. 'We didn't know what had hit us. Normally in an Admiral's house everyone is very correct in their behaviour and by about 11 o'clock start looking at their watches and making the usual noises about leaving. But on this occasion Mary had cooked the most delicious *moules marinières* we had ever eaten and we were still sitting around the table at about midnight when Caspar got up, rolled back the mat and started dancing over the floorboards.'

It was no great surprise that Caspar had refused the peerage offered to him by Alec Douglas-Home. His dislike of any form of pomp never deserted him, and the idea of becoming 'Lord John of Barnes', or something similar, was, in his view of things, faintly absurd. He felt that he could achieve more outside the House of Lords. He was equally unimpressed when the Fleet Air Arm wanted a portrait of him to hang in the mess at Yeovilton. If it had to be done, however, he felt it should be done well. He suggested that Graham Sutherland would be the obvious person and Sutherland agreed to do it for £1000, well below his usual fee. Plans went ahead to raise the money from FAA officers, active or retired.

Unfortunately the fund-raising proved something of a de-bacle and John Hamilton, then Flag Officer at Lee and coordinator of the project, had the embarrassing task of writing to Caspar to break the news that the full amount had not been raised. Caspar was unperturbed. 'I am sorry the Fleet Air Arm reckon I am only worth £667.17s.6d,' he wrote, 'but I would like to know who subscribed the sixpence. Don't worry, I know another artist who will do it for £600. That will leave you with £67.17s.6d for the frame.'

But though he did not see his future as being in the House of Lords, he was at first short of other ideas. 'After leaving the Admiralty forever,' he wrote, 'I was fearful of what to do. I was anxious to employ myself for the common good and looked around for opportunities to do so.' Over the next fifteen years, he was to take on nine differing jobs: within two years he was immersed in four of them – two related, two unrelated. 'Espion-age, spies, security – whatever one cares to call it,' he told John Henry Wood. 'This comes and goes unpredictably, as is natural in such an inexact pursuit. But when it comes, I have to drop everything else and concentrate. This can be disrupting to even tenor – but "they" think it better to have readily available part-time inquisitors than a whole-time imposition of yet another whole-time Government Department.'

The Government Security Commission was set up in 1964 to investigate the circumstances surrounding a breach of security, and to make recommendations for any necessary improvement or change in security arrangements. This was a three-man com-mittee; the other two members at its conception were Lord Justice Winn and Lord Normanbrook, the former Secretary to the Cabinet. During the course of investigation, the group had to interview the accused to find out what it was that made a man or woman spy against their country. Was it due to an unhappy family background, lack of money, blackmail, idealism or a complex of many factors?

Only two years previously, the Vassal Affair had broken in the middle of Caspar's term as First Sea Lord. Vassal was a senior Admiralty official who for some years had passed secrets to the Russians. Caspar had seen at first hand how a case of this kind could damage the morale of a Ministry and the reputation of those in charge of it. It is likely that this experience influenced him to accept the invitation to join the Security Commission, notwithstanding the fact that he had become highly security-conscious during his work as a member of the Chiefs of Staff Committee.

Of all the investigations of spy cases that had to be conducted during the nine years that Caspar served on the Commission, the most arduous was that of Bossard and Allen, and it was to this case that Lord Diplock referred as being the one in which his contribution had been particularly valuable when writing to express regret at Caspar's eventual resignation.

Bossard was a permanent civil servant, specializing in electronics, who had done top-secret work with the Foreign Office and the War Ministry, the Ministry of Defence and finally in the Guided Weapons Division of the Ministry of Aviation. Allen, a younger man, had access to top-secret papers in the Land/Air Warfare Directorate. Bossard supplied information to the Russian Embassy and Allen to the Iraqi: he was in it for money, Bossard's motives were more complex, though financial reward was certainly one of them. The two cases were distinct yet, so far as the security services were involved, pointed to very similar conclusions. The object of the Commission was not so much to apportion blame, which was sparingly dealt out, as to make recommendations which would prevent their recurrence. They proposed more stringent positive vetting procedures and better control of documents. But what particularly fascinated Caspar was the personalities of the people involved. All the trappings of the traditional spy story were there – dead letter boxes, assignations in restaurants, and railway stations, passwords, furtive photography of documents – but all that was left in the end were two rather pathetic misfits, drawn into betraying their country by a complex of petty ambitions and resentments. It was easy to despise, but also impossible not to pity them.

A second activity was concerned with the future of the Aerospace Industry. 'This is the Plowden outfit,' Caspar wrote. 'Hell of a sweat! Two days a week of intense detailed debate, with every discernible vested interest represented – not so much debate, perhaps, as cross-questioning, and testing one lot of evidence against another. Job for a judge maybe. Plowden is very good. One weakness – he insisted on *my* joining his team.'

Caspar had been appointed a member of Lord Plowden's committee in December 1964. It had been commissioned by the Minister of Aviation, 'to consider what should be the future place and organization of the aircraft industry in relation to the general economy of the country'. It stimulated a thorough investigation into every facet of aircraft design, development, manufacture and sales. It was the imbalance of these four factors which was the root cause of the industry's serious difficulties: the cost of design, development and manufacture was too high to be offset by sales to the small domestic market and exports were very low. The Government was faced with the prospect of having to resort to nationalization, partnership or some form of subsidy if it was to sustain a national aircraft industry.

After months of painstaking collection of information and interviewing of witnesses, the Committee produced a report which recommended, among other things, less Government subsidy, collaboration with Europe to evolve a European aircraft industry, seeking to obtain a freer market for aircraft sales to the USA, and the purchase of foreign-built aircraft when the cost of the British product was too high. It was proposed that the Government should purchase a share in the airframe manufacturing companies and that the existing bureaucracy, whether of the government or of industry, which was concerned with making and selling aircraft, should be radically overhauled. The Committee, however, stopped short of recommending the total nationalization of the industry.

These recommendations paved the way for the eventual regrouping of the British aircraft companies and for collaboration with European countries which, in turn, led to the production of aircraft such as Concorde, Tornado and the Airbus.

'A third activity,' Caspar told John Henry Wood, 'is concerned with our old friend the FAA/RAF relationship. This is a three-man committee with Gerald Templer as boss, to try and sort out what the Chiefs of Staff have ducked recently. Was the father of the RAF [Lord Trenchard] right when he said (in an unguarded moment) that the single Air Force would be a passing phase, and that history would see the return of individual air forces to the Navy and Army?' The work of the Committee itself only lasted for the first six months of 1965 but Caspar never lost sight of the problem.

In a letter to *The Times* in March 1966, during the continuing controversy over the future deployment of Britain's air and sea power, Caspar wrote:

> I ended as First Sea Lord from 1960–63 with an honest but unsuccessful endeavour to get the Royal Navy and the Royal Air Force to see eye to eye on the matter of the deployment of the nation's tactical air power.
>
> I wanted them to pool their resources and to cooperate in a sensible and up-to-date manner by sharing each other's facilities – carriers afloat and airfields and depots ashore.
>
> I also pursued identical aims for the first six months of 1965 as a member of a Committee set up by the Chiefs of Staff. This committee produced what was in my opinion a thoroughly workmanlike report which I judge would have resulted in a practical get-together of

these two great services, with a welcome end to the time- and energy-consuming controversies which have bedevilled their relationship for so many years and made decisions on their future so difficult.

I have never regarded aircraft carriers as more than an important alternative means of operating aircraft – i.e., as mobile floating air bases complementary to and not in competition with static air bases ashore. These ships are not just naval gimmicks, nor are they, as some people believe, a form of status symbol to which the Navy clings for its own narrow prestige purposes. As long as the Navy has an all-round role worldwide, these ships are part and parcel of it for reconnaissance, attack, and to supplement guided missile air defence.

From this view he never budged, but though he was prepared to weigh in from time to time with some lapidary statement of this kind, it was part of the past. Even when well past sixty Caspar looked to the future. The Templer Committee, closely concerned though it was with a problem that had been at the heart of his life, dealt with something that was now somebody else's responsibility and with which he had no desire to meddle. 'This activity really bores me stiff,' he told John Henry Wood, 'and does more than either of the other two to take my mind off the main ball of Housing.

'Housing intrigues me no end,' he went on, 'not only because it is something new and intensely challenging to one's powers – also because it seems to me one of the major (insoluble) problems facing this dis-United Queendom.'

It was the formidable Dame Evelyn Sharpe, Permanent Under Secretary at the Ministry of Housing, who got in touch with Caspar to arrange a meeting with her minister, Keith Joseph. Joseph told Caspar that he was looking for someone of Whitehall experience, but not necessarily with any knowledge of housing problems, who knew a thing or two about running large, complex and diverse organizations – a definition that seemed to sum up the Royal Navy pretty neatly. The job he had in mind was Chairman of the as yet unfounded Housing Corporation. Evelyn Sharpe expanded the proposition – what was involved was the organization of a new method of financing the building of houses throughout the land, which would involve close co-operation with the local authorities, as well as planners, architects, builders, solicitors, estate agents and the Treasury. The concept fascinated Caspar and he accepted the offer almost without stopping to think. 'Overnight I had become a civil servant with wide powers of introducing something brand new and sensible for the long-suffering would-be occupier of property.'

His appointment as first Chairman of the Housing Corporation caused quite a stir in professional circles and was much discussed on radio, television and in the newspapers. On the whole the reception was friendly, though some doubts were expressed as to whether an Admiral could possibly be the right man for the job. 'You might as well put an architect in charge of the Navy,' remarked Jo Grimond.

'I suppose it is a bit baffling for people to understand that a brain trained at sea and in the air can be adapted to solve problems on land,' Caspar wrote resignedly from his hideaway in the Cotswolds. 'We shall see.'

The main function of the Housing Corporation was to lend money to housing societies which had been formed by groups of people up and down the country, who saw that there was a demand for particular kinds of dwellings in a particular district. With a loan from the Housing Corporation a housing society could go ahead and purchase land, develop its scheme and subsequently manage it. By 1968 and following the Housing Act of 1964, seven hundred such societies had been formed up and down the country. The idea had caught on in a big way: 'I am flooded out with fan mail,' complained Caspar, 'from individuals who reckon I am a magician who only has to wink, and the dwelling of their dreams will spring like a mushroom overnight, JUST where they want it!

'I find this adventure fascinating from two points of view. First it is clearly such a "good thing" for people to get together to solve at least part of the housing problem *themselves* – and not wait chewing their fingernails in the hopes that a non-existent "they" will do it for them. Second, the tremendous practical problems involved – land in particular – I find these immensely challenging to one's wits – or whatever one will have to employ to solve them – probably a bit of everything.'

No one can be involved in the procurement of highly expensive equipment without being aware that patriotism and a disinterested pursuit of the greatest efficiency are not the only motives which inspire manufacturers and middlemen. Caspar was no innocent, even though he sometimes liked to play the simple sailor. 'You find there's a bit of money to be made at every street corner if you are not careful,' he remarked of the Housing Corporation's work. 'There are many questionable people in the game, as there are honourable people, because money is very much involved in land purchase and so forth.' He did not in the least deplore the profit motive, indeed recognized it as an inevitable and desirable element of the society in which he lived and probably any other society as well, but he was determined that in so far as he could control the Corporation's workings, no unwarrantable profits should be made at the expense of the taxpayer or the would-be house owner. On the whole he seems to have succeeded rather well.

Caspar worked harmoniously with Keith Joseph, who largely left him in peace to run his ship in his own way, but things deteriorated when a Labour government came to power in 1964 and Anthony Greenwood became Minister of Housing. The differences were as much personal as ideological. Caspar found Greenwood 'a weak character, blown this way and that by the latest speaker'. He objected strongly to what he saw as attempts to interfere in his work, and to influence the Corporation on the basis of irrelevant political criteria, and grew splenetic about the Minister's 'new mob of sycophantic civil servants, and all the trimmings of "experts" and "advisers", which clutter up common sense in Whitehall.' When, following a disagreement with Greenwood, Caspar resigned in the autumn of 1968, he at least had the satisfaction of knowing that the Housing Corporation was well established: 'Once the Corporation has, say, fifty thousand happily occupied and well-managed dwellings, people will wake up to the fact that in Housing Societies lies by far the best answer to "mobility" – and there is *no* subsidy involved, other than the same tax relief which an owner-occupier receives. We must wait for the first fifty thousand (today the figure is twenty thousand) before people will *believe* that here is something which – even if *new* – is right up their street. Ideas – however good – and jam tomorrow just don't persuade. People need to see and touch – as Old Thomas!'

His resignation left him feeling rather lost, although not for the first time. 'I feel just a bit distraught,' he had told John Henry Wood in 1965, 'not badly – but just a bit at sixes and sevens. Not good at sixty-two. Only because I see and experience so many nonsenses. But I reassure myself that this is all part of the 'Democratic way of life' in support of which we have twice destroyed a generation in the last fifty years. To introduce any sense of precision or unemotional qualification in the conduct of our affairs would run quite counter to our oft-proclaimed unwritten constitution. We endanger ourselves by the licence of individuality and by the licence of looking backwards (Empire etc.) – and by the licence of remembrance of the hideous history of the Industrial Revolution.'

Meanwhile work for the Security Commission came and went unpredictably – 'Have just completed five days on an international espionage affair – all very James Bondish!' – as did his teenage children. 'Their comings and goings have baffled me – and them!' he wrote. 'The kitchen at this moment is chock-a-block with them, and their supporters, of all sexes. From Greece, from Italy, from France.' And the future of Needlehole was now in the air. There was a new landlord who might well want to claim it for a farm worker. As it turned out, he was content to renovate it but on the basis that Caspar should foot the bill and thereafter pay a rent. Caspar decided to look elsewhere.

Mary had spent the summer of 1967 in a little-known part of North Wales, among the Berwyn Mountains a few miles inside the Welsh border west of Oswestry. She fell in love with the area: valleys and streams, hills, mountains, wild flowers and rare birds. 'Most of our acquisitions of houses were done at lightning speed,' Mary recalled. 'I had two weeks to find the house in Barnes, and the Welsh place was bought instantly. "No point in a deposit," I said to the farmer, and he agreed, so I wrote out a cheque on the bonnet of the car which apparently isn't the done thing. I rang Caspar, and he went along with me – he always did when it came to buying houses.' Caspar was glad at the prospect of being able to have periods of solitude in Wales. 'I have undefinable emotional ties there,' he wrote, 'probably partly so often going there as a kid, part Papa's ancestry, and part – a big part – antipathy to Whitehall (this is a negative tie – but so strong as to metamorphose itself into something *positive*).'

Moving from Gloucestershire to Denbighshire (present-day Clwyd) proved a long drawn-out business: the cottage, named 'Ty Draw' ('the house yonder'), was derelict, without water or electricity. It would have been possible to carry on the lifestyle of Needlehole, which was like camping, except beneath a roof and not in a tent, but for the long term it seemed better to modernize the house. This took about two years.

It was during this period, in July 1969, that Dorelia died. She died peacefully, asleep in her four-poster bed at Fryern Court. 'I saw Dodo a couple of days before she died, luckily,' Caspar wrote to me, 'and had a very nice chat sitting on her bed. I think she felt she had had enough, and resented having to be looked after so much. Mentally alert but physically exhausted . . . She wanted cremation, so we organized that at Salisbury. Quite a gathering, apart from family. Many tears, Fryern nearly flooded out. So, the end of a generation and the end of an era . . .'

Dodo had outlived Augustus by eight years. In her old age she was still beautiful and mysterious; gliding silently across the dining room floor in her long dresses, or sitting at the head of the long refectory table at tea-time, smoking a cigarette and laughing softly at some long-past absurd adventure with Augustus that she would sometimes retell. But she found old age trying, so that she was often snappy, especially with her daughters and grand-children. She was a formidable grandmother – not one of her grandchildren would have dreamt of calling her 'Granny' – but she was generous and appeared to be concerned about their futures. Caspar had always held her in great respect, and had become very fond of her.

Fryern Court had to be sold; no one in the family would have wanted to live there after Augustus and Dodo, even if they could have afforded it, and so began the long sad business of emptying it and dealing with all the hundred and one things that follow a death. This preoccupied Caspar for some time, as the aftermath of Augustus's death had done. Indeed, Caspar was never to be free of the complications that arise from the life of an important creative artist. Together with his half-brother Romilly, and in consultation with the others, his first task had been to work on the arrangements for the two-day auction of the contents of Augustus's studio at Christie's in 1962. Then came the fund-raising concert at Burlington House for the memorial statue; a grand affair, thronged by the rich and titled, at which the Amadeus String Quartet played, with Amaryllis Fleming, in the midst of the marvellous Bonnard exhibition. Later came the unveiling of the completed statue on the banks of the River Avon at Fordinbridge. Caspar invited Mountbatten to officiate at the ceremony. As Mountbatten let the sheet drop, two swans took off from the river. It was a moving moment, marred only by the statue. It was strange to be confronted with this huge, awkward bronze figure of a man I remembered walking about at Fryern Court, with white hair flowing and puffing on a pipe.

Caspar supported from the start Michael Holroyd's project

217

to write a biography of Augustus and gave the author much help over the five years of his researches. He always retained lurking suspicions, however, fearing that 'biography' was dangerously close to 'journalism', than which no word was more filthy. He was in some ways dismayed by the portrait of his father which emerged, but admitted its essential justice: 'It *is* sad to read of so much misdemeanour on A.J's part,' he wrote, 'built-in faults which he had no incentive to correct because of the forgiving characters of Ida and Dorelia – separately and in unison.'

'There is some quite exciting news about the National Portrait Gallery's interest in a John show linked with Holroyd's biography,' he wrote in 1973. He took a great interest in the organization of what developed into a major retrospective of Augustus's work, and made his views quite clear if he disapproved of any of the arrangements. 'The exhibition, in the main, is beautiful,' he wrote, 'and covers the whole broad span of A.J's talents, but there are some stupid flaws.' Most of them were later ironed out, though Caspar complained that one still needed a prayer mat to read some of the captions. Caspar found increasingly that he felt protective of his father's reputation. He was outraged when Germaine Greer wrote 'a filthy article on Augustus and seems to have her knife into him . . . People seem to prefer paying for and reading articles ("opinions") of degradation rather than enhancement. We live in a mildewed age.'

*   *   *

'Lolly harder and harder to obtain or rather easier and easier to spend on less and less,' Caspar had written in 1966. He was frequently appalled at the state of the country, and had little respect for any of the politicians, Tory or Labour. 'If these political twisters had any guts and leadership they would discard the economic crisis and substitute character crisis – it only requires a sensible attitude of mind by employer and employed for solvency to return almost overnight. It makes me physically ill to read of the railwaymen's attitude to liner trains, of the Tilbury dockers' attitude to modern timber discharge methods, of the persisting question of who drills what hole where. Quel shambles!'

He was thinking of emigrating. First he considered Brazil, then he looked still further afield. 'I rode on top of a 137 bus the length of Oxford Street . . . I was *staggered* by the *multitude* of people struggling along the pavements – all well dressed – all carrying a prepossessed look of anxiety. Sheep? Certainly following indifferent standards, rather than getting good ones. I am making some headway on my proposition to emigrate to Western Australia. Effort and shillings here bring *no* worthwhile encouragement, let alone reward. How depressing!'

For some time Caspar seemed serious about leaving the country; certainly it dominated the conversation around the kitchen table at home. But would anyone go with him? No one seemed in the least attracted by the idea, and eventually it evaporated; it was too late in life, and there were too many commitments, with more on the way.

In 1967 he was shortlisted for the chairmanship of the BBC, but withdrew before the final decision was made. 'Of course the BBC would have been fascinating to have a bash at, but again totally, and wrongly, involved in political choice, and although on short list of three names, I doubt my name would have emerged from the hat, even had I not said "count me out".' He might have left his name in if he had not at that point still been involved with the Housing Corporation and anxious to set it properly on its feet; 'another year at least – and then I'll probably get the boot, certainly if Anthony Greenwood stays on. He likes to spread patronage of jobs for good leftist socialists, irrespective of ability or suitability.'

Caspar's views about government and country darkened from year to year. 'I hope you realize that you are now living in a Christian Community in reverse,' he wrote in 1967. 'To him who hath it shall be given . . . I'm all *for* helping the less fortunate, but I'm all *against* helping the idle and indolent, other than with physical inducement to work. Vote Wilson, and give up every honourable standard of behaviour. Vote Brown and become reviled, hated, despised and friendless in the world.' The following year, 'What a staggering shambles we have been dragged down to. Tories at their very worst could not have done as badly.'

It was this sort of sentiment which led him to take on the chairmanship of the ill-fated and slightly absurd 'I'm Backing Britain' Campaign. This originated in Surbiton, when five typists working for Colt Heating and Ventilation decided to work an extra half-day, unpaid, in the first week of 1968. Within that first week the gesture spread into a movement and was institutionalized by the Government. On 8 January the Industrial Society – an organization financed by industry and trade unions and acting as a catalyst between the two – took it over, with the responsibility of setting it up as something economical and long-lasting. Several things about the Campaign appealed to Caspar: it wanted to make something realistic out of an idea; it was attempting to solve problems of inefficiency and lack of effort; he felt that the various organizations which had existed for many years and which in theory had the means to do what the Campaign was planning – Trade Associations, the Confederation of British Industry, the Institute of Directors, Chambers of Commerce, etc. – had wholly failed to appeal to individual effort; he was enthusiastic about the spirit it was intending to provoke. 'Men and women want to become personally involved in rescuing Britain from the slippery slope to nonentity,' he wrote at the time. 'We aim to stimulate an upheaval of thought and action from the people of Britain.'

But though he felt there was a good idea at the basis of the Campaign, and a spirit behind it which deserved encouragement, he had few illusions about what it might achieve. He foresaw that it would probably fizzle out in a year or two, and only hoped that it would achieve some modestly useful results in the meantime. He refused to have anything to do with the 'Help Britain Committee', led by Captain Robert Maxwell, because the main objective of this body was to persuade the consumer to 'Buy British'. He saw no point in buying British goods unless they were as good as and no more expensive than similar goods from abroad – to buy them irrespective of quality and price would merely encourage inefficiency and remove any chance of developing the export trade.

With the onset of the 1970s, Caspar remained as scornful as ever about the state of the country, particularly its *systems*. 'My word, our railways really are *hell* – ditto roads – ditto "sidewalks" – in fact all transport seems to me quite headless. If the Navy were run like that someone's head would be on a public charger. But there always seems some safe excuse if one's a civilian, which keeps the fat salaries in incompetent hands.' Caspar's journeys by British Rail never ceased to amaze and horrify him. On one occasion he took the train from Devon to London. Afterwards he told John Henry:

> We were only 50 minutes late at Paddington. At one moment in the journey we proceeded backwards for a timed (on my watch) five minutes – must have covered a couple of miles quite fast! No one told us from what we were retreating – maybe we had missed our way. It took some time to recover our nerve at a leisurely forward pace, by which time all the occupants of *my* cattle stall had lost their tempers. No doubt all the rest of Beeching detractors felt the same on that train. What is so infuriating is that there is no attempt at – indeed *no* method of – explanation. I asked the Ticket Collector – a fine old-style Great Western Railway man – why we should be subjected to this treatment. He nearly burst into tears, and said, 'All we are after is your money, nothing else matters; make the railways pay, that's what we're told to do.'
>
> I judge the future of this country will rest on a number of isolated communities – with luck anarchistically ordered – only able to communicate by radio/telephone plus or minus future forms of helicopter or hovercraft.

When, by 1970, all three children had gone off to college and university, Caspar began to spend more and more time in Wales. He valued the solitude and had established a rapport with the local Welsh: he understood them and on several occasions he sang in the village pub. Gardening had been an erratic occupation for many years; 'My Meconopsis B. *is* blooming,' he once reported to John Henry. 'What a thrill! Peruvian daffodils on the other hand are still hibernating – I suppose they've missed the point that it's a bit further North for them up here. Acidantheras well on the move,' . . . and a year later, 'Camellia bloomed for first time, but blossom weak in the stem and fell off early. Why? Himalayan Poppies look promising. Also Peruvian daffodil. Ethiopian Acidantheras now well established. So my little UNO Nature study flourishes in spite of veto.'

But he felt restless, and though he would not have admitted it, underemployed. Mary and he were constantly crossing the country on their separate missions – across the Welsh hills, up to London, east to Norfolk, or south to Sussex, where Mary's mother was pushing into her nineties and craving attention from her loved ones. 'Mary, who is more restless than me, asks, "Why don't you stay still?" I reply, "I don't want to stagnate and I live for change."' In 1973 he decided to buy a cottage in Devon, on the outskirts of Dartmoor, not far from his great old FAA friend John Henry Wood, and made it his base for the next few years.

Caspar had taken on new work; this time as chairman and fundraiser for the Back Pain Association, a body set up to initiate the research into the causes of back pain. He set up shop in a bungalow in Bath. 'A few of us started to put together the jigsaw puzzle with no picture,' he wrote. Sympathizers from the University of Bath and the Royal Hospital for Rheumatic Diseases joined in the effort and after a few months the organization moved to London under the auspices of the Institute of Directors in Belgrave Square, 'who gave us muscle in the form of the Director General, Sir Richard Powell'.

Caspar did an immense amount of work trying to get chiro-practors to agree with osteopaths – 'almost impossible' – and raising money, which meant tearing around interested parties, 'including Elizabeth Taylor at the Dorchester Hotel'. Once again he became immersed in a new effort, this time on behalf of the neglected millions of back-pain sufferers. 'Am deep in the mysteries of the spinal column and its surrounds,' he told a friend, but because the cause lacked dramatic appeal it was sometimes difficult to persuade people to donate sums of money: 'My experience of handling the begging bowl these days is that individuals and institutions want detailed chapter and verse before they will ante-up.'

Some of his responsibilities fell away but others persisted. Marshal of the RAF Sir John Slessor persuaded him to take over as chairman of the Governors of the Star and Garter Home at Richmond for disabled soldiers, sailors and airmen. Physical fitness had always been of importance to him; the sight of a potbelly appalled him, and he remained as thin as a beanpole all his life. He kept up a keen interest in athletics, becoming chair-man of the Milocarien Club, a tri-service organization which promoted a common rather than individual approach to the sport. He became an honorary liveryman of the Worshipful Company of Fruiterers and took advantage of one of their dinners to tell the Lord Mayor and assembled company that 'fruit would perhaps be in very short supply if "they" did not cough up more support to keep it buoyant on its journey oversea ... I sensed that the penny dropped,' he concluded, 'but I doubt if it will reach the Royal Navy.'

His most enduring commitment during these years was the establishment of the Fleet Air Arm Museum at Yeovilton, in Somerset. This museum provides an opportunity for members of the public to see and touch the aeroplanes which the Fleet Air Arm used in the course of its history. Caspar was in at the birth of this institution, helped raise money for it and was one of its main directing forces.

13

The final chapter

One January morning in 1978, Mary and I met at St Mary's
Hospital, Paddington, to await the verdict of the surgeon who
had just operated on Caspar's leg arteries to find out whether his
vascular trouble could be successfully checked. He broke the
news to us that the right leg would have to be amputated above
the knee, and that the left leg was also in danger. Caspar had
complained occasionally of pains in his feet during the previous
autumn, but had not let on the full extent of his suffering either to
his doctors or to his family. Now it was too late. A blood clot had
lodged in one of the arteries, impeding disastrously the already
clogged blood-flow to the feet. Mary had now to consider
what practical problems might lie ahead if he were to survive
the ordeal – this she was very good at. Caspar himself got on
with the business of accepting his fate and asked for some
brandy.

From there it was only a matter of what seemed like an
interminable ambulance ride to the naval hospital at Plymouth,
Stonehouse, and preparations for the first amputation. Caspar
made an extraordinarily spirited recovery and was in no time
practising walking on one leg with crutches; but it was useless.
The remaining leg was giving him so much pain that he consented
willingly to the second amputation, which was performed barely
six weeks after the first.

'I think it will be a wheelchair existence for me, which I find intriguing rather than daunting,' he wrote in a letter to a friend.

It was one of the harshest winters in years. Devon lay under snow for weeks on end, and as the wounds healed and Caspar thought only of learning to walk again on false legs, we hurtled up and down the twenty miles of the A38 between Buckfastleigh and Plymouth, delivering hot homemade soups and bottles of brandy. The slush turned to ice, then slush again, followed by fresh and very heavy snow throughout the period of convalescence. But by the time the warmer weather came and the early days of shock had passed, Caspar was bracing himself to master the use of artificial legs in the hospital gymnasium.

It was at first a matter of balance. He had previously been six feet one inch tall; on a pair of 'rockers' he stood about five foot three inches. The gym was very long, and it was, he said, 'the devil of a sweat' to get from one end to the other – first with the aid of a walking frame, then with two sticks, then, triumphantly, with only one. 'I am a mixture of anxiety and elation,' he wrote in July 1978. 'One day things go well and I am bucked up – the next day all is wrong and I am despondent. However, on the whole I am cheerful that I shall win the battle to walk again properly.' As he progressed he was put on to higher 'pylons' – false legs suitable for beginners with curved bases to ease the action of walking without a real foot. He was put up four inches in July and the design of his permanent false legs began to be considered. By the time these arrived – they were made of aluminium with holes drilled into them to lighten their weight – Caspar had become increasingly impatient and it was felt that it wouldn't be long before he could regain his independence; though I could not quite see at this stage – and it was talked about – how he would be able to drive a car again. It would of course be manually controlled, but would he be able to get in and out of the driver's seat, awkward enough with one's own legs? At the end of walking practice in the gym, his face would glow with the effort and took

225

on the same look he used to have after chopping up a load of logs while on holiday in the Cotswolds, when sweat ran down his neck and he would drink a pint of beer. There was one memorable occasion when he walked – with great difficulty – into the Packhorse Inn at South Brent, stood at the bar – five feet seven inches tall – and ordered a pint. Someone opened a bottle of champagne, and it felt, fleetingly, as if he would soon be rejoining the regular Saturday morning gathering at the Packhorse which he had used to attend, and where he had been much missed.

Once the first difficulties with the false legs were partly overcome, it was decided to have a change of scene. He was showing signs of becoming used to hospital life, and the family were worried that he no longer looked forward to weekends at the cottage; rather, he seemed to anticipate with pleasure returning to his spacious room at Stonehouse on Sunday evenings. The precision of hospital timing suited him, and while everything was done to encourage his walking, with intense physiotherapy, visits from Douglas Bader and moral support from those around him, it became clear that it was going to be a long, painful and arduous process. Already he had been at Stonehouse for over a year. So, in the summer of 1979, the break was made and he travelled by road to Wales, to the family home on the Welsh/Shropshire border.

Here, isolated in the beautiful setting of the Berwyn Mountains and wide open valleys of the Border country, he battled on; always in pain, and with many debilitating difficulties, usually connected with the straps and sockets of the cumbersome tin legs. Age was no longer on his side, and frustration often got the better of him. Physiotherapy sessions continued at the hospital in Oswestry, fourteen winding miles away. The general opinion on the medical side was that he was attempting the impossible, because of his age, now seventy-six. However, nothing was going to stop him, and he remained determined in the face of terrible problems.

He had become adept at shifting from bed to wheelchair; and

with frequent use of an overhead rope his arm muscles developed so that they became immensely strong. He started gardening from the wheelchair and, as always, kept up a steady correspondence, much of it at this time concerning the design and modification of false legs, wheelchairs and related equipment for the disabled. It was hard at first to accept the term 'disabled', for he was mentally very sharp, and one could sometimes be fooled into thinking that the physical abomination he had endured was but a minor visitation – a small setback in his view of things.

Cruelly – or perhaps mercifully – the struggle to learn to walk again ended that summer. An excruciating pain in the stomach suddenly developed one night; within two days he was undergoing an operation to remove three feet of intestine where a blood clot had lodged, and for the ensuing month he lay on his back unable to eat, move about, speak or read a book.

He made a miraculous recovery. It was expected that he would remain in hospital for up to three months. Instead he was allowed home after four weeks, where he was nursed back to strength by Mary's constant attention to diet. He had been reduced to a very weak state, and decided there and then to abandon the whole wretched business of attempting to regain independence on a pair of tin legs. He never talked about walking again.

A new problem now occupied the family; where to live. From now on the wheelchair, and attendant technicalities, were to influence, sometimes dictate, decisions, whether over movement around the country, or the layout of objects in the home.

For some time the offer of a 'grace and favour' home had been under discussion with the Navy (he had in fact been offered such a house at the end of his term as First Sea Lord, but it was declined). Now, an apartment in the grounds of Hampton Court Palace was under consideration. We went to inspect it. The ground-floor rooms, at the time stacked with Prince Michael of Kent's furniture, were majestically high, but they were dark and gloomy. This, and the prospect of living in what seemed to us a somewhat artificial environment, convinced us that it would be better to manage on our own resources.

Meanwhile, an old family friend had turned up with the news that a suitable house was for sale in Mousehole, the village on the Cornish coast which Mary and Caspar had kept ties with since they had lived there in 1950–2. It had not been spoilt by development, and a core of old friends from the 1950s still lived there and around the Penwith peninsular.

With the move to Cornwall in October 1979 began a new life which was to last almost a full five years – on wheels, or as Caspar wryly put it, 'three feet nearer the ground'. There were parties, accidents, quarrels, fish-feasts, a lot of drinking and many visitors who would travel hundreds of miles to see Caspar and Mary.

A lift was installed ('awkward bloody thing'), steps and ridges in the floor vanished and concrete slab paths were laid in the garden. Once outside the garden gate there were few restrictions and Caspar could manoeuvre more or less freely around the streets and alleys of the little village. There were no pavements and therefore no kerbs – ideal for a wheelchair. He'd enter the Ship Inn down a narrow passageway, fling open the back door and dock at the bar to a general greeting of 'Aye, aye Cap'n'. Cars became his enemy – and he'd curse the drivers; threshold steps and narrow entrances to friends' houses became points of great significance. The ramp suddenly became a most valued feature.

It wasn't always plain sailing out there in the village. The chair's battery, which was heavy and had to be recharged during the night, would occasionally die on him so that he'd shudder to a halt, but there was always someone around who'd come to the rescue. More seriously, and always unexpectedly, he'd somehow fall out of the chair; once or twice in the village but more often at home in the house or garden. He nearly always escaped unhurt, and far from feeling sorry for himself, he'd laugh at his predicament. One hot summer day I returned to Trethewey after a swim off the rocks to find him sitting in the herb bed on a bush of thyme. It was a strange feeling to have to lift up one's father. Mary once had to pluck him from the roses. When he circulated in the garden his wheels would sometimes catch the earth in the flower beds; infuriated, he'd spin the wheels and sink lower into the earth, listing dangerously, until someone came rushing to the rescue and dragged him on to firm ground.

About twice a year, he'd fly to Essex to stay with friends. The Admiral in charge at the Naval Air Station, Yeovilton, would give permission for his aeroplane, 'The Admiral's Barge' as it was called, to be used on these occasions. And he would fly to London, where one evening he attended a reception at Buckingham Palace for the principal donors and trustees of the Fleet Air Arm Museum. This was followed by dinner held in a restaurant overlooking the Thames. He left as the dancing started.

Although he looked remarkably fit, and became more independent than at one time seemed possible, his physical troubles never went away. He was plagued until the end by excruciating phantom pains – the pain he had endured before the operations persisted, and he talked often of a painful foot which did not exist. These phantom pains, for which doctors have found no cure, were caused by the severed nerve endings in the stumps which continued carrying messages to the brain, undeterred by their truncation. Neither pills, electronically wired painkilling pads, acupuncture, nor physiotherapy could numb the phantoms. But gin did. 'Juniper juice', as Caspar called it, was to become, in a sense, his saviour from mental frustration and physical torture; and it became the bane of Mary's life, indeed of anyone who was in charge. After seven too many, he would be unable to get into bed; four extra arms were needed and a 'one, two, three'. The moment was a trying one and recurred often enough, but it was brief, and he'd awake early each morning, alert as a bird, prepare breakfast and head down to the harbour to buy the newspapers. He was able to bath on his own, clean out the fire and fetch the coal, tidy up and, of course, grow his beloved lilies and a variety of vegetables from seed in the greenhouse.

He had never been a clumsy man, and retained great dignity in the face of his physical abomination. But in fits of anger he would swerve violently around the ground floor, scattering people and animals, bang into doorways ('too damn narrow') and chairs ('always in the way'), cursing his environment. Sunk into black despair, he'd slump with his head in his hands without stirring. Nobody was welcome; he wanted to be left alone and anyone who approached was told to go away. He had to endure these blackest of black moments on his own. All he wanted to do was to die; but he was not born to give in. There were bouts of rage, but never of self-pity. He began to collect material for his autobiography – an operation he found deeply uncongenial – and never lost interest in the world outside. The Falklands War both angered and saddened him, but the event that caused him greatest grief, far more than his own plight, was the loss of the Penlee lifeboat in December 1982. He telephoned me in London to give the news. 'All drowned . . . Charlie, Trevelyan . . . there's been a tragedy . . . I must go back to my crying.' Trevelyan Richards, the coxswain of the lifeboat, had been one of his closest friends in Mousehole. As the money for the relief fund began pouring in, Caspar, who had become a kind of elder statesman in the village, was ready to give advice when sought and to listen to the sorrows of his neighbours.

*　　*　　*

'I think you'd be surprised to know how the Term feels about its most illustrious member,' wrote Geoffrey Gowland, a fellow member of Hawke Term who had later entered the church. 'There is a tremendous depth of real sympathy and sorrow.

'The mental battle must be *very* testing: there is so much that seems beyond rational explanation. It seems so cruel to tell a chap in your situation that his courage and suffering and patience and endurance and sheer willpower to carry on are an inspiration for thousands of ordinary folk, besides similar sufferers . . . and that such gallantry . . . has a quality of great good against the blackness of evil.'

His eightieth birthday approached, and we talked about throwing a party. At first he strongly resisted the idea: 'I am not sympathetic to the figure of eighty,' he wrote, only six weeks before. It was a bit of a gamble, knowing that Caspar's energy faded three times each day. Since he always got up at six, he needed to rest mid-morning, then again after lunch and by seven or eight he was ready to retire to bed. In the event – 22 March 1983 – nearly a hundred people came to celebrate at the flat in Covent Garden where I was living. We divided the party into two sessions, but by far the greater number came in the evening, and although the party was planned to end at 8.30 p.m., the last guest did not disappear until midnight. At 4 a.m. Caspar woke up, and unable to sleep I came and sat with him amidst the aftermath of the party – my brother asleep on the floor nearby. He was clearly thrilled at having seen so many old friends; but what had meant more to him than anything else were the flying visits from old Whitehall colleagues.

More than a year later, on 31 May 1984, Caspar was again staying in Covent Garden when he developed pneumonia. After a few weeks in a London hospital, when he seemed perilously close to death, he recovered sufficiently to be transferred to the naval hospital at Plymouth. This was one step nearer home. The journey, which normally takes three and a half hours, took six, because the ambulance was not legally allowed to travel over sixty m.p.h. Caroline was there and had put slabs of chocolate and a punnet of strawberries by his bed. Here he stayed for some two weeks but begged us to be allowed to go home.

Finally it was agreed that it was safe enough, though he was by now quite weak. Despite the glorious Cornish weather – palm trees in bloom, roses everywhere, blue sea and sweet air, the atmosphere in Trethewey became tense. Caspar slept a lot during the day now, and the long light evenings were confusing his sense of time. Then one evening, he sat up very straight in bed and made an announcement: 'I'm dying.' The strain was too much for my mother – she was frightened he might fall out of bed amongst other things – and he was admitted to St Michael's hospital in Hayle, next to the exotic Bird Sanctuary.

On 9 July I visited him and stood crying in his room while he slept on. When he awoke, he was incoherent but now and again words emerged: 'Nearer my God to thee'. . . 'Buck up!' . . . 'Why don't you help me?' He was so weak that he was unable to sit up or use his hands. He was so thin that when you put a hand on him to help him to move, you felt hard bones. Mary and I spent the following night at the hospital. This was torment. That afternoon while under sedation, he suddenly opened his eyes and raised his hands. I held his hand very tightly and told him that everything would be all right . . . He could hear; without opening his eyes, a single tear rolled down his cheek. It was the only sign that he could hear and that he knew someone was there.

On the afternoon of 11 July, Caspar died without recovering consciousness.

BIBLIOGRAPHICAL NOTE

Primary source material was provided by Caspar John's own writings, his papers and correspondence, and the contributions of others who are named in the foreword.

For background on family and childhood, I am indebted to Michael Holroyd's biography *Augustus John, Volume I: The Years of Innocence* (Heinemann, 1974; Penguin, 1976). For further reading see Augustus John's autobiography, *Chiaroscuro* (Cape, 1952) and Romilly John, *The Seventh Child* (Heinemann, 1932; Cape, 1975).

It would be inappropriate to list all the books concerning Caspar John's career, but I cannot refrain from mentioning a few books which I found of particular value: Hugh Popham, *Into Wind, A History of British Naval Flying*, with a foreword by Admiral of the Fleet Sir Caspar John (Hamish Hamilton 1969); Geoffrey Till, *Air Power and the Royal Navy* (Jane's, 1979); Stephen Roskill, *Naval Policy Between the Wars: The Period of Anglo-American Antagonism 1919–1929* (Collins, 1968); Arthur Marder, *From the Dreadnought to Scapa Flow: The Royal Navy in the Fisher Era, 1904–1919 Volume I: The Road to War 1904–1914* (OUP, 1966); A. Cecil Hampshire, *Just an Old Navy Custom* (William Kimber 1979).

INDEX

de Havilland Sea Vampire (aircraft),
148
de Havilland Sea Vixen (aircraft),
159
de Roebeck, Admiral, 53
de Wiat, General Adrian Carton, 126
Deniken, General, 51
Deutschland, 125
Devanka, 85
Dickenson, Lieutenant-Commander,
64
Diplock, Lord, 209
'Dodo' *see* McNeill, Dorelia
Dostoyevsky, Fyodor, *The Possessed*,
85
Douglas-Home, Alec, 207
Dragon, 131
Duchess of Bedford, 127
Dunlop, Colin, 186, 191, 193, 199,
207
Dunn, Sir James, 103, 185

Eagle, 190
Eccles, Sir John, 174
Edward VII, 17
Elizabeth II, 175–6
Elizabeth, Queen, the Queen Mother,
172
Epstein, Jacob, 24
Evans, Mrs, 32
Exeter, 111, 185

FAA *see* Fleet Air Arm
Fairey Firefly (aircraft), 150
Fairey IIID (aircraft), 75
Fairey IIIF (aircraft), 83, 87–8
Fairey Swordfish (aircraft), 114, 121
Falklands War, 230
Festing, Field Marshal, 189
Firbank, Ronald, 85
Fisher, Lord, ('Jackie'), 39–40, 70
Fleet Air Arm (FAA; *formerly* Royal
Naval Air Service): development,
11, 196; discussions on future of,
66; CJ on history of, 70; CJ joins,
71; officers on board *Hermes*,

82–3; CJ's career in, 95–6;
Ramsey and, 116; 'hymn',
117–19; and division from RAF,
122–3; and Taranto, 129; rapid
build-up of, 137; equipping, 158;
reduction in size, 161; training for,
163–4; RAF and, 195; museum,
223, 229
Fleming, Amaryllis, 127, 217
Fleming, Peter, 127, 130
Fulmar, 156
Furious, 71, 78, 104

General Strike, the, 75
George V, 175
George, Prince, *later* Duke of Kent,
53–4, 108
Gissing, George, 85
Glorious, 116, 121
Glory, 161
Gloster TSR (aircraft), 114
Gogarty, Oliver St John, 100
Gogol, Nikolai, 85
Gorky, Maxim, 85
Greenwood, Anthony, 214, 219
Greer, Germaine, 218
Grimond, Jo, 213
Guevara, Alvaro, 33, 93

Haggard, Henry Rider, 35
Hahn, Kurt, 156
Hamilton, John, 200
Hardy, Thomas, 33
Harrington, General, 62, 64
Harris, Air Commodore, ('Bomber'),
123–4
Harrison, Jane, 25
Hawke, Admiral, 43
Hawker Sea Hawk (aircraft), 158
Hayes, Joc, 197
Hellcat Night Fighter (aircraft), 124,
150
Henderson, Nigel, 147–8, 151
Hermes, 71–2, 80–2, 85–7, 89–90
Holroyd, Michael, 104, 217–18
Hope-Johnstone, John, 32, 34
Hornet, 158